RESULTS
COACHING

RESULTS
COACHING

THE NEW ESSENTIAL FOR SCHOOL LEADERS

KATHRYN KEE
KAREN ANDERSON | VICKY DEARING
EDNA HARRIS | FRANCES SHUSTER
Foreword by **Dennis Sparks**

A Joint Publication

CORWIN
A SAGE Company

learningforward

For information:

Corwin
A SAGE Company
2455 Teller Road
Thousand Oaks, California 91320
(800) 233-9936
Fax: (800) 417-2466
www.corwin.com

SAGE India Pvt. Ltd.
B 1/I 1 Mohan Cooperative
  Industrial Area
Mathura Road, New Delhi 110 044
India

SAGE Ltd.
1 Oliver's Yard
55 City Road
London EC1Y 1SP
United Kingdom

SAGE Asia-Pacific Pte. Ltd.
33 Pekin Street #02-01
Far East Square
Singapore 048763

Printed in the United States of America

Library of Congress Cataloging-in-Publication Data

RESULTS coaching : the new essential for school leaders / Kathryn Kee . . . [et al.] ; foreword by Dennis Sparks.
    p. cm.
A joint publication with Learning Forward.
Includes bibliographical references and index.
ISBN 978-1-4129-8674-8 (pbk.)
    1. Educational leadership—United States. 2. Personal coaching—United States.
3. Teachers—In-service training—United States. 4. School administrators—In-service training—United States. 5. School improvement programs—United States. I. Kee, Kathryn.
II. Learning Forward.

LB2805.R475 2010
371.2'03—dc22   2010017649

This book is printed on acid-free paper.

10   11   12   13   14   10   9   8   7   6   5   4   3   2

Acquisitions Editor:	Arnis Burvikovs
Associate Editor:	Desirée Bartlett
Editorial Assistant:	Kimberly Greenberg
Production Editor:	Amy Schroller
Copy Editor:	Jeannette K. McCoy
Typesetter:	C&M Digitals (P) Ltd.
Proofreader:	Eleni Georgiou
Indexer:	Judy Hunt
Cover Designer:	Michael Dubowe

Contents

Foreword

By Dennis Sparks

I have known Kathy Kee and Karen Anderson for many years. I respect them as human beings, and I admire their work. So I take notice when they use the word "essential" in the title of their book to underscore the link between successful schools and leaders' use of RESULTS coaching skills.

In *RESULTS Coaching: The New Essential for School Leaders*, Kee and Anderson, et al. point out that changes around and within schools require that leaders think and act in fundamentally different ways. Because it is essential that teaching and learning change to successfully prepare students for a world very different from the one we now inhabit, a different form of leadership is required that the authors call RESULTS coaching.

The way in which the future will be fundamentally different than the past was literally brought home to me recently when workers replacing the steps of my front porch found a horseshoe that had been beneath the old steps since they were put in place more than a century ago. My mind immediately turned to the world the horseshoe last saw when horses were as common in Ann Arbor as horseless carriages.

I imagined myself telling the German tradesmen who built the home at the turn of the 20th century about the world of the 21st century in which the horseshoe was again seeing the light of day. I showed them the small "digital camera" I was using to photograph the horseshoe and told them I was going to "upload" my photo to my "computer" and send it via the "Internet" to friends all over the world, all of which these tradesmen found quite bewildering, at least in my mind's eye.

I asked the 21st century workers who uncovered the horseshoe to return it to the place they found it before they poured the new steps, and I tried to imagine what the world would be like 50 or 100 years in the future when the horseshoe might again be found, a world in which the cumulative effects of successful, unrelenting waves of innovation will far exceed anything previously known to humankind. It was a task that far exceeded the boundaries of my imagination.

While the accomplishments and nature of the next century may exceed my imagination, it is, nonetheless, the world for which we are preparing students who will live to see the 22nd century. En route, they will have experiences we can only anticipate in broad outline. And the task of teachers and school leaders is to prepare students to successfully navigate that world as engaged citizens and economic contributors, a task that in my view represents a moral imperative for this and future generations of educators.

Ron Heifitz uses the term "adaptive challenge" to describe such daunting tasks for which no guidebook exists. They require that school leaders shape cultures and create systems that continuously invent and reinvent teaching and learning across teachers' careers spans, or as the authors point out in their Introduction, "that the school principal is the force and catalyst to make positive results happen."

Leading school communities to create continuous improvement in teaching and learning to prepare students for a largely unknowable future requires transformation built upon a paradigm shift in leadership the authors describe this way: "Being a 'coach-leader' is a key competency, a new identity, for anyone in the business of developing teachers, staff, and students. . . . On a daily basis, coaching challenges the leader to walk the talk—to continuously grow and improve before modeling and leading others."

THE NEW LEADERSHIP ESSENTIALS

The authors provide a thorough description of the mind and skill sets that comprise the "new essentials." Coach leaders, they say, possess language and communication skills founded in high levels of emotional and social intelligence that "realize the critically important shift in leadership from telling and directing to creating meaning and empowering confidence and ownership in others. This new mindset is a new identity of the leader as a transparent, respectful partner, co-creator, and supporter of others through committed listening, believing, affirming, and eliciting the best in others."

Coach leaders, the authors point out, use their language and communication skills to engage in "conversations that will dramatically impact results and outcomes while building and maintaining trust and relationships." These conversations, according to the authors, are founded on leaders' clarity, respect, integrity, and sense of appreciation. And they have as their goal the development of deep understanding, a shift from disabling beliefs to those attuned with the school community's most important intentions and values, and the communication of deep respect for the capacity of the school community to take action on a small number of highly-leveraged fronts.

Coach leaders offer hope and release energy founded in their deeply held belief in the school community's capacity to create its desired future. They explain, "Whether we are working with students or teachers and staff, the critical new essential is believing in people's potential in such a way that we stop telling them what to do and teach them how to decide what is the best action to take or task to do given the standards, the expectations, the rules, or the outcomes."

Because the "new essentials" require a substantial shift in the thinking and practice of many educational leaders, they are founded in the acquisition of new habits of mind and behavior. The development of such habits requires intention, a great deal of practice, and a way of determining the effectiveness of the new habits in the continuous improvement of teaching, learning, and relationships in schools. While creating new leadership habits requires effort, discipline, and persistence, leaders have no other choice if schools are to enable young people to thrive in the unknown world that is their future.

—*Dennis Sparks*
Emeritus Executive Director
Learning Forward (formerly the National Staff Development Council)

Preface

In 1985, when Kathy (Harwell) Kee attended her first Cognitive Coaching training, she sensed she had found a special home. She intuitively knew that this new coaching offered the potential of accelerating the productivity and results of her fellow educators. Kathy's passion for coaching was introduced, shared, and taught to her fellow authors. Kathy began by training teachers to coach each other, which led to the first state alternative appraisal process that used Cognitive Coaching as the process for teacher self-reflection, evaluation, and goal setting.

Through the years, more teachers flocked to this process that respected their knowledge and skills and honored their ability to think and problem solve. Soon, the process moved to principals and central office administrators. In the ensuing years, many districts found Cognitive Coaching to be a valuable process and utilized its concepts and skills in many ways. But as is so often the case, once the initiating administrator moved to other positions or districts, the commitment was lost to the traditional, more objective process and method of goal setting and growth appraisal.

Many lessons were learned in those early years. The first lesson was how using a coaching process demonstrated respect and connected teachers to reflect on their goals and growth. Teachers valued the opportunity to talk about teaching and learning using this reflective process. A second lesson was that quality thinking and processing takes time. While scarce, the time spent pays dividends in building relationships and results. Another realization is that change is hard, and when barriers arise or difficulties are encountered, the tendency to return to old patterns is predicable. Brain research of today confirms the restraining nature of people and their systems to pull back to what is most comfortable. The most important lesson of all is that once people experience the power of coaching, they unleash their potential for great change and success. Neuroscience has provided the proof that the nature of coaching and its impact on the brain holds the most important avenue for deep change and learning. Therefore, coaching is our new *essential*.

Each of us as authors has experienced, first hand, the power of coaching and has realized our life's purpose is this work. Our dream is that all educators will have the experience of having a coach who supports their leadership transformation from directing and judging to RESULTS Coaching.

HOW WE CAME TO BE

In the spring of 2000, Learning Forward, or, as it was known then, the National Staff Development Council (NSDC), selected 27 educators from around the nation to participate in a special training with Dave Ellis and his Brande Foundation for the purpose of becoming coaches to educators. This training was designed to provide the knowledge and skills to support principals, superintendents, and other school leaders in successfully meeting the challenges of working with diverse student populations, high stakes accountability, and the ever increasing demands of school leadership. When the experience ended, some knew this was their life's work. Those educators are an alliance of dedicated professional educational leaders from across the United States—now known as Coaching for Results—who are trained in leadership coaching processes. Coaching for Results, Incorporated is dedicated to helping school leaders achieve extraordinary results, both professionally and personally. We support and foster confident, competent, courageous school leaders who lead their schools to high performance.

Notes

- Throughout this book, readers will thrill in the success stories and coaching experiences of the authors. Each one is based on our work that has taken place over a decade. Because of the confidential integrity of coaching, the names and districts have been changed, but the words and examples are real.
- Educators in this book who receive coaching are called clients. They are superintendents, assistant superintendents, principals, central office staff, assistant principals, and teachers.

Acknowledgments

To Robert Garmston and Art Costa for their gift of Cognitive Coaching. Special appreciation for being Kathy's first teachers and friends. Your legacy will live forever in the legacies of countless educators.

To Dennis Sparks for bringing Life Coaching to a national group of educators in 1999. The collaboration with the Brande Foundation and Dave Ellis offered a coaching experience to hundreds of superintendents and principals over several years and began our commitment to promote coaching for school leaders across our country.

To the hundreds of superintendents and school leaders who have provided the opportunity for us to realize our vision. Their courage, trust, and confidence have provided our stories and our most profound learning.

To the hundreds of coaches, authors, and consultants who over 10 years have focused our work and thinking on the critical need for coaching in schools; our bookshelves are full of their books; our heads are spinning with great thoughts and connections.

To Reba Schumacher, our friend and coaching colleague, whose support, essential stories, heart-centered knowledge, and joyful collaboration will forever be cherished.

To Coaching for Results, Inc., Marceta Reilly and Diana Williams, and all our colleagues who share our passion and who contributed experiences and insights to this work.

To Dave Ellis and his wonderful team of coaches who ushered us into the professional world of coaching, and to Dave, who so generously gave us his strategies and tools to expand our work and especially his three by five cards to dream big and without limits—then double it!

To David Rock, author of Quiet Leadership, who connected the dots to our beliefs and neuroscience evidence and who inspires us with every article.

Shirley Hord, scholar emerita, who continually asked, "How do you know?" and collected the data that supported the findings of our early work.

Francine Campone, MCC, ICF for fine tuning our skills and work toward our ICF certification and continually supporting our growth through professional development.

Ginger Cockerham, MCC, ICF for supporting our journey by providing professional growth to us in the beginning stages of our work that accelerated and focused our goals and skills.

NSDC for feeding our minds for years, linking us all together in coaching, and providing connections to systems to do our work.

Our editor, Leslie Blair, for helping us successfully navigate the process of preparing our work for publishing.

Our proofreader, Connie Dodd, for her generous time and tender feedback.

To our families who generously supported us and gave us the time to complete this dream—our own three by five goal card!

Publisher's Acknowledgments

Corwin gratefully acknowledges the contributions of the following individuals:

Jennifer Baadsgaard, Principal
Ed White Middle School
San Antonio, TX

Randel Beaver, Superintendent
Archer City ISD
Archer City, TX

Marie Blum, Superintendent
Canaseraga Central School District
Canaseraga, NY

Margarete Couture, Principal
South Seneca Central School
    District
Interlaken, NY

Robert Frick, Superintendent
Lampeter-Strasburg School District
Lampeter, PA

Michelle Gayle, Principal
James S. Richards High School
Tallahassee, FL

Kathy Tritz-Rhodes, Principal
Marcus-Meriden-Cleghorn Schools
Marcus and Cleghorn, IA

About the Authors

 **Kathryn (Harwell) Kee** is an International Coach Federation (ICF) Professional Certified Coach (PCC) and conflict mediator. With coaching as her first love and passion, currently Kathy is honored to serve as a leadership coach and consultant to numerous elementary, middle, and high school principals, assistant principals, and teachers in schools in Texas and across the United States. As an educational consultant, she is a national trainer for Cognitive Coaching; Adaptive Schools, Carolyn Downey's Walk-Through for Reflective Practice; Supervisory Language for Accelerating Results, with Dr. John Crain; Mentoring and Coaching Skills from Teachers to Superintendents, Powerful Communication Skills, and multiple educational leadership topics. A special joy for Kathy is her service as an adjunct professor at the University of North Texas where she supports new promising administrators during their final classes and internships.

Kathy served as assistant superintendent for curriculum and instruction, director of staff development, director of gifted education, campus instructional dean, department head, reading specialist and teacher in rural, urban, military, and suburban school districts during her 40 years in education. She has a BA in psychology and sociology and a MEd from Louisiana State University and Southern University. In addition, she has worked on a doctorate in public administration at the University of Texas at Arlington and received numerous certifications from Texas Woman's University, University of Oklahoma, and Southwest Missouri University.

Her greatest honors include serving as the first president and executive director of the Texas Staff Development Council and serving as board member and president of Learning Forward (formerly the National Staff Development Council) from 1994–1999. She is a founding member of Coaching For Results, Inc., and serves as one of its board directors, responsible for the Teaching and Learning Division. She serves as a trainer and mentor to coaches. Kathy has written numerous articles, including, "Say It Like a Coach" for NSDC and "Why the Brain Needs Coaching" for *Coaching School Results*.

Karen Anderson is an ICF Professional Certified Coach (PCC) and learning facilitator who is passionate about coaching educators to higher levels of performance. Karen's clients report greater clarity, goal achievement, and improved results for staff and students. She has been a public school educator for over 41 years. Her expertise is facilitating groups focused on working collaboratively to discover solutions and improve processes and delivery systems. She is a national trainer and currently serves as an adjunct faculty member at Texas A&M University-Commerce. From 1996–2004, she served as the executive director of the Texas Staff Development Council and was recognized as the recipient of their Lifetime Achievement Award.

Karen is a founding member of Coaching for Results, Inc. (CFR) and is currently responsible for the Teaching and Learning Division. Her responsibilities include the design, development, and delivery of internal and external professional learning experiences that provide ongoing growth for CFR coaches and those desiring to become coaches. She also serves as a CFR trainer, facilitator for coaching labs, and mentor for those developing their coaching skills.

Karen completed Dave Ellis' life coach training from Falling Awake, is an active member of the ICF, and holds certification as a PCC. She is also a member of the North Texas–ICF Chapter. She has authored numerous articles, including "Coaching for High Performance" and "Leadership Coaching for Principals."

Vicky Dearing is an experienced educator, leadership coach, and consultant with more than 42 combined years of successful experience in both public education and the business world. She holds a MEd from Texas Woman's University, with a major in supervision and a minor in gifted education. She has been a teacher, central office administrator, and principal and has been recognized at the district, state, and national levels. She has directed gifted and talented programs for two school districts and served as elementary principal for three schools, leading each to increased academic achievement and state recognition. One school received a National Blue Ribbon School of Excellence. After retiring from public education, Vicky moved into the business arena working for a national education company. During her eight years with the company, she advanced from National Director of Training to Senior Vice President of Training and Implementation responsible for the development and delivery of training and implementation services to teachers across the United States while working directly with some of the largest school districts in our nation. After retiring from her work with the national education company, she served as lead evaluator and co-evaluator of products associated with a large urban education service center. Recently, she served as a consultant and member of the leadership team for the American College of Education.

Vicky is passionate about learning and living a life of intention and integrity. She is a committed member of her church, serving in multiple leadership roles, including chair of the Church Administrative Council and facilitator of women's Bible studies, which led to the challenging and rewarding opportunity to provide training to incarcerated women. Having studied under Art Garmston and Bob Costa and Coaching School Results, she has been involved with coaching for more than 12 years. While serving as a principal, Vicky was a district level trainer for Cognitive Coaching and also served on the district level team that implemented a coaching alternative to the state level teacher evaluation process. Vicky describes her work in coaching as a "transformational and life changing." She says, "Once you experience the real power of coaching, you're hooked for life." As a CSR Coach, she coaches school leaders from across the United States and Canada and consistently receives high ratings for her work. She serves on the Board of Directors of Coaching For Results, Inc. and is certified as a Professional Certified Coach (PCC) through the International Coach Federation.

Edna Harris has worked as an educator in several large suburban school districts for more than 30 years. She has experience as a teacher, supervisor, reading coordinator, principal, and staff developer. She has developed curriculum and training materials for several organizations and school districts. She has presented training sessions for numerous professional organizations and universities, primarily in the area of implementing effective staff development programs.

In 1992–1993, Edna served as president of the Texas Staff Development Council. She was named Texas Staff Developer of the Year in

1997. She has served on a variety of national- and state-level task forces designed to promote effective staff development practice, including teacher certification and legislative policies. In addition to the growth opportunities she has had as a consultant and school district administrator, she serves in a variety of leadership roles in her church. She continually strives to enhance her skills in the areas of group facilitation, understanding and sharing the link between teacher training and student success, coaching, and leadership development. Edna is a founding member of Coaching for Results and is certified through International Coach Federation as a Professional Certified Coach (PCC).

 **Frances Shuster** has been professionally coaching for more than 10 years in the areas of leadership development, transformational change, executive effectiveness, and strategic thinking and planning. In addition to guiding her clients to develop insights, she partners with them to co-design positive actions that lead to acceleration of goal achievement.

She is a founding member and president of the nonprofit organization, Coaching For Results, Inc., an active member of the ICF, 2006 president of the ICF, North Texas Chapter, and credentialed as a PCC. She is a faculty member and supervising coach in the University of Texas at Dallas School of Management ICF Accredited Coach Training Program and a coach in the Executive MBA program.

In addition to coaching, Frances is an international presenter and expert facilitator. Prior to becoming a coach, she was a director of staff development and a national literacy consultant. She has written and delivered numerous leadership training programs. Publications include tips booklets for teachers—*Effective Parent Conferences and Time Management for Teachers.*

Frances obtained her BS from the University of Texas in Austin and her MEd from the University of North Texas. She received her coach training from the Center for Cognitive Coaching, Breakthrough Enterprises, and Coach U.

Introduction

"There are two ways of spreading light: to be the candle or the mirror that reflects it."

—Edith Wharton

"It is essential in relationships and all tasks that we concentrate only on what is most significant and important."

—Soren Kierkegaard

The modern world has brought many new essentials to our 21st-century way of life. What was previously not widely known or yet invented 100 years ago has now become essential. The examples are endless.

A United States passport was previously required only for travel to continents outside of North America. Current world conditions and border issues have now made a passport essential for travel even to our bordering countries of Canada and Mexico.

Paper tickets are now rare when traveling by air. What was once essential is now outmoded. E-tickets are everywhere. By checking in online and printing our own boarding pass, we can move to the front of the line for upgrades or notifications of flight cancelations. Obtaining an e-ticket and checking in online are essential to a smoother air-travel experience.

When cell phones first became available during the last part of the 20th century, they were a luxury. Now, they are essential to 21st-century life in all parts of the globe—even the most remote and least populated. Public phones and pay phones have literally disappeared. Heaven help us if our cell phones die, get lost, or are left behind. Being accessible by cell phone 24/7 has become an essential expectation in today's world.

For many, access to a latte has become a new essential, replacing the morning cup of coffee or tea. In fact, it's become so essential that Starbuck's is now a point of interest (POI) on our GPS (Global Positioning System).

Results, having always been important, have today become essential to survival. For years, small businesses have come and gone quickly for failing to achieve the needed financial results. In the last decade, schools have confronted a commendable new reality where it is no longer acceptable for some students to fail or for only a few to succeed. Our nation is committed to high quality education for all children. One might wonder how anyone would not be committed to this noble result. It becomes clear that embracing the lofty expectation depends on a specific class or a specific teacher. When my class or my school has numerous children with no parental involvement or supervision; when my class or my school has numerous children with no boundaries set at home for sleep, structure, behavior, or even drug use; when my class or school has several special-needs children who require special differentiated instruction; suddenly the word "results" goes from concern to anxiety and soon to a feeling of fear of responsibility for every child's mastery of learning. For the first time, the leader's job and identity is on the line, hanging on the success of every single child in less than 195 days. Is it right? Yes. Is the responsibility monumental? Yes, it is—in so many places and with so many children for so many teachers and principals. A "standardized test" has become a new essential; it has become high stakes accountability!

We celebrate Michael Fullan's moral imperative that we must get results in our schools today, and we know that the school principal is the force and catalyst to make positive results happen. In many instances, structures and processes for getting results have not changed in years or even decades. We seem to be dealing with the same issues over and over with new names and faces as the players. And the results stay the same.

A case in point is the story of Jana, one of our clients who is a principal. The story is shared by our colleague and coach, Reba Schumacher.

I had coached Jana for several months prior to her first assignment as a school principal. I had, in fact, coached her through the process of applying for and accepting that first principal position. Things were progressing predictably during her first few months (typically known as the honeymoon stage) in her new role. Then one day in the middle of March, Jana called my home office desperate for coaching. She began by listing the conditions and issues at her campus that were keeping her awake at night, and she was unsure of the best approach for addressing her situation. She went on to say, "I would love any advice or words of wisdom you can offer."

I asked Jana to tell me more, and she responded with a stream of frustrations beginning with, "I know great schools are made of great teams. Out of my five grade-level teams, three have positive attitudes; however, two teams do not, and those two teams are really putting a damper on the entire campus." She went on to lament that adults were not following district and campus policies and guidelines, including violating the adult dress code, consistently arriving late for work, and allowing children free rein of the campus. She added that since adults were frequently violating the rules, students did not seem to be compelled to follow the rules either. Even though teachers were reluctant to enforce the student-behavior policy, they did expect Jana to single-handedly control student classroom behavior from the principal's office while simultaneously increasing the campus's crucially low adult and student attendance rates. She was now on a roll.

Without taking a breath, Jana launched into her next level of concerns, which revolved around the lack of challenging, engaged student learning and authentic assessments. She emphasized that ubiquitous and numerous worksheets and student art work created with dyed popcorn, paper streamers, and dried beans were not her idea of meaningful assessments. She mused that many of the teachers seemed hesitant to raise standards for students, fearful that it would require more work from them.

Just as suddenly as she had begun, Jana stopped, seemingly exhausted from the months of bottling her concerns. As I offered the gift of silence, waiting to see if any other concerns were coming, she pleaded tentatively, "I need your advice. Did you ever go through the same things?"

In a flash, I thought back to a day 21 years earlier as I sat with my superintendent, filling her ears with the same stories of sleepless nights and lack of teacher accountability. Because life is a series of ironies, I am now coaching Jana, who is currently the principal of the school where I began my first principalship 22 years earlier. As I reflected on her litany of concerns, I realized that in the midst of many technological and life progressions, some things in schools never change. Jana is reliving the challenges I had faced all those years ago.

What is changing is what I offer to Jana today that I did not offer even six years ago. The difference is coaching, my new essential. When she asks me for advice and words of wisdom, I offer committed listening, powerful questioning, and a space for her to create her own solutions.

This story invites us to consider the degree to which schools have substantially changed through the decades. It reinforces the definition of insanity: "Keep doing what you've always done and expecting different results." Leaders' mindsets and actions must profoundly change in order to positively affect the dynamics for success inside schools.

What's at stake? At stake is a future full of hope and possibility, resulting from a high quality education for all students. As schools serve more and more students from all walks of life—from the poorest to the most privileged, from the most challenged to the most gifted, from the most unlikely to the most likely—high quality schools are *essential*. High performing schools keep hope and possibility alive and create the necessary energy for preparing students to contribute to our society. The dedicated school leader's mission is to achieve different and broader results. Because school leaders have the responsibility to deliver results, what is required is a new essential skill of leadership.

Until the individuals who lead our schools develop the attitudes, behaviors, and skills necessary to elicit the best from each staff member and student, lasting change is elusive. Schools must become, from top to bottom, places where everyone is respected for what is possible from within. Schools need to move from places that "correct" to places that "connect" for development and growth. Coaching provides the venue, rich with language and skills, to seek, find, and develop the best within. Coaching offers the pathway for new responses, new awareness, new results. Winston Churchill reminds us that "It's not enough to do our best; we must do what is required." *Powerful coaching skills are required; they are essential to transforming individuals, schools, and entire organizations.*

RESULTS Coaching is the new essential for today's school leaders. Being a "coach-leader" is a key competency, a new identity, for anyone in the business of developing teachers, staff, and students. Because coaching language and skills require alignment of the integrity of one's attitudes and behaviors, coaching continually strengthens emotional intelligence for self-awareness, self-control, motivation, social awareness, and skill enhancement. On a daily basis, coaching challenges the leader to walk the talk—to continuously grow and improve before modeling and leading others.

Why RESULTS Coaching?

RESULTS Coaching . . .

- is the navigation system for impacting new thinking and solution finding at every level of school systems.
- creates new pathways in the brain, resulting in new energy and motivation.

- teaches the power of articulated clear and established standards and expectations that are the springboard for the majority of conversations.
- teaches language that builds trust and scaffolds confidence and competence.
- models thinking processes that move people to action.
- focuses on goal clarity and multiple options leading to action and achievement.
- slows us down while allowing the brain to speed up. Reflection equals connections!
- promotes discovery and the illumination of the brilliance within each of us.

RESULTS Coaching offers a mnemonic scaffold or blueprint that guides a leader through conversations that will dramatically impact results and outcomes while building and maintaining trust and relationships. This scaffold creates the "turbo charge" to both small and dramatic changes that create new models of professional collaboration and ultimately results for kids. The model accelerates deep thinking and unleashes multiple ways to succeed. Quite simply it is as follows:

R . . . Resolve to change results

E . . . Establish goal clarity

S . . . Seek integrity

U . . . Unveil multiple pathways

L . . . Leverage options

T . . . Take action

S . . . Seize success

In the upcoming chapters, new pathways for joyful success and rewarding results will be revealed. Our commitment and deep passion for coaching as a process that holds the promise to transform leaders in powerful and essential ways will become transparent. We believe that if you resolve to embrace, practice, and integrate the ideas and processes in this book, your leadership will be transformed, and you will achieve the results you want for yourself, your teachers, and your students.

Chapter 1. The Coach Leader Mindset: The Cognitive Shift prepares the leader for a paradigm shift in supervisory roles and explains how and what the leader can be and do to transform a school community.

Leaders will realize the critically important shift in leadership from telling and directing to creating meaning and empowering confidence and ownership in others. This new mindset is a new identity of the leader as a transparent, respectful partner, co-creator, and supporter of others through committed listening, believing, affirming, and eliciting the best in others.

Chapter 2. Intention: Being Purposeful focuses on the power of intention and provides a new way of thinking that moves our intentions to amazing actions as a result of being purposeful. Using the Intention Pyramid as a tool for moving from intention through attention to action, leaders will realize how being intentional and purposeful dramatically impact targeted results. How we "show up" in our work is examined through the lens of "having," "being" and "doing."

Chapter 3. Leader as Coach: The RESULTS Coaching Navigation System presents a powerful metaphoric visual of the RESULTS Coaching Navigation System that provides evidence of the significant complexity of the art and skill of coaching. Each component of this intricate system creates clarity for leaders as they walk in the role of today's Coach Leader. Each component part is examined in a way that will provide understanding, examples, and benefits to the leader and those they inspire and support.

Chapter 4. Language: The Essential Connector educates readers about the power of a new language for leaders. The four concepts of levels of language, speaking the truth, making and keeping promises, and requests versus requirements hold the potential for dramatically changing the way leaders do their work. When understood and used intentionally, these concepts become the essential connector for today's leader.

Chapter 5. Communication Skills: The New Essentials delves into the essential skills of coaching. Readers will learn about the communication skills of committed listening, paraphrasing, presuming positive intent resulting in powerful questions, and reflective feedback. For each skill, an opportunity for practice and deeper understanding is provided. To gain total integration of these new essentials, practice is a must!

Chapter 6. The Leader's GPS: Guided Pathways for Success introduces a tool, which like the GPS in a car, becomes the roadmap for powerful conversations. Whether the conversation is solution focused, goal focused, planning focused, or reflection focused, readers can follow the pathway to the intended destination with permission to recalculate when needed!

Chapter 7. RESULTS Coaching Plan for Action: Essential for Unleashing Promise and Possibility helps build the leader's internal resourcefulness and capacity to impact change. The RESULTS Coaching framework is described as a tool for transforming work in schools. It causes conversations to focus on the most important outcomes in a way that brings clarity, insight, and energy to action.

Our goal is to provide a guide that will inspire and motivate school leaders to commit to the use of new essential coaching behaviors for greater results for their schools and relationships.

> "When educators speak with clarity, possibility, and accountability, and when they interact with others in respectful and mutually satisfying ways, they empower themselves and their organizations to produce extraordinary results.
>
> Such interactions add purpose, joy, and energy to our lives and the lives of those with whom we relate and increase the organization's capacity to engage in demanding, complex tasks and to sustain that effort over time."
>
> —*Dennis Sparks*

The Coach Leader Mindset   1

THE COGNITIVE SHIFT

If you picked up this book on coaching, you are probably searching for a more influential and inspiring way to interact with others to achieve the expected high level of results for students today. As a school leader, you have perhaps functioned in a variety of capacities—mentor, advisor, supervisor, counselor, facilitator, and consultant. You might be curious about this role of coach. How does it compare to these other roles? You may be asking, "What is coaching all about?"

Roles that have been present in our business for years include the following:

- Supervisor
- Consultant
- Presenter or Teacher
- Mentor
- Advisor
- Specialist
- Counselor

Every role has the intention of helping the student, the teacher, or a staff member to more successfully function in their roles or responsibilities. Sadly, many of the terms and titles have become muddled with a wide variety of uses and purposes. While all the roles have a specific intent and purpose, there is only one role that can enhance all roles—that of the coach.

As schools today prepare students to compete in this new world that is interconnected, ever changing, and dynamic, new skills and intentions are required. We must prepare students to be thinkers who think what they have never thought before, who do what they have never done before, and who can be what they have never been before. We must prepare them to find solutions to questions never faced before; we must prepare them to assess multiple forms of information and draw accurate and new conclusions; and we must prepare them to communicate effectively and respectfully in many languages with many different points of view, attitudes, beliefs, or backgrounds. This kind of education requires new habits of mind, new language, and new skills. It requires the mindset of coaching.

Webster's defines mindset as a "frame of mind; mental or intellectual climate." The mindset of coaching often relates to our past knowledge of and experience with athletic coaching. We have incredible stories of amazing coaches who influenced and motivated others to incredible results. We bring that spirit, energy, passion, and knowledge to our new role of "thinking" coach in schools, a mindset that believes deeply in the potential of others and believes that hard change is possible if we provide time and structures for focus, repetition, reflection, and reflective feedback.

One challenge for the "new essential coach leader" is the "way-we-have-always-done-it" attitudes and beliefs. The following gorilla story provides a powerful example of how hardwired behaviors and actions become.

This story starts with a cage containing five gorillas and a large bunch of bananas hanging above some stairs in the center of the cage. Before long, a gorilla will go to the stairs and start to climb toward the bananas. As soon as he touches the stairs, all of the gorillas are sprayed with cold water. After a while, another gorilla will make an attempt with the same result: all are sprayed with cold water. Every time a gorilla attempts to retrieve the bananas, each is sprayed with cold water until he quits trying and leaves the bananas alone.

One of the original five gorillas is removed from the cage and replaced with a new one. The new gorilla sees the bananas and starts to climb the stairs. To his horror, all the other gorillas attack him. After another attempt and attack, he knows that if he tries to climb the stairs, he will be assaulted. Next, the second of the original five gorillas is replaced with a new one. The newcomer goes to the stairs and is attacked. The previous newcomer takes part in the punishment with enthusiasm.

Next, the third original gorilla is replaced with a new one. The new one makes to the stairs and is attacked as well. Two of the four gorillas that beat him have no idea why they were not permitted to climb the stairs or why they are participating in the beating of the newest gorilla.

After the fourth and fifth original gorillas have been replaced, all the gorillas, which were sprayed with cold water, are gone. Nevertheless, no gorilla will ever again approach the stairs. Why not?

Because that's the way it's always been done.

Source: Excerpted from "A Trainer's Companion: Stories to Stimulate Reflection, Conversation, Action" by Walter R. Olsen and William A. Sommers, PhD. (2004). Reprinted with permission. All rights reserved. www.ahaprocess.com

THE COGNITIVE SHIFT

The mindset of coach leader shifts reframes from responding "how we have always done it" with new possibilities never thought before. A coach leader is one who will challenge his or her educators to break away from the norm, to be creative, to use their imagination, to initiate something new, to act in new ways. A coach leader is a facilitator of a new mindset that is critically needed in schools today. Principals and teachers must model this new mindset for a generation of students for whom it will mean survival.

The coach leader mindset reflected in the chapters of this work include the following:

Shift From		To
Listening to respond with one's own point of view		**Listening to understand** with others' point of view
		Listening to hold up standards-based expectations
Shift From		**To**
Using Language		**Using Language**
Not to correct	but	to connect
Not to confront	but	to respect
Not to tell	but	to bring self-insight
Not to provide constructive advice	but	to encourage other's assessment
Not to ask questions relying on familiar habits	but	to ask questions that provide clarity and stimulate great thinking

The coaching mindset is about using powerful new strategies, skills, and scaffolds that support another human being in reaching his or her greatest potential and accomplishments. The authors of this work desire to rekindle and reconnect us to our deep belief in people. We see this so clearly when our country is threatened and people rally to fight to defend our basic freedoms; when there is a natural disaster, and people everywhere open their homes and wallets to help those in danger or need; when a child goes missing and citizens step up to seek and find our most precious. Where is it more essential to believe in others than in our schools? As teachers, we know our ability to teach and influence is greatly diminished if we do not believe in our students, regardless of the challenges each may have. The same is true of leaders. We must believe in the potential best of every member of our staff. Either we must hire those who share our vision and goals, or when we begin a new leadership of a campus or district, communicate at the start our beliefs or expectations so all staff members have an opportunity to choose if this workplace is aligned with the beliefs of the leader or system. If there is someone who does not adhere to the expectations or standards of our system, our coach mindset is not to demean or belittle but to offer workplaces more aligned with the individual's beliefs and goals. Moreover, for those who have similar goals and beliefs, the coach leader's belief in them must be seen always in actions and language. Some examples might include the following:

- "Knowing this is a staff who always puts what is best for our kids first—what targets do we want for this year that align with our beliefs?"
- "Since we have a covenant with one another that 'failure is not an option' for our kids, what strategies are you thinking will take us to the next level?"
- "I know how important it is to you that your students have a strong foundation in math, so I'm looking forward to hearing about your next steps to accelerate their skill development."

LESSONS FROM NEUROSCIENCE

The work of David Rock (2006) and the field of neuroscience offer research that has brought new discoveries about the way people think. We have recognized that if we really want to increase results and improve performance, our leadership language must be refined to increase and improve people's thinking about their work. For years, we have known that the brain has trillions of layers of connective wiring. We often thought that as we learn new things, that wiring is, over time, replaced with new wiring. Today, we know that the wiring always remains. As we learn, we are creating new wiring that informs our emotions and actions. The bad news is that change is difficult because we cannot change the wiring; we must change the thinking about that wiring, and in doing so, we create new wiring with new behaviors. The good news is that new wiring can be created that provides connections with new choices for thinking and behaviors. It just takes time, repetition, and positive feedback (Rock, 2006).

Think about the student who was repeatedly told by his parents and teachers as he was developing into a young person that he was not very smart. Then at a pivotal time in this young person's life, a teacher lovingly peels away the layers of insecurity and introduces the student to a special gift or talent he never knew he had. He soars in his knowledge and skills and goes to college and into a vocation. As a young man, when the boss reprimands him for some mix up or problem, the young man perceives the boss's words in such a way that his brain goes directly back to when he was a child. His insecurities reemerge and replace his confidence with doubt and a sense of failure. Through the good fortune of a special teacher's influence, our student was creating new wiring about his confidence and capabilities. However, always lurking deep in the brain is the old wiring of insecurity that will emerge when the environment or language of fear and doubt reconnects to that "old time and place" wiring.

Another example is that of the smoker. After smoking for many years, the person learns about the damage to her health and long life. She decides she wants the health benefits more than the addiction of smoking, so she quits. Her habits and behaviors change as she builds new wiring for a healthy life style. One evening after dinner with a group of old friends, some people light up. Instantly, she feels the urge and desire to smoke. The environment and old habits rekindle the old wiring.

THE ESSENTIAL MINDSET

There is a mindset about coaching. People are attracted to coaching because they believe in the capabilities of people—those talents and abilities that are often unknown even to the person. Coaching draws to it those who either believe deeply in the potential of others or have witnessed transformation within themselves or others. Coaching offers a safe place to think, to reflect, to speak truthfully, to ask questions—about self and others. Very few places is that a possibility in this world. The authors' mindset questions why the environment of education is not this place.

What has happened along the way that changed the halls of learning to a road race to accountability? We know part of the answer. The answer is that along the way, our egos forgot that our focus was the children, not the adults. We celebrate that the difficult journey of accountability in education means every child will experience meaningful teaching and learning, we celebrate that no children are left behind, and we celebrate that there are no more excuses for why every child does not learn at high levels. Now is the time when we must scaffold and support those with the responsibility to teach and motivate while they inspire, care, and guide learners of all ages to a new place and time in society—a time when all children experience high levels of learning.

Our new world today, as so many have described (Gardner, 2006), is not like any we have ever known before. Our world is interconnected and interdependent. There is instantaneous knowledge and information. It is a world with its ubiquitous search engines, multipurpose devices, invisible banking, faceless relationships, paperless photos, satellite maps—all requiring knowledge and skills that before were for the few geeks, not for every person walking through the corridors of education. We are in this new world; we must act in new ways; we must respect differences and tolerate different points of view. We must talk to one another in new ways, as collaborators and partners, not workers or children.

Since the quest for the magic bullet has not turned up cures or even changes, let us return to the new basics of 21st-century knowledge. First, is a review of the new knowledge of how we learn and change and then a description of the type of intelligence required for this new world. In education, we have spent a decade sharing what we have learned about the brain, how the brain works, what it needs, why we forget, and what we need to remember. With all the information, presentations, trainings, and book studies, it shocks us when we see so little application of this groundbreaking knowledge. In the most recent years, neuroscience is teaching us the central ideas about how to change human behavior. Neuroscientists today are providing information to us that has the power to fundamentally rewrite the rules for nearly every human endeavor involving thinking and learning, including how we educate our children, how we train our teachers, and how we develop our leaders (Rock, 2006).

The greatest challenge in education is positive openness to change—change in how we view teaching and learning, change in how we determine structures for learning, change in the roles in schools, change in the purpose of schooling, and on and on. In all our efforts to improve performance, we continue to focus on processes that produce results. Today, we know from neuroscientists that if we want to improve performance, we must improve thinking. Learning to think critically, problem solve, or predict outcomes rarely comes from a kit or program. It comes from real interactions that continually model the expectation of thinking to achieve results. Therefore, whether we are working with students or teachers and staff, the critical *new essential* is believing in people's potential in such a way that we stop telling them what to do and teach them how to decide what is the best action to take or task to do given the standards, the expectations, the rules, or the outcomes.

For years, we have known that the brain is a connection machine. Our thoughts, skills, and knowledge are big connectors or "maps" joined together via complex chemical and physical pathways. In that wonderful head on one's shoulders, is the wiring of the house. To understand the complexity of this wiring, add wiring for every memory, every word learned, every relationship, every experience, and every meaningful encounter. Thus, every thought, bit of information, skill, and capacity we have is a complex wiring of connections between pieces of information stored in many parts of the brain. When we are thinking, we process our thinking by comparing it to the trillions of pieces of information we previously have connected to thought patterns. Subconsciously, in a fraction of a second, we look for links for similar patterns. If we find a link, we create a new connection that becomes part of our massive brain wiring. Because the brain loves order, it will then reorder the connections in a way that makes us feel comfortable. We get a sense of the "gestalt." When this happens, we learn to predict and differentiate.

Remember our first cell phone with all the features and how we read the directions over and over or had someone show us all the features and how the phone worked. Now, you are probably on your fourth or fifth cell phone, which is more than just a phone. Notice how you glided through the operation of it and probably didn't have to read the directions or have much of a lesson on how to use it. That's your wonderful brain; it has ordered all those similarities from the simplest wiring into a huge core of "fiber optics." It's amazing, and oh, so taken for granted. When we make those connections and have those "aha" moments, we form new neural pathways, and with that new insight or epiphany, comes a burst of energy. When we make new pathways, we feel motivated to do something. Our eyes and face light up. There are small "aha" moments and big aha moments—simple things made clear or powerful revelations.

When we think new thoughts, work through a problem, unravel a delicate issue, or process a new skill, we are creating a new wiring or map in the brain. It is important to know that this is still the case if we are told what to do or what we should do. Unless that "to do" or "should do" fits with our wiring, we will have to expend the energy and effort to create our own map or new wiring. Today, neuroscientists are reporting the following:

1. To truly be committed to a new course of action, people need to have thought through issues or situations for themselves.

2. The act of having those moments of insight and epiphany give off a kind of energy needed for people to become motivated and willing to take action.

3. From the energy burst that has been expended on the new motivation, a degree of inertia can be expected.

This brain sequence also gives meaning to what Michael Fullan calls the "implementation dip," which is the small setback that often occurs when you begin implementing something new or a change in practice— the small setback in momentum during a change process. You must work through that "dip" or setback in order to make real progress. Eva Wong's (Wong & Heifetz, 2009) research at Harvard illustrates how coaching is the process that sustains the change during the critical time typically encountered before dropping or returning to old habits.

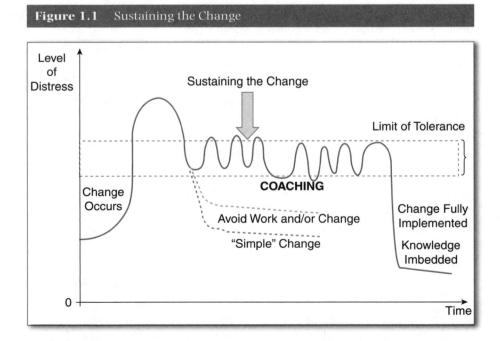

Figure 1.1   Sustaining the Change

Source: Adapted from Eva Wong, President, Top Human Technology Ltd. China and Ronald A Heifetz, Co-Director of Center for Public Leadership, Harvard University

This new learning about what is happening in the brain offers great insight for understanding. People aren't being difficult; they are not losing motivation; they are requiring the additional support moving from insight to continued action. Conversations about first steps and reflecting on potential and possibilities offer support during that natural tendency to lose motivation or guard for the many other initiatives pulling on time and effort.

MAKING A DIFFERENCE

Educators come into this field because they want to make a difference. What we say and do can change patterns in people. Throughout our history, there are thousands of stories of how teachers have impacted the lives of children. We all have a story. We hear the stories of others. Wouldn't one guess that a huge percentage of *Chicken Soup for the Soul* stories are about teacher or student situations?

Kathy Kee tells the story of her own child, who struggled in school, particularly in math, and the tutors and specialists who supported her during elementary, middle, and high school years. She was a child who did not think she was smart, but several teachers saw her organizational skills, her interpersonal skills, her flair for the dramatic. Even with the continual and constant belief in her from her parents, it was her theater teacher who, by putting her on stage in front of an audience and by giving her events to organize, changed her doubts to confidence. The more her teacher asked of her and told her she could do, the more she did. Even as she went off to college, even when she encountered obstacles with her math requirements, her belief in herself was now different. She knew she could, and therefore, she did. Her resume today includes television journalism, video editing, working for Steven Spielberg, working for Universal Music, and working for Steve Jobs as senior producer at Apple iTunes. What kept her going? She had been told she "could" so many times; she had been praised for her selected skills; she had learned that if she worked hard enough, she could do whatever she desired. Her brain was rewired through the positive language that surrounded her and the experiences given that supported her for success. As a result, this insecure child became the competent and capable adult she is today.

The new essential skill for educators today is a renewed mindset. It is a mindset of believing in the best of mankind. Our journey as educators has taken us through many concepts, theories, and studies that have ultimately formed and defined our core values about people.

When Kathy Kee began her career teaching remedial eighth graders—each seemingly eager to disrupt, disengage, and drop out—it was William Glasser's books from *Reality Theory* (1965) to *Choice Theory* (1998) that proposed a new approach to reduce school failure, an approach based on increased involvement, relevance, and thinking done by the student that brought success to an unlikely classroom. Learning that her students were trying to satisfy the genetically driven need for power that only human beings have, unlike all other living creatures, she was able to satisfy that power need by respecting her students through learning and using language of choice.

Somewhat later, Robert Greenleaf (2002) developed his concept of *Servant Leadership*, an approach and philosophy that asserts that when we look after the needs of followers, through our respect for their knowledge and thinking, employees reach their full potential and motivation toward the work. Steven Covey (2006) supports Greenleaf's concept as he reminds us, "the old rules of traditional, hierarchical, high-external-control, top-down management are being dismantled; they simply aren't working. This has changed the role of leader from one who drives results and motivation from the outside into one who is a servant leader—one who seeks to draw out, inspire, and develop the best and highest within people from the inside out. Leadership becomes an interdependent work rather than an immature interplay between strong, independent, ego-driven rules and compliant, dependent followers" (Covey, 2006, p. 1).

Another powerful strategy that has been successful with parents and teachers is *Love and Logic* (Fay & Foster, 2006). This approach of choice teaches that each intervention technique with children must preserve or enhance the child's self-concept. It is based on the research that one's view of self has significant motivational influences on behavior and cognition. The research further proposes that one's self-efficacy comes directly from one's cognitive appraisal of difficulty, one's abilities, and whether effort or struggle will yield success. The key concept guiding this program is that children only develop problem-solving skills under two conditions:

1. When they are required by the adults around them to think about and solve the problems they create

2. When the adults teach problem solving by modeling and instruction

A very important message for educators was found in the research examining the behavior change process: When the rigid applications of behavioral principles were applied to human relationships, there was no long-term, positive change. However, when behavioral principles of change were combined with high levels of trust, empathy, and warmth, students were more likely to be cooperative and copy the modeled behaviors of adults (Fay, 2010).

Another gift to Kathy Kee was the book *The Gift of the Promise* by Gary Smalley (1993) that takes sound biblical doctrine and applies common sense to how we should regard children. It offers a powerful model of how educators might view children—not as empty vessels but as promises to be unfolded.

Smalley reminds us, in one of his five elements, that words have incredible power to build us up or tear us down. It is critically important that children, husbands, wives, partners and co-workers hear words of love and acceptance. Words are powerful. *The Gift of the Promise* reminds us from the core of those we love most, the critical importance of seeing the promise in each other and in our children—our future.

In recent years, the evolutionary concept of Appreciative Inquiry (AI) has also become part of our mindset. AI deliberately seeks to discover people's exceptionality—their unique gifts, strengths, and qualities. It teaches that by recognizing and amplifying successes and strengths that already exist, new images of the future can be created that are so compelling that we consciously and unconsciously move toward it. As AI has come into schools, it has brought the fundamental approach of seeking to discover, honoring the person, and emphasing what works. The results are being seen at all levels, with individual students, teacher-student relationships, classrooms, schools, school districts, and communities.

One example in our world of high stakes accountability was at Shaw High School in urban northeast Ohio. Shaw's graduation rate was less that 65%, and less than 40% had passed the mandated test for graduation. A pilot project identified 25 students who had failed the exam at least three times and whose teachers gave no hope of graduating. Using the AI approaches to discover and spotlight the abilities each student already possessed, the AI consultant designed a rigorous program for their core subjects and study skills. At the end of the five-week, five-hour-a-day program, 19 of the 22 who stayed in the program passed the tests on the first try, and all said they were going on to college. The greatest insight of the pilot was that years of failure can be turned around when the focus is on strategies for successful achievement of a goal (Henry, 2003).

RESULTS Coaching aligns with the core value and philosophy of believing in the capabilities of people from quality schools to AI. Coaching aligns with what years and decades of research continues to support: that as human beings we do our best, think our best, and work our best when others believe in our best. Once evidence of our best stands on solid confidence of what we can rather than what we can't, the world becomes the recipient of our best—our students, our schools, our future.

Coaching is the new mindset to get us there. . . . Let's consider a few definitions that demonstrate this new mindset and inspire the opportunity to support others through the power of coaching.

- Coaching is partnering with clients in a thought-provoking and creative process that inspires them to maximize their personal and professional potential (International Coach Federation, 2009).
- Coaching is unlocking a person's potential to maximize his or her own performance. It is helping him or her to learn rather than teaching him or her (Whitmore, 2002, p. 8).
- Coaching is an ongoing relationship, which focuses on clients taking action toward the realization of their visions, goals, or desires. Coaching uses a process of inquiry and personal discovery to build the client's level of awareness and responsibility and provides the client with structure, support, and feedback. The coaching process helps clients both define and achieve professional and personal goals faster and with more ease than would be possible otherwise (ICF, 2009).
- Professional coaches provide an ongoing partnership designed to help clients produce fulfilling results in their personal and professional lives. Coaches help people improve their performances and enhance the quality of their lives (Ellis, 2006, p. 3).
- Coaches are trained to listen, to observe, and to customize their approach to individual client needs. They seek to elicit solutions and strategies from the client; they believe the client is naturally creative and resourceful. The coach's job is to provide support to enhance the skills, resources, and creativity that the client already has (International Coach Federation, 2009).
- Coaching closes the gap between where you are now and where you want to be. A coach points out things you can't see, motivates you to be your absolute best, and challenges you to go beyond where you normally stop. A coach helps you tap into your greatness and enables you to share it with the world (Miedaner, 2000, p. xvii).

Coaching believes and assumes that every person has untapped, inspiring potential. Within this core of potential—which is derived from past and present capacities of achievements, assets, innovations, strengths, elevated thoughts, opportunities, high moments, lived values, traditions, stories, expressions of wisdom, insights into the soul, visions of a future—all of these possible elements tap into the core of potential for change. Every person has potential, much like an inherent talent. Talents must be recognized and practiced in order to develop. As our confidence grows, our trust grows, and we begin to listen and to be open to other possibilities. This new energy, these new connections, insights, and "ahas" free people to be open to possibilities. When that happens, they become mobilized to change in ways never thought possible.

It has been evident that the role of a leader is to help people make their own connections and pathways. What we find is that most leaders spend their time and energy telling people what to do or doing the thinking for them. The "results" seem to keep education going in the same circle it has for hundreds of years. The new essential is a new mindset concerning how people change. This mindset is learning a set of skills for the coach leader, which does the following:

- Creates the environment and scaffolding for thinking in new ways
- Creates environments where deep thinking is sought and valued
- Facilitates processes of dialogue for deep thinking and expanding one's insights and experience from different points of view
- Presumes the best in thinking and doing in others
- Amplifies the strengths and successes of others
- Communicates clarity of visions and goals and supports the success of all who take up the call
- Holds up the standards and expectations of the profession to guide solutions and decisions
- Respects other values, models, and assumptions as effects of experience and knowledge
- Believes in the best self that is within each of us
- Uses language of appreciation, respect, possibility, and clear expectations and outcomes

The skill of coaching offers a vehicle where by every level of our society can connect with the best of self. As Barack Obama began his first days as the 44th President of the United States, he wrote a letter to his two daughters, Malia and Sasha. He said,

I ran for President because of what I want for you and for every child in this nation. I want all our children to go to schools worthy of their potential—schools that challenge them, inspire them, and instill in them a sense of wonder about the world around them. I want them to have a chance to go to college—even if their parents aren't rich. And I want them to get good jobs; jobs that pay well and give them benefits like health care, jobs that let them spend time with their own kids and retire with dignity. . . . These are the things I want for you—to grow up in a world with no limits on your dreams and no achievements beyond your reach, and to grow into compassionate, committed women who will help build that world. (Obama, 2009, p. 2)

The world described is the world courageous and dedicated educators desire for all children. What will it take to get there? It will take a way of speaking and teaching to each other, a language of possibility and belief in each and every child in our world.

SUMMARY

RESULTS Coaching—the new essential—offers a new (or perhaps a renewed) mindset that is about honoring educators where they are and walking with them as they polish their brilliance toward accomplishment, competence, and unlimited results for our future, our children.

The essential mindset of the coach leader is to

- support another person taking action toward his or her goals;
- be a partner with another person to plan, reflect, problem solve, and make decisions;
- be nonjudgmental while giving reflective feedback;
- use highly effective skills of listening and speaking;
- focus on the assumptions, perceptions, thinking and decision-making process; and
- mediate resources, clarify intentions, and identify multiple options for self-directed learning and optimum results.

In order to have this mindset, it is nonnegotiable that the coach leader must

- believe in another's ability to grow and excel,
- recognize that "Advice is Toxic!" and
- use intentional language that aligns with his trust and belief in others.

All that is required is to

- set aside or suspend unproductive behaviors,
- see each person as whole and capable, and
- be a model of committed listening and speaking.

How prepared is your mindset to focus totally on another and support his or her goals?

Intention   2

BEING PURPOSEFUL

"We learn and grow and are transformed not so much by what we do but by why and how we do it. Each decision we make, each action we take, is born out of an intention."

—Sharon Salzberg

It appears the technological revolution is far from over. On any given day, we discover yet another way to interface with others across the globe via our computers. While social networking has been around for years, the emergence and ever growing popularity of social media platforms, such as My Space, Facebook, Plurk, LinkedIn, and others, began with the intention of connecting people. In reality, that intention has changed the face of how we interact and work in today's world because the scale of our possibilities for connection has been transformed from a small rather controlled group of contacts to the possibility of connections around the world.

Now, we are suddenly faced with a friend request, a recommended professional contact that we can accept or deny, the option of writing on someone's wall, posting a picture, completing a profile, keeping up with organizations by becoming a "fan" or a "follower," and so on. The options seem to be endless. So, how does one decide the level and degree of connection he or she wishes to have?

Just as with the creators of the platforms, intention is *essential* to our initial and ongoing decisions to engage. What is our purpose? Why are we using the platform? How will we personally connect and engage in this new way of "being" with others? What level of access do we want others to have with us personally? When we step back, intention becomes an *essential* driver of when, how much, and why we interact with social media—whether we want to obtain a solution, to share a personal story, to have a conversation with colleagues, to access technical assistance, or to post pictures of our family.

Likewise, intention has forever been an *essential* for the school leader. It shows up in the leader's resolve and determination to act in a certain way. Intention suggests clarity and greater deliberation to act and behave in specific ways. It presupposes a carefully calculated plan that is focused and goal directed.

From the moment you decided to become a school leader, at some level, you were acting on intention. Did you want to change the world? A specific school? The nature of how teaching and learning is approached in school settings? To see if what you knew intellectually about leadership and leading really worked in the real world? Or was it the next step in your journey as a human being in the world of work? Were there just simple pragmatic issues involved, such as higher pay?

Whatever the reasons for beginning this work as a school leader, your intentions for how you proceed matter each and every day. As a 21st-century leader, being purposeful about the results you expect and the best ways for achieving those results is an inherent expectation of your role. Being intentional means that you are prepared to respond in an effective manner before the need for that response occurs. Without intention, in critical moments, your response will most likely be the one you are most familiar or comfortable with rather than the one that will bring about the results you want.

The purpose of this chapter is to take a closer look at intention and the potential for how it can change the way we do our work. By examining the following three concepts, we will create clarity around the importance of *intention* as an *essential* for our work as leaders.

1. Having, doing, and being

2. Life purpose

3. The Pyramid of Intention

The following is an instrument offered for pre-assessment of your current status with regard to intention. Based on the descriptions provided, indicate a rating that best describes your current knowledge and practice around each indicator.

Intention Self-Assessment

	1	2	3	4	5	
I assume that everyone knows how we do things around here.	1	2	3	4	5	I set clear expectations about desired results and make overt agreements about ways we work together.
I frequently make decisions or take action impulsively and then deal with what happens.	1	2	3	4	5	I seek and attain clarity about intended outcomes and communicate my intentions to others.
I hold my thoughts and feelings closely, only sharing with a few close colleagues.	1	2	3	4	5	I share intentions and feelings openly, which frees up energy and expands possibilities.
I tolerate mediocrity by couching my language in vagueness and niceness and by skirting issues regarding less-than-desired performance of staff.	1	2	3	4	5	I intentionally and effectively address attitudinal, performance, or behavioral issues and create multiple pathways for positive change.
I focus on activities and reasons why it is not possible to achieve desired results.	1	2	3	4	5	I purposefully focus on results and accountability at every level in the organization.
I micromanage instead of leading. There's no leadership development.	1	2	3	4	5	I intentionally coach and delegate to develop high quality, future leaders.
As a leader, my job is to dispense advice.	1	2	3	4	5	I routinely seek input and involve people in goal setting and solution finding.
It's important that I convince others that my point of view and course of action are correct.	1	2	3	4	5	I explore multiple points of view and multiple options for action, which leads to better results.
I protect my staff from many of my leadership decisions, enabling them to do their jobs.	1	2	3	4	5	I share challenging situations with my staff, empowering them to contribute to the process of goal attainment.

HAVING—DOING—BEING

What leaders say and do is critically important. Yet another, often missed, aspect of leadership is how leaders "show up" to do their work. The most effective leaders bring intention to all three aspects of leadership and leading—having, doing, and being. They demonstrate congruence between their own values and the actions they engage in on a daily basis. There is a clear connection between who they are, the goals they set, the actions they take, and the results they attain.

Leading with intentionality and purpose means you make choices both long-term and in the moment that are aligned with who you are. Most of our choices fall into the categories of having, doing, and being.

Figure 2.1 Having, Doing, and Being

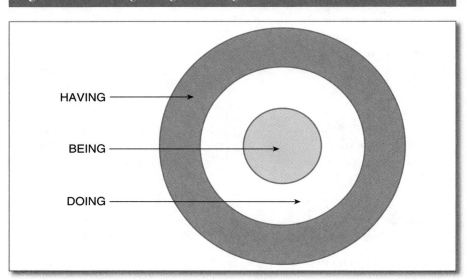

Source: Coaching School Results, 2009

Having refers to the tangibles and intangibles we want to "have" in our lives. Tangibles may include such choices as having a nice house or car, a good job, and the latest electronic gadgets, while the intangibles may be such choices as having a happy family, a caring and competent staff, a high performing team, or outstanding student learning and achievement.

Doing addresses choices about what we want to "do." It represents "doings" that include contributions and accomplishments and answers questions like, "What activities merit my time?" "What will be my contributions to the world or to my school?" "What have I accomplished or do I wish to accomplish for myself and/or my school or district?"

Being is who we want to "be." It emanates from our center or core; it is our essence, and it affects our choices of doing and having. Consideration of our being points to what we want to pay attention to as we achieve our goals. In addition, it is how we want to show up in our work. An example is our intent to be respectful when working with staff, students, and parents. Other examples include an intention to be thoughtful, calm, or balanced as we accomplish our goals.

What we *do* flows from who we *are* (our being). What we *have* flows out of what we do. Who we *are*—our being or essence—determines our *actions* (doing), and our actions determine what we *have.* In general, we are more aware of what we want to have and what we want to do than who we are or who we want to be.

"Being" merits our attention for the purpose of gaining clarity about who we are or want to be as leaders. Collectively, we as educators have perfected the art of goal setting (having) and generating strategic actions (doing). We have a very strong tendency to move directly from our goals to actions without consideration of our "being"—how we want to think, act, and behave in specific situations.

Consider the leader who has the goal of improving the morale of his school. With certainty about what he wants, he moves immediately to action by determining strategies for improvement of morale in his school. Without consideration of the question, "How do you want to be?" as he works to achieve this goal and takes action, the school leader may lose his grounding in the purpose and intention of the original goal. Without acknowledging his intent to be collaborative and to build trusting relationships as he improves morale, he can actually work in ways that interfere with the achievement of his goal. For example, being directive and telling others exactly what to do, can work at odds with improvement of morale.

We can illustrate this process by looking at the word *behaving*: *be— have—ing*; "Be" (our essence) "have" (goal) "ing" (actions). With clarity about what we want to have, we can purposefully determine how we want to be in order to achieve the goal. Then, we can choose the actions that are in alignment with who we want to be as we achieve our goal. Alignment of our thoughts, actions, and behaviors keeps us in integrity as we move toward goal attainment.

There are a number of ways to get clear about core being. One way is to invest time and thought into writing our life purpose. A brief and clear statement of purpose serves as a guide for all of our goals and actions. Life purpose defines our intention both moment to moment and long-term. It becomes the gauge or barometer for alignment of our actions with the things we hold as essential to our core being.

LIFE PURPOSE

Entire books, such as Rick Warren's (2002) *The Purpose Driven Life*, have been written about the significance of knowing and acting on one's life purpose. Executive coach Richard Leider (2004) offers this quotation:

"The purpose of life is to live a life of purpose."

Purpose is that which ignites the human spirit and makes our heart sing. It drives our full engagement in life and fills our soul. Discovering what we want in life comes from our clarity around life purpose. Knowing our life purpose becomes the touchstone for clear intentions and defines our being, doing, and having.

Finalizing a life purpose statement is not usually accomplished in one sitting. Revision and editing over time allows for deeper reflection and greater clarity. Your life purpose creates the big picture that answers the question, "Why am I here?" Here are some possibilities:

- My purpose is to live, love, and laugh.
- My purpose is to serve.
- My purpose is to ensure that all students have opportunities for success.
- My purpose is _____.

Reflection

Take a moment to be intentional about writing or tweaking your life purpose statement.

My purpose is . . . .

_____

_____

_____

_____

While being aware of our overarching purpose is critical, there is also great value in identifying purposes for various aspects of our life. The benefit is congruence between our intentions and our actions. Knowing our work purpose can add great value and meaning around the day-to-day doings. For example, when our work purpose as a leader is to think collaboratively with others to find solutions that will benefit all students, designing staff meetings takes on greater significance. It helps us align our purpose for staff meetings with our intentions and actions of promoting thinking and collaborative solution finding with others.

Acknowledging our intention changes the way we work from the inception of a need for a meeting, to the design of the meeting, to the execution of the meeting. It changes how we show up for the meeting and the processes we use to accomplish thinking and collaboration during the meeting. In the end, it allows us to leave the meeting knowing if our purpose has been met.

When we are clear about life purpose, work purpose, and various other purposes, we can keep in focus what we want to have, do, or be. Intention allows us to filter out activities that do not move us in our desired direction. We become more thoughtful as our intentions become a compass for the direction of our actions and keep us in integrity with how we spend our time. It gives us courage to make better choices—to say "no" to actions that are out of integrity with our intentions. When we are purpose driven at both the macro and micro levels, we are much more likely to achieve our goals.

Reflection

In what ways can you bring intention to the day-to-day aspects of your life, such as attending meetings, working with parents, or designing professional development opportunities?

_____

_____

_____

_____

One of the most helpful tools for ensuring alignment of intention with action is the Pyramid of Intention described in the next section.

THE PYRAMID OF INTENTION

The Pyramid of Intention is a process that is useful in gaining clarity about intended outcomes and getting the program RESULTS we want. What we learn here forms the basis for the RESULTS model discussed in Chapter 7.

Offered through the Adaptive Schools work of Robert Garmston and Bruce Wellman (1999), the Pyramid of Intention provides a visual representation of the dynamics of intention. When we determine our intention, that determination focuses our attention, which results in actions aimed directly at the achievement of our goal. Intention serves as the foundation for what is important to us—aligning with what we want to pay attention to—thus opening the door for action aligned with our intention.

Figure 2.2 Intention Pyramid

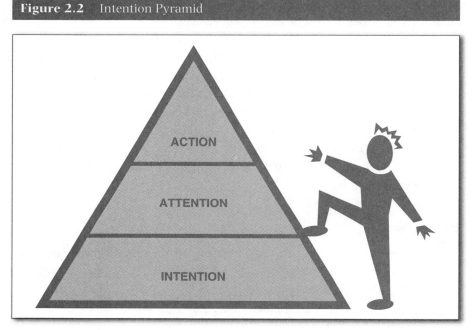

Source: R. Garmston, & B. Wellman (1999).

The space within the pyramid gets smaller as we move up from intention to action. This signifies that our intention or goal serves as the base or foundation of the pyramid. It is the beginning point and sets the direction for the steps that follow. It also suggests that as our intention moves through attention, gaining clarity, the strategic actions of greatest leverage potential become more focused because they are aligned with our intention.

INTENTION

It is important to continue to clarify one's intention until we are certain without question that our goal is achievable. When our intentions are clear, we use more precise language to describe it, and we know how it will be measured. When someone questions our actions, we can explain why we made that decision because our intention is clearly defined.

Intention refers to what we have discussed earlier in the chapter as what we want to "have," that is, "I intend to have a slimmer body," or "I intend to have a more balanced life." These can also be "I want" statements, like "I want to have a high-performing team." The intentions stated here are still broad in nature and difficult to measure in terms of accomplishment. For example, to bring greater clarity to the intention of having a slimmer body, we might say, "In three weeks, I want to lose at least six pounds." When our intention is clear, we know exactly what our target is.

Here are additional examples of moving intentions from being broad in nature and difficult to measure to being measurable and achievable:

Broad and Difficult to Measure	Specific, Measurable, and Achievable
I want to have a school where differentiating instruction is the norm.	In one month, I will see evidence in my learning walks of differentiation being used in every classroom.
I want to meet with my instructional coaches (assistant principal) on a regular basis.	Each month, I will meet with my instructional coaches (assistant principal) to focus on the essential skills of becoming a coach leader. (How are we using listening, paraphrasing, presuming positive intent, and reflective feedback in our conversations weekly?)
I want to improve the morale of my school.	Over the next five months, I will implement at least three strategies targeting trust building with resistant teachers.

Reflection

How would you change the intention of having a high performing team to a clearer, more measurable outcome?

_____

_____

STRATEGIES FOR GAINING CLARITY OF INTENTION AND GETTING RESULTS

In conversations with other people regarding organizational goals, the intentional leader who practices committed listening will discover that people will often state what they want. However, the more the leader questions them about their stated goal, the more it becomes obvious that they really want something else. Helping others get clear about what they want ensures a greater likelihood that the goal they have set will get the intended results.

When leaders assist teachers to set outcomes for children based on state and district goals and expectations, becoming crystal clear about the meaning, it increases the likelihood that results for students will be realized. In some cases such as goals related to student mastery on mandated testing, this clarity becomes illusive or fuzzy. The real goal, ensuring that students learn to read proficiently in order to continue to unlock more complex meaning, becomes lost in the goal of passing the test. So looking beyond the original goal into the deeper, underlying goal, often changes the original goal, which changes the actions that have the most promise for accomplishing it.

Following are six strategies designed to help the leader get clearer about what she wants and to help others do the same. The purpose of these strategies is to refine the intention or goal, making it more specific and more measurable.

Strategy 1: Begin With the End in Mind

One option for ensuring that proposed goals are clear is to practice what Covey (1989) says, "Begin with the end in mind." Describing what goal accomplishment will look like and sound like when achieved is a great way to bring clarity to your goal. If this is an organizational goal, it is effective to describe what teachers and students will be saying and doing when the goal has been implemented and the change institutionalized.

Using the indicator from the self-assessment, "I seek and attain clarity about intended outcomes and communicate my intentions to others" as an intention, the clarifying question could be, "What will teachers and students be saying and doing when this goal is accomplished?" Sample responses could include the following:

- "Teachers will be working toward the outcomes that have been clearly articulated and will also be communicating those outcomes in their classrooms and with parents."

- "When there are questions, I will ask for additional information that will give me clarity; I will listen and consider input from others."
- "I will immediately communicate any changes and choose language that communicates my intentions as concisely as possible."
- "There will be open communication throughout my organization built on the trust that comes from clarity of intention and language and the actions that follow."

Strategy 2: Hypertext

Another strategy that brings goal clarity is envisioning the key words in the goal as a hypertext feature on your computer. As you click on each word, details describing the meaning of the word appear. These additional words can bring a deeper understanding to the words selected, thereby enhancing the meaning contained in the goal. Global concepts, such as improving morale, creating high performing teams, and using effective strategies in all classrooms, can often be fuzzy, vague, or too big. Using the strategy of hypertext asks you to explain, define, or describe the words for meaning and clarity of thought. You can use those words as long as you (and others, if involved) are really clear about what they mean. Goal statements should align with your intended outcome. This seems simple, but it is a complex and deep process when done well.

Strategy 3: "Which Means?"

For this strategy, the leader continues asking, "Which means?" Each time you ask, "Which means?" you are able to get more depth and clarity around your stated intention. This strategy is a way of deepening and clarifying your own language and meaning toward your goal. If your goal is to seek and attain clarity about intended outcomes and communicate your intentions to others, you can select the word *communicate*, and ask, "Which means?" Communicate means let others know by speaking clearly. "Which means?" Allow questions from others that clarify meaning for them. "Which means?" Everyone who is impacted has a common understanding. "Which means?" There are numerous conversations utilizing committed listening and speaking with clarity.

Strategy 4: Physical Timeline
(Modified From Dave Ellis as Offered in Training)

A tool for getting clear about what you want is the use of a physical timeline. Physically walking through a timeline of success and steps to getting there is powerful beyond words. It never ceases to amaze educators at the clarity they have about what they need to do after using this simple process of walking and talking through one's journey to success.

Reflection: Physical Timeline Process

- Think about one of your goals, issues, problems.
- Be prepared to use physical movement to enact the process of examining your goal.
- If this is done in a group setting, ask others to enact the process in their heads.
- Create an imaginary timeline in front of you by indicating a point that signifies "now" and a point that signifies the "future." (You will determine the exact date.) (Label chairs or points that you can stand by for each designated mark.)
- Position yourself on the timeline *in the future*, and identify when that time is. This place will signify the time of accomplishment.*
- "Describe what you are seeing, feeling, doing, being, and so on that specifies that the goal was accomplished."
- Ask guiding questions such as the following:
  - How does it feel?
  - What are others saying about this?
  - Who are you telling about your accomplishment?
  - What were the two or three most important strategies that got you here?

*It is important to stay in the future long enough to really feel the success and accomplishment, see the body language, the energy, the excitement.

- Then, project two or three months in the future. Say . . ."You have achieved your goal. Now, that you are reflecting back on this achievement, what strategies would you do again and what strategies would you do differently in achieving this goal?" Optional questions include the following:
  - What first steps have you taken?
  - What barriers have you encountered?
  - Who have you enlisted to support you?
- "Now, come back midway between today and your goal achievement."
  - What has occurred to get you to this point?
  - What first steps have your taken?
  - What barriers have you encountered?

- "Come back on the timeline to the present. Ask these processing questions."
  - Now that you have walked the timeline of success, what will be your first action step? Who will help you?
  - What do you want to learn to be successful?
  - What will you want to take with you into this journey?"
- Share the first step on the timeline and describe where you are and how you feel.
- Step off the timeline and talk about your experiences.
- Ask others to comment about the experience of doing this activity internally (if done in front of a group).
- Celebrate your future accomplishment!

Strategy 5: Write It

There is always power in the act of committing our intentions to writing because you begin to live them. It's not about magic; it's about getting crystal clear about what you want. The clearer one is about what he wants, the more likely he is to get there. It accelerates progress toward the goal.

Strategy 6: Elicit Input From Others

Asking a trusted colleague or friend to answer questions like, "What do you think I mean by this goal?" or "What do you think I will accomplish if I meet this goal?" can assist us in gaining clarity. When teachers ask these questions of each other in a sharing, collegial environment, teacher "think" is reinforced, and energy and excitement about new possibilities erupts.

Organizational goals such as improved morale, better relationships, or less conflict are evasive and hard to measure. Details that describe exactly what the leader wants will ensure that the next steps in the planning process will be aligned with what he really wants. If the goal is improved morale, what specifically do you want to see happen? For example, do you want to see teachers sharing more ideas during faculty meetings? Teachers coming to school on time? Teachers having positive conversations with parents and community members? Get specific about your morale concerns and how you will know that the intervention you employed is successful. Often, there is discreet data available to help you pinpoint exactly what variable of morale is the target for improvement.

Once your goal has been clearly defined, write it as if you were recording it in the intention area of the pyramid. This serves as the foundation of your pyramid.

Reflection

My goal of intention is . . .

_____

_____

ATTENTION

In the center of the pyramid is *attention*. Attention returns our focus to our state of being or how we want to be, what we value. It serves as the context for the environment or climate we wish to create. For the school leader, this section addresses what she wants to pay attention to—those "being" behaviors that will help the leader reach the desired goal. The leader matches her intention with the mindset she has adopted about the change she has resolved to accomplish.

Two questions help the leader address this issue of attention. The first one revolves around the leader. The question is, "How do I want to be?" Generating a list of adverbs or adjectives describing how she will be in this situation is a great way to stimulate a response, such as calm, excited, supportive, collaborative, stern, determined, pensive, open to new ideas, thoughtful, decisive, encouraging, and so on. See yourself as you want to be.

It is imperative to note that this step does not focus on how you want others to see you. If a school leader focuses on other's perceptions, actions become inauthentic and are perceived as phony, dishonest, and manipulative. Simply show up as the "you" who you are becoming. Operate from your own integrity.

The second question is, "What do I want to pay attention to as I accomplish my intention and/or goal?" This sometimes involves the physical environment of the interaction. For example, where will people sit? How will the furniture be arranged? If the leader is trying to create a collaborative working interaction, how the furniture is arranged is totally different than one in which the leader is trying to be forceful, bold, in control, or directive. In addition to paying attention to the environment, it also involves what you want to pay attention to as you accomplish your intention, such as tone of voice, body language, emotional state, eye contact, openness to alternative outcomes, data that supports the goal, risk-taking behaviors, or what's underlying the issue.

In the example, "In three weeks, I want to lose at least six pounds," perhaps I want to pay attention to being healthy and being mindful of what I put in my mouth. If my intention is to conduct a meeting with input from all participants, I may want to pay attention to active listening as people speak.

This step is often neglected or skipped completely. When we leave out *attention*, we leave out the essential essence of goal achievement—that personal part of ourselves that holds our passion and character in alignment with our goals and activities. Very often, *attention* is the personification of what the leader brings to any situation that has the greatest leverage for change.

In general as leaders, we move from intention—our goal—immediately to action or what we want to do without considering how we want to be. This is a strategy of *ready—fire—aim*. To reverse that and bring intention into our work, an alternative is to move from intention to examination of how we want to be or what we wish to pay attention to. This holds us in integrity as we practice the sequence of *ready—aim—fire*.

Attention reminds us of who we are or who we are becoming. It serves as the filter between what we want to have, our intentions, and the third section of the pyramid—our actions.

Reflection

I want to be _____.

I want to pay attention to _____.

ACTION

Finally, we get to what we do so well—designing actions. People are often trapped when they generate only one or two pathways or solutions to an issue they want to resolve or a goal they would like to attain. As a result, they may develop a false sense of security and be open to tremendous disappointment. When leaders have multiple pathways, they will be more successful. There is always more than one way to get the job done. Creating multiple options promotes empowerment, thinking outside the box, and allows leaders to be creative and flexible in their thinking. It prevents leaders from getting stuck and frequently results in innovative solutions.

There is great wisdom that comes from this Chinese fortune cookie. It reads,

"The best way to get a good idea is to have many ideas."

Idea Generation Strategy

This idea generating process capitalizes on the idea offered in that fortune. It begins with the leader recording as many ideas as possible to accomplish the stated goal or intention. Generating multiple ideas will help you reach your goal. Remember, the concept is not to figure out the one best idea but rather to generate as many ideas as possible. Take off any censoring device you may have in place. When you hear your mind saying, "That's insane!" or "That will never work!" or "We don't have the resources for that," or "I don't know how to do that," write down that idea anyway. Refrain from asking "how," as it puts a lid on thinking rather than opening it up. List things you would never do and wish you had the courage to do. Think outside the box; come up with some wild and crazy ideas. At this point, the goal is not quality of ideas but quantity. Just write the first things that come to your mind.

Reflection

You have one minute. Think of at least five options that would lead you toward the attainment of your intention.

1.

2.

3.

4.

5.

You have one more minute. Now, think of five more.

6.

7.

8.

9.

10.

You have a minute and a half. Now, add some really wild and crazy ideas.

11.

12.

13.

14.

15.

You have two minutes. Push yourself to come up with even five more.

16.

17.

18.

19.

20.

This activity will be repeated in Chapter 7 when you learn about the RESULTS Coaching Plan for Action.

Sometimes, leaders use the strategy of generating options to unlock their thinking and to move into possibility thinking. They may not be ready to develop a plan for action, yet they want to think about how they might do things differently.

For example, Edna had a client who was a principal of a low socioeconomic middle school. She was planning a back-to-school night and wanted to explore ideas about how to get the parents involved. She thought of many of the usual things—notices posted around the community, placing an ad in the community newspaper, sending letters home to parents, posting a notice on the school billboard. Then, she laughed as she said she could pay them to come but of course that was against district policy, and she didn't have the funds anyway. It was that crazy out-of-the-box idea that prompted her to think about holding a clothing drive in conjunction with the meeting. The school had lost-and-found items left over from the previous year. She knew that teachers would also contribute. Perhaps she could get businesses to contribute prizes for drawings. Her creative juices were flowing. She left the coaching conversation with a renewed vision and spark. She worked with her staff to develop the plan. The event was a huge success. Parents visited classrooms and talked with teachers before they selected clothing. The principal had over 50% of the families in attendance, up from less than 10% the previous year.

Only now are you ready to decide upon the actions that will best lead to the accomplishment of your goal. Before leaders finalize their plan for action, they will want to examine all the options generated and select those that have the most potential for accomplishing the stated intention.

In other words, leaders are narrowing the list of options to include those they are serious about trying. An advantage to generating multiple options for action is the depth of strategies available if your top ones fail to bring about the desired result.

Now is the time to determine the top two or three strategies that have the greatest potential for making a difference. This often involves organizing, prioritizing, and categorizing the options previously generated in order to design strategic actions for realizing the intention.

Reflection

Of the twenty options you generated, which ones hold the greatest promise for success for you and your intention?

_____

_____

_____

_____

The Pyramid of Intention allows our actions to become more purposeful—more meaningful—and to ensure achievement of the intended RESULTS from the plan. Actions then become the "doing," the process, or the plan by which we accomplish our intention or our goal. It brings alignment to our work and keeps us in integrity. In summary, we have a tool that reflects our

- *intention* or what we want, passing through
- *attention* which is a commitment of how we want to be or what we want to pay attention to, followed by
- high leverage *actions* or the processes that are aligned with our intention—what we want to do.

ANGELA'S PYRAMID OF INTENTION

At the conclusion of this chapter is a Pyramid of Intention co-created with a coach and an elementary principal. It springs from the principal's intention, "students are engaged in meaningful work every day." You can see the evolution of the principal's thinking as she reached goal clarity. Her original goal was "for teachers to provide engaging work for students every day." Through the strategy of hypertext, she was able to define three areas of clarity: what teacher behaviors would look like, what student behaviors would look like, and what meaningful work would look and sound like. Work on the intention statement spanned two coaching conversations.

Considering the two questions characteristic of the *attention* section of the Pyramid, she addressed what she wanted to pay attention to and how she wanted to "show up" for the teachers. While she wanted teachers to feel supported and listened to, she was clear that she simultaneously wanted to be the instructional leader who was knowledgeable and a resource to them. This was accomplished in one call, reviewed and modified in a second call.

With her "being" in mind, she moved to strategic actions. Notice that she generated 20 strategies. Her second step was to prioritize the possibilities using the strategy of five–three–one; assigning five points for her highest leverage strategy, three points for her second, and one point for her third strategy. In addition, she color coded her top three actions that she chose from the ones that had the most points—gray for first, teal for second, and green for third. Her final step was to move this information to a more traditional "Action Plan" with the columns of "Action Step," "Resources Needed," "When Completed," "Who's Responsible," and an "Indicator(s) of Success."

SUMMARY

Intention is like the blueprint for building a house. Everything is created twice, once in our mind or on paper and again in reality as the house is being built. The concepts of intention explored in this chapter—having, doing, and being, life purpose, and the Intention Pyramid—are the blueprints for getting the planned RESULTS we want. When practiced, they bring clarity, resolve, and determination to our goals. Keeping the *essential* of intention in our work as leaders, assures that we remain in integrity so that what we have and what we do aligns with who we are. It aligns with the legacy we want to leave in all areas of our lives.

Figure 2.3   Angela's Intention Pyramid

Actions

#1 Action= ★

#2 Action= ■

#3 Action= ▲

- Model best practice by consultant from Schlechty Center (5)
  Plan with Design Team at May Retreat for next year (5)
- ■ Observe engaging work by teacher observation of one another (5)
- Align walk through form with Schlechty work (3)
- ★ Ensure that Campus Design Team meets more frequently (5)
- Send more to the WOW Conf. (3)
- Make sure student engagement terminology becomes a part of our everyday language (5)
- Publicly recognize those who facilitate and/or produce engaging work (3)
- Visit with students about their work (1)
- ★ Attend more team planning sessions (5)
- Ongoing PD follow up (3)

- Walk into a class and see if kids are engaged at 80% (1)
- ▲ Provide a forum for constant display of student work (5)
- Influence the number of times teachers invite me into their classrooms (3)
- Be more clear in regard to instructional expectations (3)
- Continue to network with other principals with/regard to what works with WOW (3)
- Effectively utilize data (3)
  Enrichment Friday – half day blocks every nine weeks; provide subs for extended planning (5)
- ■ Take more teachers to see WOW schools (5)
- Observe teachers planning in WOW schools (3)

Attention

I want to be . . .

Supportive	Knowledgeable
Patient	A listener
A resource	An instructional leader
A guide	A cheerleader

I want to pay attention to . . .

- Work that students are producing
- Feelings that students have about their work, their classroom, and their interactions with adults
- Efforts that teachers are putting forth
- The use of resources and their effectiveness
- What's not on the surface; underlying

Intention

~~For teachers to provide engaging work for students every day~~ became –
Students are engaged in meaningful work every day

Teachers:
Design lessons with other teachers
Take into account student interest
Reflect on student work samples
Assess success of lessons (what would replace)
Encouraging students to work together
Review data to see if lessons are
   resulting in academic growth

Students:
Put forth a valiant effort
Acquire information and retain it
Are on task and motivated to participate
Work together
Excited about their learning

Meaningful Work:
Has a purpose and is aligned with TEKS*. Students make connections to other TEKS, the world, and to self. It is interdisciplinary, project based at times, and is differentiated to meet individual needs of students. There is a clear reduction, if not elimination, of worksheets.

*TEKS – Texas State Curriculum – Texas Essential Knowledge and Skills
*TAKS – Texas State Annual Assessment – Texas Assessment of Knowledge and Skills

Figure 2.4 Action Plan to Support Angela's Intention Pyramid

Intention: Students are engaged in meaningful work every day.				
Action Step	Resources Needed	When Completed	Who's Responsible	Indicator of Success
1. Ensure implementation of more engaging work including use of terminology • Campus Design Team – meet more frequently ○ half day every nine weeks ○ Parents sub ○ Purpose – to guide the campus on WOW • Team Planning – attend more meetings ○ Design lessons together ○ Review student work ○ Using protocols				
2. Observe engaging work Internally-campus Externally-WOW Schools				
3. Provide a forum for constant display of work				
*WOW – Working on the Work (Schlechty)				

Source: Coaching School Results, Angela's Action Plan, (2009).

Leader as Coach

3

THE *RESULTS* COACHING NAVIGATION SYSTEM

"The winds and the waves are always on the side of the ablest navigators."

—Edward Gibbon

After months of shopping for a new car, you have made a final selection that is perfect for you. Imagine that you are sitting in the driver's seat ready to take possession and leave the dealership. The instrument panel is before you with all its lights, buttons, signals, and flashers that represent the car's navigation system. You may be excited about the possibilities of the components of this system, such as the electronic unit that includes power locks, power windows, flashers, automatic windshield wipers, or driver's seat position memory switches. Or maybe it's the state-of-the-art audio component that thrills you with its speakers, radio, and CD capabilities, and in some cases, satellite or HD radio. Then, there is the GPS (Global Positioning System) element with a back-up camera, a Points of Interest (POI) directory, and destination and direction abilities complete with maps and audio assistance. And we haven't even mentioned the other parts of the system that afford the driver cruise-control options, air bag safety, security through automatic locks, automatic air conditioning controls, traction control, lumbar support, adjustable pedals and steering wheel, odometer, and trip meter indicators. The list goes on and on.

The navigation system also has feedback capabilities. It tells us when we need maintenance, or when something is not working to the expected standard of excellence. The system tells us when the engine needs oil replacement, the fuel gauge indicates when our fuel level is low, and the engine coolant temperature gauge warns us when the engine is too hot. We can also get a read from the warning lights that tells us the windshield washer fluid is low, the engine oil level is low, or the antilock brake system is working to return us to safe driving conditions. Most important, the navigation system is consistent and persistent in reminding us to use our seat belts.

Just as the navigation system is essential to the high performance of a car, a navigation system is *essential* for the leader who aspires to be more coach like when leading. A clear picture of what coaching is and is not can assist the leader with navigation from being one who tells and directs to becoming a leader who elicits the thinking of others, builds capacity in their ability to act on their own behalf, and empowers them to hold the standards and expectations of teaching and learning that get the best results for students.

The definition of a navigation system is the process of reading and controlling the movement of a craft or vehicle from one place to another. It also refers to specialized knowledge used by navigators to perform the tasks associated with navigation. All navigational techniques involve locating the navigator's position compared to known locations or patterns.

Leaders are responsible for the process of reading and controlling the movement of a district, a school, or a classroom from one place to another. We have specialized knowledge, such as common standards and expectations based on research and best practice that assist us as we perform our navigation tasks. Data analysis is a technique that we use to determine our position or location, identify patterns of performance, and chart our next move.

The purpose of this chapter is to focus on the role of leader as coach. Through examination of the RESULTS Coaching Navigation System, including the standards and expectations for the leader as coach, we will identify a pathway for becoming more coach like in our behaviors as the leader.

STANDARDS AND EXPECTATIONS FOR THE LEADER AS COACH

The drop dead nonnegotiable for leaders is to clearly articulate the standards or expectations of the work of schools. As the coach leader "holds up" the standards and expectations that have been determined from a solid research base of "what works," it focuses the work on making decisions and acting in ways that have the potential to most dramatically impact results. When we work from a "standards based" body of research, the possibility of an aspect of the work becoming someone's personal preference or expectation is diminished. The federal government requires that teachers are "highly qualified" and that all students make adequate yearly progress (AYP) (US DOE, 2005). States and districts demand that students are taught a "guaranteed and viable" curriculum (Marzano, 2003). Leaders' responsibility is to maintain focus toward the goals and articulate expectations found within the profession. Just imagine the potential of conversations on the day the contracts are offered if the standards and expectations are reiterated and reviewed as a condition of signing the contract. What if conversations sounded like the following?

"Good morning, Mr. or Ms. Teacher (or Principal). I am pleased to offer you a new contract for the next school year. I would encourage you to review it yourself, and I want to take a few minutes to highlight the major areas found within the contract. When you sign this contract, you acknowledge you understand the expectations of the contract and are committed to meeting the expectations as a condition of your position.

The federal government and our state require that you are highly qualified, which means that you will attend professional development annually that maintains high levels of pedagogical and content (and leadership) expertise. There is also a requirement that within your classroom (school), students will make adequate yearly progress. This means it is your responsibility to utilize your knowledge and skills and all the resources provided by the district and state to meet the needs of your students to master the learning objectives of the curriculum. It also expects that you will follow the mandated curriculum scope and sequence as you design and plan for (or monitor) quality teaching and learning in your classroom (school). If these expectations are acceptable to you, please sign, and we can look forward to another successful year."

What impact on how we spend our time would result from more conversations like this one? What conversations could be avoided? What would conversations be more focused on? Why do we keep having the same conversations year after year that keep demanding but seem to do little to change practices within classrooms and schools? In *Trust in Schools* (Bryk & Schneider, 2002), the authors identify three kinds of trust.

One is contractual. So, what if we had contracts that were more than something put in a mailbox to be signed and returned. What if the contract was more ceremonial, more renewal? What if it became a covenant of the standards and expectations of our work? I wonder what the impact would be.

Some of the most common standards and expectations that have repeatedly been found and supported from school improvement and best practice research include the following:

- High levels of learning for students
- Continuous improvement for students (AYP)
- Teaching, monitoring, and assessing the mandated state or district curriculum
- Using high yield, research-based "best practice" instructional strategies utilizing high levels of student engagement for high gains, transfer, retention and acceleration of learning
- Creating and maintaining safe and trusting learning environments
- Working as collaborative teams and communities of learners, also known as Professional Learning Communities (PLCs)
- Building partnerships and trust with parents and community
- Adhering to the "educator code of ethics"

In schools, it has taken almost 30 years to understand that in a world of high stakes testing and accountability, a viable and guaranteed curriculum is required for all students. It is not an option! We all know the elements of the triangle shown in Figure 3.1 must be aligned for effective instruction and continuous improvement for students.

Figure 3.1

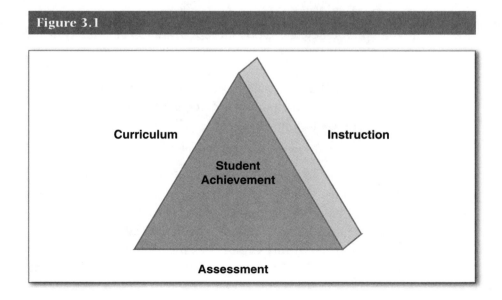

What this means in education is that teachers are hired with the expectation they will teach the state- or district-mandated curriculum that is aligned to high yield strategies and formative and summative assessments that document student progress and growth. It also means that all leaders must identify for their staff or district what guiding standards or expectations will be articulated and become the focus of all conversations. When expectations or standards are fuzzy or unclear or poorly communicated, it is difficult to know exactly where to focus. When there are so many expectations, people get lost much like students who have too many rules to follow. The first point of clarity is in knowing what expectations or standards guide our decisions and thinking as leaders. As a result, conversations immediately have purpose because they all point in the direction of how to meet the standards or expectations. It moves from what a certain principal or curriculum director wants to standards based on sound, solid knowledge of impact.

Listen to the difference in the two conversations that follow, one without clear expectations and the second with clear and articulated expectations.

Conversation 1

Teacher: Cooperative learning is just too time consuming. My kids start talking and get off task and just simply won't pay attention. I can have full attention when I lecture and demand their quiet behavior.

Principal: Cooperative learning will allow students to work together to learn more and enjoy it more. The research on the benefits is overwhelming. I need to see more student engagement when I am in your classroom.

Teacher: Well, it might work for some teachers, but it is just not my style. You will see what I am doing is making students pay attention and learn.

Principal: You really need to stop lecturing so much and engage your students. I will expect to see more when I am in your classroom again.

One wonders if there will be any change in this classroom. The leader is directing and telling the expectations in a way that is fuzzy and mandatory. He is telling and ordering the teacher rather than promoting thinking or solution finding on the part of the teacher. The teacher will only be annoyed, and the principal will continue to get more frustrated with each conversation. Contrast that to the language used in the next conversation, where the standard or expectation is conveyed by the principal throughout the conversation.

Conversation 2

Principal: I have had the opportunity to be in classrooms a lot this semester and am excited about the use of best practice in all the department classrooms. Kids are engaged at high levels (standard and expectation) because they are talking together in small groups about their learning and progress. They are enjoying learning because they are verbalizing their learning goals and monitoring their progress (standard and expectation). And a couple of students said the class time must have been shortened because time goes so fast. What exciting results are you seeing from your students as you put best practice strategies in place in your room?

Teacher: Well, I am trying, but it is really hard to let go of the control and risk students misbehaving.

Principal: Yes, changing from a teacher-directed classroom is scary (standard and expectation). Yet I know how much you care about the high levels of learning for your kids and that it is your goal to keep trying other high engagement strategies every day (standard and expectation). How did the "think-pair-share" strategy that we used during professional development work in your class this week (standard and expectation)?

Teacher: Well, I probably need to try it this week.

Principal: Absolutely, and let me know how much your students enjoy working together in a structured way (standard and expectation). You will be so proud of their behavior and interest in your subject. Can't wait to talk to you next week.

The language of this leader is to simply convey or *hold up* the standards and expectations for the teacher. There is no need to preach or beg; the standards are there because they are known to work for kids. This leader also sends the strong message of belief in the teacher to do those things that will best support kids and learning. The language is clear, unwavering, and clearly demonstrates belief in the teacher to use best practice.

Cognitive research reminds us that when we ask others to change, we are asking them to give up something they probably view as a good thing that works for them. In order to change to something else, the person must understand the relevance or importance of what it will do for them first and then for their kids. Teachers surely would not trade in their computers for the typewriters of years ago. They have accepted at some level the value and importance of technology in the navigation of our world today. When we are given opportunities for conversations about what we have learned about the new practices we are asked to put into place, it affects our thinking and emotions and allows us to consider the benefits.

Another important benefit from simply holding up the standards and expectations is that it is not about one person's belief or opinion. It is based on what works in schools and classrooms. So, as a campus leader, I can stop begging teachers to use the aligned curriculum—it is not for me to beg, plead, or win someone over to an idea—it is a contractual standard and expectation. The language of the conversation might sound like the following:

- "Charlotte, how is the new curriculum assisting you in planning lessons for your students?"
- "Harry, what are you finding to be the most helpful from your use of the new curriculum, the lesson designs or the instructional strategies?"
- "Victor, as you use the new curriculum, what are you discovering are some of its best features? What elements, if any, does the curriculum team need to revise?"

The leader's language clearly communicates there is an expected standard. And what we know is that people want to live up to their leader's expectations! The magic of language is the vehicle for making it happen!

Wow, what a relief for the leader. No more nagging, just holding up the expectations in everyday conversations.

- "What successes are your PLCs seeing in analyzing their assessment data?"
- "As you create a safe environment for learning in your class, what are you noticing in your student responses?"
- "What strategies have you found to build the best relationships with your parents?"
- "What are the most beneficial aspects of the time your team spends planning together?"

REFLECTION

What are your district and/or campus standards and expectations?

_____

_____

_____

_____

In what ways have you articulated these standards and expectations?

_____

_____

_____

_____

With the nonnegotiable standards and expectations set and articulated, the leader is ready for full integration of coaching behaviors into his repertoire. The RESULTS Coaching Navigation System, described in detail in the next section, becomes the mental model for transformation of the leader into the identity of coach leader. Specific skills to support this transformation will be the topics of the remaining chapters.

RESULTS COACHING NAVIGATION SYSTEM

The RESULTS Coaching Navigation System is a visual representation of coaching. It serves as the compass for what we do as coaches, giving us feedback on our own performance as coach leaders—what's working well, what needs our attention, and what might need maintenance. We work with others to bring out the best in ourselves and in them. The navigation system helps us gauge the temperature of the relationship giving us feedback on RESULTS—ours and theirs.

During our journey, we have learned that a picture can do more to explain an idea or concept than words. This discovery is reinforced by the cognitive research showing that the brain loves color and pictures over words. Discovering just the right visual to depict what occurs in coaching interactions is not an easy thing to do. We have explored several representations of what coaching looks and sounds like. One was a continuum that suggested you progress in a hierarchical order from one point to the next. We realized right away this did not show the flexibility and fluidity of coaching, that the most effective coaching is not sequential in nature. There is not a recipe or set of steps to be followed. It is not linear in terms of first you do this, then you do this, then you do this. So, we continued to search for a more appropriate model.

This RESULTS Navigation System model is depicted in full color on the inside, back cover of this book. It serves as a valuable framework for the role of coach and is based upon the coaching mindset and intention that we spoke about in Chapters 1 and 2. The Navigation System clearly delineates what coaches do and do not do; suggesting how the leader navigates toward integration of coach-like behaviors into his role as the leader. Some of the premises upon which the model is built can best be illustrated by the following two quotations. The first is from David Rock (2006), author of *Quiet Leadership*, and the other comes from Galileo who offers wisdom from ages ago.

- David Rock says, "If you want to improve performance, the most effective way to do this is to start to improve thinking." (p. xxiii)
- Galileo understood what coaches should realize when he said, "One cannot teach a man anything. One can only enable him to learn from within himself." (BrainyQuote, 2010)

Because our goal for coaching is to support another person's best thinking, action planning, and goal achievement, this RESULTS Navigation System offers a structure for that goal. The concentric circles hold the concepts or ideas for each of the possible zones we encounter during coaching. Color is added to the mix—violet, red, yellow, and blue-green—to indicate appropriate movement as a coach leader. Violet is the nonnegotiable, never violate zone. Much like the signal light, red signifies *stop*, yellow represents *caution*, and the warm, blue-green area says, "*go*," clearly supporting the mindset for an effective coach leader.

In the next section, the four zones are explained in detail, assigning attributes to each area of the Navigation System. By distinguishing between coaching behaviors that fall within the coaching zone and those that do not, we will bring clarity to the identity of coach leader.

VIOLET ZONE—VIOLATE COACHING CODE OF ETHICS

The outer ring of the RESULTS Navigation System, represented by a violet color, is Violate Coaching Code of Ethics. This refers to the International Coach Federation (ICF) Code of Ethics that is the standard and expectation for all coaches with regard to conduct at large, conflicts of interest, professional conduct with clients, and confidentiality and privacy. Violation of the code is a nonnegotiable, a never-go-to area. For more information, visit www.coachfederation.com to review the code of ethics in its entirety.

As you think about this area of the Navigation System, what are attributes you would expect to see included?

You are correct! Trust and confidentiality would be at the top of the list. This circle is very important and is sometimes minimized or taken for granted. Honesty and professionalism are other attributes of this circle. In this case, professionalism is defined by the ICF Code of Ethics, therefore, clearly setting the standard and expectation and leaving no room for personal speculation or judgment. For example, under the confidentiality and privacy portion of the code, it states, "as a coach I will maintain the strictest levels of confidentiality with all client and sponsor information" (ICF, 2009). This means the coach leader guards the information learned through coaching conversations much like a sentinel guards the safety of his troops. Heightened sensitivity to this zone ensures the integrity of the role is protected so that RESULTS through coaching remains a reality.

RED ZONE—BE DIRECTIVE AND/OR GIVE ADVICE

Moving to the next circle inside the Navigation System is the red zone of being directive and giving advice. Recalling the colors of the signal light, we know this is an area where we *stop*! And we acknowledge, especially for leaders, that this is easier said than done. In our work with school leaders, we find this to be one of the most significant areas of dissonance. Because we have all been promoted to our current positions, due in part to our ability to solve problems, this concept is often a difficult pill to swallow. Yet we know this to be true: when you are a great problem solver, people bring you great problems to solve, over and over and over again!

We have fully developed brain hardwiring around solving problems. In fact, before a person can complete a description of the issue, our brains are already working to give advice based on our own success and experience. And what we know for sure is that our success and experience is not the same as the person with whom we are speaking. In addition, we create a relationship of dependency when we are the chief problem solver. Think about the role of principal. If the culture depends on the principal to solve problems and make final decisions, what happens when he is absent? Does problem solving and progress come to a standstill until the leader can return? Not only is this gate keeping; it is ego stroking. Admit it—it's fun and powerful to be the solver of problems for others.

So, how do we counter this long-standing habit? David Rock (2006) suggests we create new wiring around the notion of helping people think better rather than telling them what to do. Presuming that we have the answers to a problem that is specific to another's context robs them of the ability to do their own thinking and problem solving to find the solution that is a perfect fit for their issue or concern.

In a coaching conversation, advice has no value. That conclusion is backed up by recent studies in neuroscience that assert that it changes little. We feel so strongly about this that we say "advice is toxic" in an effort to make the point. Resisting giving advice and giving answers empowers others to think, to act, and to achieve. Admittedly, others will notice that we are responding differently and may tempt us to return to our typical behavior of supplying answers. When we hear the push back, "just tell me what to do," we simply acknowledge to ourselves that this is a trap of the hardwiring on both sides and re-commit to the coach-like behaviors of the Navigation System.

This is the danger zone. As we work to improve our identity as a coach leader, we replace advice-giving behavior with the essential skills taught in the remaining chapters of the book. We listen, we paraphrase, and we presume positive intent. We offer reflective feedback, and our questions mediate the thinking of the other person so that they discover the answers that were always present but not recognized.

REFLECTION

In what ways has this section provoked your thinking about being directive and giving advice?

_____

_____

_____

_____

What are your strategies for responding to the trap, "Just tell me what to do"?

_____

_____

_____

_____

What is your resolve?

_____

_____

_____

_____

YELLOW ZONE—OFFER OPTIONS AND/OR TEACH

Now we move to the yellow area of caution in the Navigation System: offering options and/or teaching. Just as with the signal light, it does not mean we don't go here; however, it does mean that we are cautious about being here. Occasionally, there is a moment where a concept or strategy might offer support to the other person. For example, when a principal is preparing for a difficult conference with a teacher by rehearsing what she might say, a coach notices the principal appears to hold an assumption that the teacher does not care or try hard enough. So, the opportunity presents itself to ask the principal if using a positive presumption would be helpful. When the principal responds that she is not sure what that is, the coach asks the principal for the opportunity to teach a concept or to practice language that might be helpful. The key here is that the coach asks for permission to teach by saying, "Would it be helpful?" Other examples that may be opportunities to teach include concepts around mental models, point of view, or a skill or strategy that the person does not know.

As coach leaders, we monitor how much time we are spending in this zone. Checking frequency and length of time in the yellow zone is one of those temperature gauges of the Navigation System. Another example of how this looks comes from our work with instructional coaches, especially those working with new teachers who have encountered a trouble spot. We go to the yellow zone to take advantage of that teachable moment and then we head back into the coaching zone as quickly as we can.

The idea of teaching a little and returning to the coaching zone is pretty clear. However, the idea of offering options requires more clarity.

Some people wonder why offering options is not the same as advice giving. First of all, the plurality of the idea suggests one reason it is not the same as giving advice. Options imply choice—you are not telling another what to do. Options offer up possibilities so that the person can make his own personal choice of action to take. It's not "the" answer. It communicates that there is not one way to do it and doesn't present the solution as " my" way to do it. The person is doing his own thinking, which empowers him to think about what would work best in his situation.

It is usually when people get to a place where they are stuck or fresh out of ideas that the "pull" to the yellow zone opens up. This is like the traction control feature of our car's Navigation System. When we begin to skid into the yellow zone, the antilock brake system takes over and returns us to the safety of the coaching zone. What would this look like for the coach leader?

Example 1

A teacher says, "I can't generate another idea; I'm really stuck on this." If this is a response pattern that appears before any ideas have been generated, the coach leader may say, "What strategies have you tried so far?" or "When you think about your most successful experience with this issue, what strategies did you use then that could apply here?" When we have been conditioned to come to someone else for answers, we default to not knowing and may need a "jump start" to get our thinking going again.

If the teacher says this after generating several ideas, the coach leader may say, "I will offer two ideas or possibilities, and then we'll come back to you for an additional idea." So, I go to the yellow zone, offer one or two ideas, and come right back into the coaching zone. I don't offer options as *the* answer; they are possibilities. When it comes time to decide what options will work, the teacher makes the decision.

Example 2

Let's look at another example. This one shows how I can coach from the role of mentor. I'm a mentor, and I'm working with a teacher who is having difficulty with order in the classroom; things are out of control. As I prepare for the conversation, I determine the mindset I want to bring to the conversation. I want to be helpful, and I want to hold up the district and campus standards and expectations. After showing some personal regard, I ask, "How helpful would it be to go over some of the expectations we have in our district around having a discipline management plan?" As we talk about the expectations and look at samples, I'm teaching the non-negotiables of the district, for example, to never demean, humiliate, or embarrass students. My language may be, "Given these nonnegotiables of the district and these options for classroom management plans, how do you want to set up your class?" or "Given all these possibilities, which ones are you thinking you want to choose?" or "How do you want to set up your classroom so that it meets the requirements of the district?"

Example 3

Let's say I'm a principal concerned because the teacher continues to have teacher-centered instruction 95% of the time. I've been in the class several times, and in our professional development, we've learned about best practices and the importance of high student engagement. As the coach leader, I could say, "As you are thinking about high engagement strategies and best practice for mathematics, what strategies hold the greatest possibility for you to increase the level of engagement for your students?" Someone might say, "I don't really know what that is." If so, that becomes the teachable moment. However, as in this case, it serves to reinforce the standard of what is expected during the teaching and learning process.

Example 4

Perhaps I'm working with a principal who reports his leadership team has trouble moving great ideas into action. I might ask, "Would it be helpful to look at a few formats or protocols that could offer your leadership team some advancement in their work?" After the principal says, "Yes," we review several options discussing the discrete attributes of each. Finally, I say, "Knowing your team and each member's individual needs, which of these formats or protocols is best for you and your team's work?" When the teachable moment emerges, we go there, teach a little, then step back and offer people the power to consider what will work best for them. Doing so conveys our belief and confidence in their ability to find their own solutions and to know what will work best for them given their circumstances.

REFLECTION

What strategies will assist you to resist the "pull" of the yellow zone?

_____

_____

_____

_____

How will you monitor frequency and length of time in the yellow zone?

_____

_____

_____

_____

BLUE-GREEN ZONE—COACHING ZONE

This zone, which fades from blue to green, represents the Coaching Zone of the RESULTS Navigation System. It encompasses everything we want to focus on, do, and practice as we improve our identity as coach leaders. In the warmth of this zone, there are no warning signals, flashers, or emergency alarms. This area is the heart of the model where the Navigation System is working to perfection, all components are running at top-notch speed, and are evident as there is movement from one destination to another.

Coaching Presence: Ethical Standards, Trust, Integrity

Surrounding this inner circle, almost as a buffer to the other zones, is coaching presence that includes the critical elements of ethics, trust, and integrity. This is part of what makes a coaching conversation different from other conversations. The coach leader is open and fully present for the conversation with the other person. While he may have a general idea about the nature of the conversation, the coach leader remains flexible, dancing in the moment. He honors and accesses his intuition when something presents itself, refraining from "stepping over" issues, concerns, or emotions. He is confident in the many ways to work with the other person and takes risks by shifting perspective and considering alternative possibilities for his own actions.

Karen Shares Rachel's Story

Rachel was a teacher leader in her school responsible for heading the School Improvement Committee. As the end of the school year approached, it became the work of the committee to help deal with budgetary cuts in the form of reduction in force (RIF). As the leader of the team, Rachel wanted to conduct a meeting that was highly organized, that was fair in terms of hearing all voices regardless of position, and accomplished the goal of determining recommendations for the RIF. She wanted structures and processes that would reduce the high emotion associated with the decision and an environment conducive to the difficult decision that had to be made.

Our work was about creating a plan to meet her desired outcomes. By the time we ended the coaching conversation by phone, Rachel had designed an action plan that described what kind of leader she wanted to be during the meeting and specific actions she wanted to take to ensure her meeting purpose. We planned to continue refining the plan in our next call.

In the second call, we continued our work. About half way through the call my intuition kicked in, and I finally said out loud what was churning in me. I said, "There is a great heaviness in our call today. I wonder what that is about." The door opened up; we got to the real conversation. The RIF was going to be her. The Reduction in Force was going to be Rachel. My sense that something else was going on allowed Rachel to say it out loud. And trusting my intuition expressed through a paraphrase about Rachel's emotion changed the whole conversation so that the real concern could emerge along with the emotion associated with it. By not stepping over what existed below the surface, it became possible to develop a new plan for what was to happen next.

While coaching presence is ever present in coaching conversations, there are other competencies at work in the coaching zone that will be discussed in greater detail below. Those include the following:

- Coaching agreements
- Committed listening
- Intentional language
- Powerful questions
- Create awareness
- Plan for action
- Design action
- Manage progress

Coaching Agreements

Imperative to the RESULTS process and success of coaching interactions is the interplay of agreements made before, during, and at the end of each conversation. Before coaching ever begins at a school, the consideration for coach leaders centers on the context that is built for coaching. What standards or expectations are articulated about what coaching is and is not? What are the understandings that people hold about the role of coach versus other roles that leaders are asked to assume? What conditions will maximize the coaching relationship (including perspectives from both the coach and the person being coached)? What outcomes or plan RESULTS are expected from coaching?

In addition to the agreements made about the big idea of coaching, agreements are also made for each coaching conversation. This develops understanding for what is required in the specific coaching interaction. "In the amount of time (10 minutes, 20 minutes, etc.) we have, what would be most helpful for us to accomplish?" "Given the amount of time that we have, what would you like to accomplish by the end of our conversation?" "What would be measures of success for this conversation?"

During the conversation, the coach leader continues to make agreements by holding up the goal of the conversation, reframing the goal if direction changes, and maintaining focus on what the person has requested of the interaction. An example, "You have three big ideas you are considering. Which of the three would you like to work on first?" or "Of the three big ideas you have mentioned, which holds the greatest promise for the results you want from this conversation?" A third example is, "In the beginning, you wanted to develop a plan for differentiating your instruction. Now, you are focused on the details of differentiating for this particular lesson. Will the bigger plan for differentiation or the details of this lesson be more helpful to you?"

As the interaction develops, next action thinking usually emerges as a natural part of the conversation—something the person wants to do between this conversation and the next. An agreement is made about the level of commitment to the action. Often, the person being coached immediately picks up the agreement, "Before our next call, I want to think more about my plan of action, or I want to make my goal a SMART (specific, measurable, achievable, realistic, time-framed) goal." The coach leader, can ask, "What is your commitment between now and the next time we talk?"

Committed Listening

The critical nature and importance of this competency is obvious because of its prominence as one of the essential coaching skills identified and explained in Chapter 5. In fact, it is the most important competence of coaching upon which all other skills are built. It is the ability to focus completely on what the other person is saying and not saying, as Karen did in Rachel's story above. The coach leader is fully present for the agenda of the other person, attending to both the verbal and nonverbal cues. Effective paraphrasing is the product of active listening, ensuring clarity and understanding of the deeper essence of what the other person is expressing. Finally, committed listening is absent of judgment, allowing the person to openly and authentically work on real issues and concerns.

Intentional Language

The significance of intentional language as a competency is best illustrated by the very fact that two chapters, Chapters 4 and 5 are devoted to its full development. Beyond committed listening, how we talk to one another is an essential attribute of coaching. Three of the four essential skills we teach in Chapter 5 are about the use of intentional language— paraphrasing, presuming positive intent, and reflective feedback. The ability to communicate effectively in a positive, clear, and direct manner is essential to the leader's success. Language that assists the person to see a different perspective or point of view can lead to discovery and insight for new thinking and future action that was never possible before. The use of metaphor and analogy can illustrate a point or create an image of possibility. Here are a few examples:

- "Being named a Blue Ribbon School is like receiving an Oscar because it represents your staffs' talent, excellence in performance, and recognition by others of the untold hours you have invested in the success of your students."
- "Your classrooms are much like the passenger cars of an Amtrak train. When they are full, operating with strategy and precision, you are able to transport everyone with accelerated speed from where they are now to where you want them to be."

Powerful Questions

Skillful use of questions in coaching helps to reveal the information needed to maximize the benefit of the conversation to the person being coached. Powerful questions are a reflection of committed listening and understanding the other person's perspective that is confirmed through paraphrasing. This suggests a progression from listening, paraphrasing for understanding, and then asking powerful questions that yield clarity or mediation of thinking.

When and how we ask questions is important. This skill is amplified in Chapter 5 under presuming positive intent. Presuming positive intent is a key to increasing the power potential of the questions the coach leader asks. For example, asking, "Of all the literacy strategies you have learned in professional development this year, which one has given you the best results with your students?" instead of "Did you use any literacy strategies to get these results with your students?" demonstrates the presumptions that you have learned literacy strategies and also know which one has produced greater results.

Asking too many questions too early in the conversation can feel like interrogation to the individual being coached. Therefore, powerful questions are those that lead to discovery, insight, and commitment to action. Often they challenge the assumptions of the person speaking. Open-ended questions instead of yes or no questions evoke greater clarity, possibility, and new learning. A question about standards or expectations can often challenge assumptions and lead to discovery. In a conversation with Kathy, a school principal shared her disappointment with the quality of the lesson plans that her teachers were submitting, there was a long silence following the question, "When you articulated your expectations for lesson plans at the beginning of the year, what was the criteria that was requested?" In that moment, the principal got it. She understood that in the absence of the articulated standard, it was difficult for teachers to know what was expected. In turn, the open-ended question that presumed positive intent opened the door for possible action. Indeed, that is what happened in terms of a plan for collaboratively developing the standard for quality lesson plans with her leadership team.

Questions embedded in the present and in the future work to move the person forward rather than backwards, which forces her to justify past actions or rationalize why she is currently doing something. We only step back into the past to bring information forward into the present or future. For example, "What have you seen work successfully before?" "As you think about a very successful principal or teacher, what have you observed that he or she did that might be a possibility for you to do now?" This strategy reconnects the person to the power of success in his life, to the efficacy of being successful, so that he can bring that energy into the present.

Chapter 7 focuses on the RESULTS Coaching Plan for Action. Powerful questions are an integral part of the RESULTS process, from goal setting to generating possibilities to selection of high leverage options to determination of strategic actions. Each step in the process with accompanying questions will be fully delineated in that chapter.

Create Awareness

This competency of the Coaching Zone is about the integration and interpretation of information that has been presented to the coach leader by the other person for the purpose of creating awareness and new understandings. It includes listening beneath the surface to discern typical ways the other person perceives himself and the world, to note any discrepancies between what the person says he wants and the behaviors or actions he takes, to hold up observations of incongruent patterns of behavior that are evident over time. For example, the coach leader may note, "In the last five minutes, you have mentioned how angry you are at least four times. Would you like to talk about it?" or "Over the last three conversations, you have continued to emphasize your commitment to be in classrooms, yet you report that you have not accomplished your goal. What is this suggesting to you?" These observations focus on the incongruent behavior so the person can see the behavior with clarity and plan accordingly.

The intent is for the person to be able to visualize new thoughts, beliefs, perceptions, or emotions for herself that come from a broader point of view. The focus is on the strengths of the other person, assisting her to recognize the relationship between themes that appear, to act on insights, and to distinguish between trivial and significant issues and concerns.

Reframing is another powerful coaching tool that invites the other person to view the issue from another point of view. Often, it is as simple as moving what is said from a complaint to a commitment or goal. For example, the complaint, "Teachers are not teaching the science curriculum," becomes the commitment and/or goal, "I am committed to high quality science instruction for all students." Simply reframing what someone offers as a complaint to a statement about their commitment opens the door for thinking and action from a different perspective.

Another example of reframing is the use of a question, such as, "If you were on the receiving end of this situation, what are some things you would like to see happen?" This shifts the thinking to another's point of view. A third example is, "If this were happening to you, how would you want someone to handle it?" This type of question allows the person to pause and consider another perspective on an issue.

Plan for Action

This competency of the Coaching Navigation System implies a plan and a timeline for implementation and movement toward the accomplishment of the goal. It connects directly to the RESULTS Plan for Action in Chapter 7. The seven-step RESULTS process includes the following:

1. *Resolve . . . to change results*

2. *Establish . . . goal clarity*

3. *Seek . . . integrity*

4. *Unveil . . . multiple pathways*

5. *Leverage . . . options*

6. *Take . . . action*

7. *Seize . . . success*

Working through this process consolidates the information collected during the coaching conversation into a coherent plan with results that are attainable, measurable, and specific with identified target dates for completion. Appropriate resources are noted, and adjustments to the plan are made as progress develops.

Design Action

By following the RESULTS Plan for Action identified above, the coach leader automatically addresses the competency of Designing Action. From brainstorming possibilities or multiple pathways to leveraging options, one is considering and planning actions that will hit the mark for goal success. During this period of exploration of alternative ideas and strategies, the opportunity for self-discovery and active experimentation exists. It's a time for out-of-the-box thinking, examination of assumptions and perceptions, and trying on new ways of being and doing. It's a place for stretching and learning about new possibilities.

After many options and possibilities are present, it becomes time for selection of actions that have the greatest potential for accomplishing the stated intention. This often involves prioritizing and categorizing. It moves broad and expansive thinking to more focused and intentional thinking. Prioritizing is crucial to those we coach because it focuses how we spend our time and energy. Time is the most critical factor for why things do not happen; prioritizing is the gift of planning for success. Designing actions that are high leverage strategies ensures accomplishment of the goal.

Manage Progress

For the coach leader, managing progress means holding attention on what is important while leaving the responsibility for taking action with the person being coached. We simultaneously support the other person in designing his monitoring system and managing the process of goal achievement, including celebrating progress along the way. It means making requests that help move the person toward his stated goals. And it means if a pattern of avoidance develops, the coach leader confronts the incomplete actions. We follow up on the commitments made in prior conversations, acknowledging what has been done or not done. Without judgment, we ask what has been learned or what awareness has been created. Nonjudgmental questions, such as, "What would you like to do about what you have not completed?" or "What lessons have you taught yourself about this work?" hold up the commitment yet turn future actions over to the person. As the coach leader, keeping the goal in sight is important; however, flexing and adjusting to shifts in direction is also important.

The coach leader threads the language of progress management throughout a single coaching conversation as well as between one conversation and another. During a conversation, managing progress may show up while goal setting when we encourage the person to think about measures of success, to describe what success will look like, and to design structures for making the success a reality. Sample language includes, "When your goal is achieved, what will people be saying about your success?" "When this goal is fully implemented, describe what will be happening for students." "At the end of this conversation, what will be a measure of success that we have accomplished what you want?"

As we discuss managing progress, we move back and forth between the big picture of what a person wants and the detail of a specific aspect of what they may be working on. It evolves until we ask the person to make a commitment to action. This shows our belief in the person to make her own decisions, to address key issues in her life, to determine priorities, and to design actions with timelines that support the achievement of her goals.

In between coaching conversations, it might sound like, "Between now and the next time we talk, what actions will you take?" "How will you collect data to support progress toward the achievement of your goal?" "What is your next step?" "What small step will you take tomorrow?"

Another aspect of managing progress resembles the feedback feature of the car navigation system. Having a sense of the impact or our work—how our system of coaching is working—can keep our *coaching zone* in tip-top shape. One of the ways to do that is to schedule periodic checkups much like an oil change. Scaling questions are a strategy for gaining this kind of feedback data. "On a scale of one to five, with one being low, and five being high, how would you rate your progress toward your goal of making trust deposits with your teachers?" The same kind of question can be used for feedback on your coaching. "On a scale of one (low) to five (high), how effective has our coaching been for the achievement of your goal for improving your relationships with your teachers?" In addition, we can end each coaching interaction with a question of positive presumption that offers feedback on our performance. "Of all the ideas we have generated today, what is the most significant for you and why?" "What was of greatest benefit in our conversation?" "What question asked today provoked your thinking the most?"

REFLECTION

Using the competencies in the *coaching zone*, consider these areas of reflection:

- Coaching agreements
- Committed listening
- Intentional language
- Powerful questions
- Create awareness
- Plan for action
- Design action
- Manage progress

What competencies in the *coaching zone* are operating at full capacity for you?

_____

_____

_____

_____

What competencies may need a tune up?

_____

_____

_____

_____

What strategies will you use to ensure improved performance?

_____

_____

_____

_____

SUMMARY

The RESULTS Coaching Navigation System provides a new mental model for navigating conversations and interactions in the school house of the 21st century. Educating for the 21st century requires the leader to be intentional about being an agent of change. Our multimedia and global world demands a coach leader who believes in the possibility of every member of the school community and has and uses skills that unleash critical and analytical thinking and problem solving for this new world . . . new thinking, new literacies, new technologies, new classrooms, new integrations, new disciplines, new tolerances, new collaborations or even new communities.

Coach leaders' skillful use of the Navigation System, whose default leads from the warm, blue-green area of the Coaching Zone, centers and guides their language and action around key influencing strategies. Articulating clear expectations and goals of the work will drive agreements that support everyone's success. Through committed listening, use of intentional language and powerful questions, an awareness is created, plans are designed and implemented, progress is managed so that goals are achieved. Because the coach leader does not default to the red area, he uses the Navigation System for feedback on what is working well, what needs a tune up or maintenance, and what needs replacing. He knows that the most influential leadership conversations are collaborative and nondirective, inviting thinking, and fostering respect and integrity for those with whom he interacts. He knows the best way to influence the highest levels of performance and lead schools for the 21st century is to build the confidence, the competence, and the capacity in others to lead, thereby igniting their motivation and energy for making great things happen in our world.

Language

4

The Essential Connector

"I know you believe you understand what you think I said, but I am not sure you realize that what you heard is not what I meant."

—Robert McCloskey, State Department spokesman (attributed)

How R U? Y haven't I heard from U in awhile?
LOL. I've been 2 busy workin'.
OMG yes. It is time 4 a break!

Certainly, you have noticed the emergence of this new language—a hybrid of standard English that arrives on your cell phone from somewhere across the globe with the speed of lightning. It's a new way of communicating in quick, short passages that simultaneously convey meaning while connecting one person with another. For Karen to use this new shorthand language, she had to adapt in several ways. One, she had to rewire her brain about the words and symbols used to represent the thoughts and ideas she wanted to share. She had to get enough clarity about her message so that she could express it with the fewest symbols possible. And she had to rethink the tool that she previously had conceived was for the function of speaking only. Text messaging changed how she uses language to communicate with others.

Karen acknowledges this has been a slow process for her. Taught and encouraged by the younger generation in her family—who Marc Prensky (2001) calls digital natives—her son and niece were the first to send her text messages. After receiving the message, she would immediately pick up the phone, call them back, and say, "I don't know how to text."

One particular situation stands out vividly. On a recent trip, Karen's plane was sitting on the runway when she learned that the flight would be significantly delayed. Knowing that her young niece was driving to the airport for the first time to pick her up, it was important to give her advance notice that the flight would be arriving later than expected. Karen literally stood up, looked for a young person sitting around her, and asked him to help her send a text message to her niece.

Over time, more colleagues of Karen's age and generation are beginning to communicate by text. This has encouraged her to practice and perfect this new language. She confesses that while she is still in the process of learning this new skill, she realizes the emergence of a *new essential* that is impacting the way we all speak to one another—whether we are in the same place or miles apart.

Schools have quickly come to realize the impact and relevancy of this new essential for communication. For the learners of today, texting is their default language—the one they automatically turn to. It is transforming our place called school. What was once a nonissue now requires our attention at multiple levels.

For example, consider the teacher who capitalizes on the new essential as a means for engaging her students. When traditional ways of getting students to attend afterschool tutoring were not successful, she considered what would be relevant to her students. Picking up her cell phone, she simply sent the text, "Where R U? I'm N the CR waitin' for U. See U in 5." Suddenly, her attendance in tutoring picked up, and she was able to accomplish her goal of improvement for her students.

On the other hand, schools are finding the need for consideration of the ethical issues associated with the speed and accessibility of this new essential. Just as we had to address ethical standards when the computer and the Internet became new essentials, we must find ways to address the challenges of this new essential in a way that honors the positive potential while considering less desirable implications.

While this nanosecond language is fast and gets results quickly, it does not replace another essential—the need for deep and thoughtful communication. At the heart of who we are is intentional language. Texting works well when we are not in the presence of another, yet it does not replace our need to listen and speak powerfully with one another. In the school environment, listening and speaking take on even greater significance as critical skills for how we accomplish our work.

In the example above, the teacher was able to use texting as a way to get the attention of her students as she was also demonstrating care and concern. However, in no way did that replace the communication of teaching and learning that made her students more successful. It was the listening and "speaking" that brought about the desired results. How we speak to one another in schools is crucial.

Language is powerful. It is far more than the simple expression of thoughts, feelings, and experiences. As psychologist Lev Vygotsky (1986) said, "It produces fundamentally new forms of behavior." Language does this in several ways: It molds our sense of who we are; helps us understand how we think, work, and play; and influences the nature of our relationships.

Our words shape our identities. What we say to others can deeply affect their sense of who they are and who they might become. The words of educators have special power in this regard because we are working with children during their formative years. What and how we speak to them impacts their being and their becoming. As the leader of the learning environment, it becomes a moral imperative to embrace this new essential as we work with children and as we work with our staff. Language is the essential connector, and how we choose to use it will significantly impact the relationships and identities of those we lead.

This chapter focuses on four communication concepts that can dramatically change the way we do our work as leaders. All four concepts spring from intentionality and include the following:

- Levels of Language
- Speaking the Truth
- Making and Keeping Promises
- Requests versus Requirements

The following is an instrument offered for pre-assessment of your current status with regard to each concept. Based on the descriptions provided, indicate a rating that best describes your current knowledge and practice around each section.

CFR Communication Assessment

Below are five concepts associated with "being" intentional as a communicator. Assess your personal strengths and areas where you want to grow stronger.

**Powerful Listening
(Listening fully)**

I am intentional about listening to what others have to say. I am aware of the amount of airspace available and am purposeful about how I choose to use it. I monitor or set aside distracters that interfere with being fully present.

Low				**High**
1	2	3	4	5

(Continued)

(Continued)

Powerful Speaking
(Choosing words of power)

I am intentional about my choice of words because I know that words inspire or deflate, encourage involvement or cause retreat, invite action or inaction, lead to solutions or failures, and offer hope or despair.

Low				High
1	2	3	4	5

Speaking the Truth
(Being "real" with self and others)

I speak my truth in a genuine and respectful manner while also listening to the truth from other perspectives. Before I speak, I honor silence to gain my own clarity, choose words carefully, and I deliver my message with personal regard.

Low				High
1	2	3	4	5

Making and Keeping Promises
(Displaying honesty and integrity)

I am intentional about making and keeping promises to myself and others. Before making a promise that commits my time, energy, and resources, I thoughtfully weigh the implications based upon priorities and values. My promises reflect my intention to follow through. When I cannot keep a promise, I take responsibility for speaking the truth to myself and others.

Low				High
1	2	3	4	5

Requests Versus Requirements
(Inducing desirable responses with adeptness)

I know the difference between a request and a requirement and am clear when I use each. I lead from the viewpoint of making requests that offer options and hold requirements for those areas that are non-negotiable.

Low				High
1	2	3	4	5

Analysis of Results

One way to make sense of your data is to connect the numbers you have indicated for each concept by drawing a line from the number in one box to each of the numbers in the remaining boxes. Draw conclusions about your data. These questions may be helpful as you make meaning from your personal assessment.

- Do you have a straight line or a jagged line? What is the significance for you?
- Is your rating to the right or left of the halfway point? What does this mean for you?
- What areas stand out as clear strengths for you? Why?
- Based on what you understand the concept to mean at this point, what are areas that could be improved?

What intention will you hold as we move into a deeper understanding of each concept?

_____

_____

LEVELS OF LANGUAGE

Earlier, we spoke of the power of language as a catalyst for impacting our thinking, speaking, and acting. In the pre-assessment, we spoke about choosing words of power versus words of victimhood. So, just how important is it that we are intentional with our language?

When we listen to the types of words that we choose to tell our stories or describe our schedules, we may be amazed at how often our language demonstrates victimhood rather than our level of commitment. When we hear someone tell another, "You should . . . or you ought to . . ." what is the underlying message that we are also sending? At one level, we are suggesting that we know the answer and they do not. At another level, we are implying that we know better for them than they know for themselves.

Dennis Sparks, former Executive Director of Learning Forward (formerly the National Staff Development Council), speaks clearly about the power of language. "Our use of language can disempower or empower, enable or disable, intensify resistance or increase commitment, and inspire passion and creativity or promote resignation and passivity" (Sparks, 2006, p. 41).

How we speak to ourselves and to others in the school setting has a profound impact on our willingness and desire to rise to the challenges we must face. Adapted from Dave Ellis' (2002) Language Ladder in *Falling Awake* is a mental model that can lead to greater clarity and deeper understanding of what is meant by levels of language.

Our visual that supports this notion of levels of language is a grand staircase in a two-story building or home. Imagine one that you have known. Stand at the bottom and look up at the steps before you. Consider that each of the seven steps is a choice that you can make about your use of language moving from least powerful to most powerful.

Figure 4.1

Source: Coaching School Results, 2009

Language of Obligation

Standing on the first step is the language of obligation—words that sound like, "I should, I'd better, I have to." When you choose words at this level, it is interesting to notice how you feel. Karen shares that she has a feeling of heaviness as if someone has placed a backpack full of bricks on her. The heaviness of "shoulds" and "oughts" weigh us down. There is also a second covert message included in the statement—one that includes a hint of guilt associated with not doing what is in the message. Words at this level have less power and place us in the position of being victims. Amazingly, our choice of words can empower us or give our power away.

By just paying attention to the level of language in a school, one can learn a great deal about the sense of power and efficacy that a staff feels for their work as educators. For example, when we hear language such as, "We *should* tutor these kids because they are not going to pass the state assessment," or "You *ought* to try this classroom management strategy in your classroom," the underlying message is someone else is in control or knows better than you do. Yes, it's subtle, and because we have practiced this language for so long, we are often unaware of the impact or effect that it has on others and ourselves.

Language of Options

Return to the staircase you have imagined and move from obligation to options. Language at the options level sounds like, "I might, I could, and maybe I will." Notice how you are feeling at this point. To say that you have several options opens the door that felt closed when your language was at the obligation level. You have increased your power and added some lightness to your load.

By changing the language from "we should tutor" to "we *could* offer several options for tutoring, including before school, after school, and at designated times during the school day," shifts the power and control. When a teacher moves from "I ought to try this classroom management strategy in my classroom" to "I *could* try this strategy *or* this strategy," she demonstrates her influence on the decision-making process.

Language of Preference

Continuing our assent, we move from the language of options to the language of preference exemplified by words such as "I prefer to" or "I want to." With each step, we add energy, power, and commitment to our language. Clearly, our language at this step indicates our presence and participation in deciding what is best for us. So, our ongoing example changes from "we should tutor" to "we could offer" to "I prefer to arrive early for tutoring because I am sharpest at that time of the day." And when I am able to tell my leader, "I want to attempt this strategy over this strategy," I have shifted from obligation to option to preference. I have made the idea my own and will more likely proceed with its implementation.

Language of Passion

Moving up another level, we are now at the language of passion that brings increased energy, power, and commitment for what gives us joy. When we are passionate about something, language mirrors our feelings because we have found greater personal meaning. We hear phrases such as, "I'd love to, I can't wait, or I'm excited about." And when this passion moves from an individual to a team or a staff, the excitement becomes contagious and doubles its potential for impact. When a staff says, "We are *eager* to tutor our struggling students because we know that additional time for learning can make the difference," we are light years away from the heaviness of the language of obligation. A teacher who discovers renewed passion around implementation of strategies that will bring success to her students will be manifested through the energy in her language—"I'm excited about. . . ."

Language of Possibility

When we speak from the language of possibility, our words represent all that we intend to have, do, or be. By standing in possibility, we turn challenges into opportunities, and we turn to the future for inspiration and drive. Our language shows up as, "My dream is . . ." or "I desire to." The way we stay in possibility is to generate multiple options or pathways for achieving what we want. In Chapter 7, we will demonstrate a detailed process for how to optimize this level of language. In the case of the tutoring example, the *dream* may be for the staff to work themselves out of the job of tutoring as evidenced by mastery for every child. Another possibility is the *desire* to have every student who requires tutoring be present and working toward mastery of identified targets. For the classroom management example, the teacher may say, "I *desire* to have a management plan that is fair and consistent and meets the diverse needs of my students." A second possibility could be, "My *dream* is to be so effective with the management of my instruction that I have few, if any, discipline problems in my classroom."

Language of Plan

As we arrive at this step, our energy, power, and commitment continue to increase. We also add another dimension—that of accountability. When we use phrases like "I expect to" or "I plan to," we show more intentionality. Our language indicates that we want to do more than "talk the talk." We are ready to "walk the walk." With this level of language, we see our commitment and resolve to move to a future state that is an improvement beyond our present one. As you will see in Chapter 7, resolve is the first step to creating a Plan for Action that builds concrete support for your expression of expectation. In the tutoring example, each individual forms a team that "expects" or "plans" to see the results of his or her actions with students. Teams anticipate that there will be a desired impact from their resolve to work above and beyond on behalf of the students for whom they are responsible. In our classroom management example, when I articulate "my plan" for more effective management, I accept responsibility for ensuring that misbehavior does not distract from the learning time of my students.

Language of Promise

While there may be more steps on this staircase, our final step for now is that of promise. At this step, we see the highest level of intention that carries us forward into action. This level of language is expressed as "I will," "I do," I promise," and "I intend to." The level of commitment present at this level was absent in the language of obligation. Staff members *promise* to see that all students in the school are successful and that tutoring is but one means for ensuring that success. A teacher standing in what she will do or intends to do with her classroom behavior will harness the energy and power to make it happen.

With each advancing step, we have increased our energy, power, and commitment, as well as adding the dimensions of self-responsibility and accountability. As our intentionality and resolve have gone up, so has our commitment to act. Understanding the levels of language gives us the power to choose words most representative of our state of mind and intention. We can be passionate about something without a resolve to move to action. The steps are not hierarchical so we can literally leap over the ones at the lower levels and land on the higher levels of possibility, plan, and promise.

One key idea about choosing words with intention is the recognition that we cannot totally eliminate all obligations from our lives. When Karen first learned about the language of obligation, she made it her goal to eliminate all obligatory language. Quickly, she learned that her goal was unreasonable for there would continue to be obligations in her life. Karen represented taking action around her new learning by reframing what was previously considered to be an obligation. At the time, her 80-year-old mother was residing in a nursing home. By listening to her language, it was apparent that she was living in the arena of victim language. You might have overheard her saying to a friend, "I have to go visit my mom." Once Karen heard her language and understood the weight associated with it, she resolved to move up the levels of language to a more intentional state. "I expect to visit my mom on a regular basis because I want the remaining years of our lives together to be memorable."

We continue to have obligations, and as leaders, we often find ourselves in the position of obligating others. We can, however, choose to take on obligations out of options, preference, passion, possibility, plan, or promise rather than taking on the heaviness of obligation. When we as leaders are faced with obligations or a nonnegotiable, we have an opportunity before us. We can leave it at the level of obligation, or we can intentionally move it to another language level. What's at stake here is the energy, power, and commitment that we want to create or assign to the impact of our words. So, one option is to reframe the obligation for our self and then to assist others in adjusting their frame or view point.

Several examples that we frequently hear in education are, "We have to do this because Central Office told us to," or "We have to teach this curriculum instead of the textbook because the district says so." Consider the impact of framing these questions from a different language level.

Let's take one at a time. "We have to do this because Central Office told us to." After reading the samples provided, formulate your own response.

- "What options do we have for meeting this request from Central Office?"
- "Central Office has asked for this report by the first of next week. While the timeline is quick, it is important for us to collect accurate data because it will ultimately be helpful information about the performance of our students. I want us to. . . ."
- "Knowing that Central Office needs this information to provide support for us, what is our plan for providing them with what they need?"

What is your response? _____

_____

_____

Where does your language fall on the Levels of Language?

_____

_____

Here is the second example: "We have to teach this curriculum instead of the textbook because the district says so." Consider the examples provided and then create your own response.

- "Knowing a textbook draws on a national perspective, the scope and sequence of our curriculum may be my best strategy for teaching because it is designed to address the assessed needs of our students."
- "The textbook can be a resource to support our district curriculum when it aligns with the assessment of what we want our students to know and be able to do."

What is your response? _____

_____

_____

There is at least one caveat regarding the seventh level—promise. Often, our preferences, passions, and possibilities lead us to plan and promise more than we are able to fulfill without struggle. When this occurs, we have over promised, and thus, put ourselves back into the mode and language of obligation. "I *have* to do this because I promised that I would." We will speak more about the seductive power of over-promising in the section that follows on Making and Keeping Promises.

Knowing that our choice of language can show level of commitment over victimhood, we want to focus on another component of communication that holds the promise of dramatically changing the way we work—Speaking the Truth.

SPEAKING THE TRUTH

From the work of Bryk and Schneider (2002), we know that there is a direct correlation between high levels of trust and high levels of performance in schools. Their research, reported in *Trust in Schools* (2002) emphasizes that trust matters. Megan Tschannen-Moran (2004) defines trust as "one's willingness to be vulnerable to another based on the confidence that the other is benevolent, honest, open, reliable, and competent" (p. 17). Trust begins with being trustworthy. Trustworthiness springs from the congruence of what we say and what we do. Speaking the truth is a tenet of being trustworthy. When you can count on my word and see that my actions support my words, the door opens for the presence of trust in our relationship.

Susan Scott (2002) also writes about speaking the truth. In her book, *Fierce Conversations*, she defines a fierce conversation as "one in which we come out from behind ourselves into the conversation and make it real" (p. 67). This requires summoning the courage and willingness to speak our truth so that we can interrogate reality by examining multiple points of view, check with one another for deeper understanding, and move toward agreement and action that supports the accomplishment of our intentions.

While this makes perfect sense, speaking the truth is sometimes a challenge for many of us. We can generate a long list of reasons we resist telling the truth. Primary among those reasons is hurting someone else's feelings. It's a reaction to the adage we learned as children, "If you can't say something nice, don't say anything at all." When given the choice of delivering difficult information or preserving the relationship, we defer to the relationship and refrain from telling the truth. Sometimes, we do not speak our truth, but it is not a lie. Instead, we withhold our feelings or opinions, keeping them to ourselves. Withholding is like an untruth. Withholding entails not being authentic, and it ultimately interferes with the level of trust.

For example, I may refrain from sharing my point of view about a planned district intervention that I have reservations about. My internal dialogue may convince me to withhold. "What if this idea is not valid?" "What if I am wrong?" "What if no one cares about this?" As a result, my voice is unheard, and my silence can be misconstrued as support for something that I do not support. This creates a negative ripple effect over time. First, I refrain from speaking the truth to myself, then to my team, then to my leader, and so on.

Individuals and organizations cannot make meaningful decisions for students when real issues remain unstated and unexamined. When consensus really means "just going along," we jeopardize trust and reinforce the pattern of not speaking the truth with one another. Speaking the truth means "speaking the truth, the whole truth, and nothing but the truth." While telling the truth is not practical and it's often not easy, it has the potential to be life altering. When we can authentically discuss exactly which strategies hold the greatest potential for making a difference for our struggling students, we have created a "trusting" place where we can express our diverse points of view.

Being Honest With Self

There are different levels of speaking the truth and getting reality on the table. Naturally, it begins with us: being honest with self. It requires acknowledging our own point of view and being willing to put it on the table so that our voice is represented. It means setting aside any negative self-talk or second-guessing. It means trusting ourselves and our own intuition.

Being Honest With Others

Being honest with others is another level of speaking the truth. Finding the courage to deliver difficult information without damaging the relationship is hard work and requires a skill set that is frequently missing from our repertoire. It calls on us to develop skills that will ensure that the message is delivered and the relationship remains intact.

One strategy is to *say what we mean and mean what we say.* To do that, we may use data and the language of presuming positive intent (Chapter 5) to support our point.

> Example 1: "For the past three weeks, your lesson plans have been turned in late. Knowing that quality instruction is important to you, I'm wondering what is going on?"

> Example 2: "This six weeks, over 50% of your students failed. This has to devastate you. What strategies are you putting in place to turn that around?"

> Example 3: "I've received some disturbing news that I know will concern you as much as it has me. Both parents and students have reported use of sarcasm in your interactions with students. What are you thinking are the ways you want to approach this?

A second strategy is to *tell the truth without blame or judgment.* Keeping the "pointy finger" out of the conversation shifts the conversation to the truth rather than to the person. Our choice of language becomes extremely important. For example, the use of "you" often flames the fire and promotes an unintended consequence such as defensiveness. This strategy, coupled with data as described above, permits the information to remain objective without the presence of judgment or blame. When the heat of blame or judgment is removed, we can think and respond appropriately to the situation. When I believe that you are in this with me, it changes the dynamics and invites the trust factor into the relationship once again.

> Example 1: "A concern has been brought to my attention from a parent about not receiving her child's progress report. How would you like to investigate the situation?"

Example 2: "We committed to the goal of differentiating instruction to meet the specific needs of all students. What results are you seeing in your plan for Freddy?"

Example 3: "Professional learning communities have taught us about the power of collaboration. What benefits have you gained from collaboration with your team?

A third strategy is *not letting **our** truth get in the way of **the** truth.* When we become attached to the outcome, we close down the opportunity to hear and be heard. Believing that there is only one answer, and that answer is our answer, transforms our efforts to speak the truth to grandstanding or manipulation. This strategy asks us to remain open, to stay at the table, and to hold our truth with a "small t rather than a *big* T" until we can hear all possibilities.

Example 1: "Your perspective is that the district curriculum is like a policy and procedure book rather than a guide for planning instruction."

Example 2: "Because of the high standards of performance you hold for yourself, you are wrestling with the notion that all kids can achieve at high levels."

Often, we want to speak our truth and don't know how to go about it. We avoid these fierce conversations because we do not want the conversation to become confrontational. This has certainly hit a nerve because the field is full of resources that will help us with the development of this skill set. This list of titles of recent books attests to the interest and need for skillfulness in this area of leadership: *Fierce Conversations, Crucial Conversations, Courageous Conversations, Difficult Conversations, Compelling Conversations, Critical Conversations,* and *Confrontational Conversations.*

In the next chapter, you will find four skills that, when practiced and integrated into your conversations both within and outside of your school, can transform your relationships. These skills begin with committed listening and are supported by language that builds trust in the relationship while conveying the expected standard or expectation to be met. It mediates our thinking to move from the language of victimhood, "having to have the conversation," for example, to the language of commitment, "wanting to have the conversation."

A recent conversation with a principal focused on this very issue—delaying a conversation with a teacher about an incident that had occurred on a field trip the previous week. When the language of the principal was noted by the coach—"I *should* have this conversation with my teacher before she leaves for the weekend," coupled with the paraphrase that the principal had been carrying the weight of this impending conversation around with her for a full week, it suddenly became clear to the principal what her next action would be. She changed her language to commitment and resolved to go to the teacher's room for the conversation immediately following the call with her coach.

When we speak the truth to others and ourselves, we show our courage, and we offer a gift, a chance for us all to examine reality and plan more honestly for the future. It invites us to see if our behaviors are supporting the fulfillment of our goals and desires. As we honor different perspectives and acknowledge the data we have collected, we can investigate the world of possibility going beyond the limits we have arbitrarily set for ourselves. By speaking our truth and listening to the truths of others, conversations will be more authentic and our relationships with people will be deeper and more profound.

REFLECTION

To take stock of your current practice of speaking the truth, consider a few questions from each of the areas below.

Be Honest With Self

- If I were guaranteed honest responses to any three questions, whom would I question, and what would I ask?
- What am I pretending not to know?
- What truth do I often deny about myself?
- What truths am I able to see about myself that are difficult to own?
- In what areas am I honest?
- In what areas do I want to get back "to the truth?"

Be Honest With Others

- What conversations am I avoiding—with colleagues, friends, family, employees or myself—that if I engaged in by telling my truth without leaving an emotional wake, might transform everything?
- What have I said recently that was an embellishment or spin of the truth or an actual lie?
- Whom do I need to talk to about an untruth that I have not admitted yet?
- What promise did you make that you did not keep?

Say What You Mean, Mean What You Say

- Describe a situation when you chose not to speak honestly about your feelings and your perceptions.
- Describe a work experience when you chose to withhold your opinion or ideas.
- Describe a personal experience when you chose to withhold your opinion or ideas.

Tell the Truth Without Blame or Judgment

- In what situations do you judge others for their beliefs or actions?
- Is there anyone you have blamed for a bad situation in your life that you would like to talk to about that situation?

Not Letting *Our* Truth Get in the Way of *the* Truth

Describe someone you have difficulty talking to. How is your truth different from that person's truth? Think of how you talk to that person now and how you might change your way of speaking your truth to him or her.

MAKING AND KEEPING PROMISES

Returning to the research of Bryk and Schneider (2002) about *Trust in Schools*, one of the filters of trust identified in the study was integrity. Integrity is about honesty, sincerity, and candor. Simply, it is doing what we say, walking our talk. In leadership, it shows up as the congruency between what leaders say and how they behave. It is one of the most critical values by which leaders are measured. Trust develops based on whether they keep the promises they make—both large and small.

Our words are our major currency. You will recall from the Levels of Language that promise was the highest level of intention that carries us forward into action. When we say we will act, people accept that as truth, as a promise. When we disappoint them by not acting, our integrity is diminished. So, making and keeping promises becomes a critical way to demonstrate our integrity while simultaneously developing trusting relationships.

Sometimes, our intention is not to follow through but rather to be cordial and move on. When we say we will do something and have no intention of following through, we are being dishonest and can damage relationships with our colleagues.

Because of the strong implications making and keeping promises has for a leader, viewing this issue at a deeper level can offer insight regarding how we currently make and keep promises while affording us the opportunity to examine unintended consequences that run counter to our purpose. First, we will look at how we make promises. Next, we will look at how we break promises, sometimes unintentionally. And last, we will look at ways to make and keep promises.

How We Make Promises

People make promises in a variety of ways—overtly and covertly. Sometimes we make overt promises stating our intent for action. However, we can also make promises by signaling a promise or commitment to someone when we do not intend to make a promise. Body language figures into the equation in a huge way. Nuances take on greater significance in this arena of making promises. What might my nod or silence signal to the other person with regard to a promise?

Consider this example from an organization that thinks it has a norm of keeping promises around "being on time." George and his department chairs meet at 1:30 by agreement. They show up, put their notebooks in the meeting room, and leave if George is not in the room. To some, having their materials in the room constitutes being on time. What is your promise about being on time? What is your team's promise about being on time?

Some of the ways a person can make a promise include silent agreement, nodding, verbalizing support, withholding comment or disagreement, or consenting without the intention to act. Additional possibilities for how we make promises include volunteering others without their consent, agreeing to tasks and assignments without intention, accepting responsibilities without intention, and accommodating others' needs.

Add other ways we make promises.

_____

_____

_____

_____

How We Break Promises

Just as making promises can be subtle or obvious, so can breaking promises. Obvious ways people break promises are by failing to following through or complete tasks or assignments by the designated deadline. A more subtle way we break promises is by keeping our opinion to ourselves, especially when it is counter to the one being proposed. The speaker may assume our silence means agreement and a willingness to support the idea beyond the meeting. Often, we do not even consider the commitment to be a promise or do not know that our actions are being perceived as promises. Our failure to check this out leaves the possibility of a promise on the table.

We find numerous examples of this phenomenon in education.

- We promise that every student will be a reader by the third grade, and some fall through the cracks.
- I promise to teach the curriculum, and I continue to teach my favorite units.
- I promise to pay a contract in 30 days, and I do not.
- I promise to talk to a parent when I don't intend to.
- I promise to meet the needs of every learner when some students are not succeeding.
- I promise I will be in the classroom a certain number of times, and I am not.
- I promise to provide progress reports to parents on a regular basis, and I do not.
- I promise to get something for you, and I do not.
- I promise to meet you at a certain time, and I am late, or I do not show at all.
- I agree to follow our school norm about a warm and supportive learning environment, and I use sarcasm in my classroom.
- I promise to be fully present, and I continue to check my cell phone.

We do it in such small ways that we don't even call it breaking a promise. For example, one of the qualifications for having the Reading First Program in your school is the principal's agreement to be in the classroom a certain number of times. In many cases, even though the principal signed the contract, he or she did not keep this promise.

There are other ways we break promises. Making excuses or blaming others is a promise breaker. Either strategy, excuse-making or blaming others, attempts to shift the responsibility for breaking the promise to someone else.

Add additional ways we break promises.

_____

_____

_____

_____

How to Make and Keep Promises

To maintain the integrity of our word as leaders, it is important that we are aware of how we make and keep promises. By "turning up the noise" in our head about what we say we will do when compared to what we do, we can directly influence the level of trust we have with others. Being clear of our intention, listening to how we frame our promise, and carefully choosing our language will ensure that we can deliver. Choosing the language of intention when we are sure that we want to make a promise aligns with our level of commitment. Expressions such as "I will," "I do," "I promise," and "I intend to" signal our intent to follow through.

Leonard and Larson (1998) in *The Portable Coach* offer a strategy for making and keeping promises. They promote "underpromising" and "overdelivering." They say, "Overpromising is seduction; it makes you become either a workaholic or a liar" (p. 134). How many times have we overpromised because we were trying to keep from disappointing others, hurting their feelings, or letting someone down. Acknowledging and labeling when it is not appropriate to make a promise keeps us in integrity.

Making too many promises and making promises about things that are not our passion causes us to feel overwhelmed and ultimately places us back in obligation, which is the lowest level of language. When we hear ourselves saying, "I have" to do something, that is a sign that we have moved from promise to obligation. Saving promises for the big things ensures that we can make and keep our promises to self and others.

Leaders can promise discriminately by being clear about their priorities and goals. Goal clarity frames the promise-making process, helping one know when to say "yes" or when to say "no." If a leader is unsure about whether he wants to make a promise, he can delay giving the answer, creating time to honestly consider the request. When he has made a decision, it is important to respond to the person in a timely manner. Thus, when the leader does make a promise, he accepts responsibility and responds with intentionality to make the promise a reality.

How does the leader maintain integrity if she has made a promise and recognizes that she cannot keep it? When the leader finds she has over-committed and cannot deliver on her promise, several options can allow her to maintain her integrity. One is to renegotiate the commitment rather than to make excuses or blame. Perhaps a portion of the commitment can be kept—a draft, a section of a report, or an outline. After accepting responsibility for the "overcommitment," the leader can work with the other person or persons to modify or reexamine the expectations or time-line. Ignoring the promise or turning in an inferior product diminishes the value of our word and tarnishes our integrity. Honesty and intentionality around making and keeping our promises maintains our integrity even when we cannot deliver on the original promise.

REFLECTION

Describe your intentions for making and keeping promises.

_____

_____

_____

_____

What would be the impact in an organization if everyone kept his or her promise?

_____

_____

_____

_____

REQUEST VERSUS REQUIREMENT

Leaders also build trust by being clear in their communication. Knowing the difference between a request and a requirement can dramatically change the way we do our work as leaders. How we ask for what we want, once we have gained clarity about it, is important as we advance the conversation with others. This is sometimes very easy and sometimes more difficult. Understanding the distinction between a request and a requirement clears the "fuzziness" that is sometimes present when we are asking something of someone else. Here are some suggestions that will make asking for what you want more successful.

When making a request, the other person has an option, an opportunity to grant the request or deny it. If the person making the request can accept that either answer of "yes" or "no" is acceptable, it is a request. If we make a request of someone and react strongly when the person says, "no," then we have not made a request; we have imposed a requirement.

Leaders often ask staff members to serve on committees, attend meetings, and revise curriculum. If the leader has only one person in mind for this job, and he is not willing to consider anyone else, the request—no matter how nicely it is stated—is essentially a requirement rather than a request. If the only response you will accept is a "yes," it is a requirement. If "no" is a possibility, it is a request.

Consider the friend who wanted her husband to remove an unsightly automobile from their property. She professed to making a request, "Recognizing that you want our yard to give a good first impression when our guests arrive this weekend, are you moving the car today or tomorrow?" Her husband responded that he had no intention of moving the car. Her clue that it was not a request but a requirement was the surge of anger that surfaced in response to his reply.

In *Falling Awake*, Dave Ellis (2002) suggests that when we make requests, we use very specific language providing details that include the timeline. When we ask for what we want, we model a powerful skill that invites others to ask for what they want.

Leaders generally think that it is a requirement if it comes from their boss. However, a leader, living in integrity, who also has a good relationship with her boss, may respond to the situation differently by asking for a clarification. Is this a request or a requirement? Knowing the difference between request and requirement gives us options to consider and invites clarity in the conversation, especially with regard to any future actions.

For example, an elementary principal was asked to take over the district professional development initiative following the resignation of a central office staff member. This occurred in the middle of the year. The principal disclosed to his coach that he was not interested in taking the position. While he had served on the Professional Development Committee in the past, he did not view this step as a growth opportunity for himself. He also knew that the responsibilities would include commitments in the evening that would compete with his commitment to spend time with his young family. During the conversation with his coach, he moved from thinking he was obligated (required) to do this job regardless of his personal preferences to realizing that he loved the process of interviewing, which would support the staffing of this open position. Through the process of rehearsal with his coach, the principal found the language and courage to renegotiate the request from the superintendent to one of interviewing and hiring the person to fill the position.

Initially, the principal assumed the request was a requirement and that he was obligated to take the position without consideration of what he wanted. Ultimately, he learned that what appeared to be a requirement was actually a request because the superintendent was fully supportive of his idea.

In the school setting, our minds most often go directly to requirement. Here is another example of how knowing the difference paid off in a big way.

An assistant principal learned the power of asking for what she wanted knowing that the answer could be "yes" or "no." She wanted to request extra funding for her initiatives, staff development, and the continuation of work with her external coach. To support her case, she prepared by developing a plan based on the outcomes she expected, including evidence of past successes. She met with the head of the staff development department to lobby for increased staff development funds for the purpose of building teacher leader capacity on her campus. She supported her request with how that would benefit kids. Clear about what she wanted and how she could get there, she identified a certain amount of money for a specific purpose for particular teachers. And she was perfectly clear that this was a request.

The outcome was that she received the money, and teachers received professional development, which empowered them to lead the initiative on the campus. She was promoted to principal.

Read the next example to see how lack of clarity in language with no understanding of request versus requirement can interfere with communication as well as the relationship.

The superintendent says to Joe, "We just got these quotations from a vendor. Look them over and see what you think."

Although the superintendent thought she was clear about her requirement, Joe never got back to her about the quotations. The superintendent complained that Joe had ignored her order to review the quotations. Joe had reviewed the quotations immediately and then waited for the superintendent to invite him to talk about them. His complaint was that she threw stuff at him and never got back to him.

The superintendent is expecting a requirement, and Joe is thinking it is a request even though they do not know the language. Regardless, the result is that work does not get accomplished in a timely manner, *and* the relationship is impacted in a negative way.

Choosing language with greater specificity helps the receiver become clearer about what you want. Consider a replay of the conversation between the superintendent and Joe.

The superintendent says to Joe, "We just got these quotations from a vendor. Look them over and see what you think. Get back with me by Monday morning prior to our staff meeting, so we will be prepared to discuss our options at the meeting." or "Let's set a time when we can review these together."

Clearly, this is a requirement rather than a request. With more precise language, communication is clear, work moves forward, and the relationship remains intact.

According to Dave Ellis (2002) in *Falling Awake*, there are five effective responses to a request. One is that you can grant the request. Another is to deny the request knowing that "no" is a perfectly good response. A third possibility is to make a counteroffer, such as "I could deliver the report by _____." (This is a date beyond the original timeline that fits with your schedule and workload.) Asking for clarification is a fourth option. And the final possibility is to postpone your response by asking for more time to consider the request before making the commitment.

REFLECTION

Think of a time when you made a request and others thought it was a requirement. What happened?

_____

_____

_____

_____

Conversely, think of a time that you made a requirement and it was not honored. Write an effective way to restate your requirement, adding specifics that will clearly communicate your expectation.

_____

_____

_____

_____

In what ways will you use this concept of request versus requirement to enhance your communication with others?

_____

_____

_____

_____

SUMMARY

The four concepts presented in this chapter hold the potential for dramatically changing the way we do our work as leaders. All four concepts spring from intentionality. With each advancing step of the Levels of

Language, we add self-responsibility and accountability to our communication as we increase our personal energy, power, and commitment through the language we choose to use. Our choice of language can move us from the heaviness of obligation to the power of promise. By speaking the truth and listening to the truths of others, our conversations become more authentic, and our relationships are enhanced. Making and keeping promises maintains our integrity as a leader in a way that opens the door for development of trust, which is necessary for high performance for everyone. Finally, language that distinguishes between requests and requirements can bring clarity to the conversation so that expectations are clear and options are possible.

Language is the essential connector. Just as we are connecting in new ways via texting, it is essential that today's leader connect with staff in new ways. This chapter spoke about the power of a new language for leaders—one that delivers the message while preserving the relationship. Chapter 5 will help us develop the specific skills of language for this new way of connecting.

g2g ~ cu l8r.

Powerful Communication Skills

5

THE NEW ESSENTIALS

"The problem with communication . . . is the illusion that it has been accomplished."

—George Bernard Shaw

About 25 years ago, many of us chuckled to ourselves when we heard the prediction that by the 21st century, every home would have a computer. From our perspective, at that time, we thought it sounded like a farfetched prediction, and yet now, many of us have at least two computers, not to mention all the other things in our homes that are computer operated.

So, how did we move from being unskilled to proficient computer users? We moved through a process from the hearing, seeing, wondering stages on to the investigating, exploring, battling, and conquering stages. As we progressed through these stages, the more intentional we became in our use of the computer. We began to experience the value of this new tool, and we became much more committed to learning how to use it. At some stage during the process, the computer moved from a "don't have" to a "nice to have" to a "must have"—a true essential in our lives. We became one with the computer (at least we felt we couldn't get along without it), and we said good-bye to the no longer essential typewriter.

It's this change process that Hord, Rutherford, Huling-Austin, and Hall (1998) discuss in their book *Taking Charge of Change* that moves individuals from an attitude of investigation to an acquisition of new behaviors, if they are willing to take the journey and if they believe that the new behaviors are essential, a "must have," for them.

As school leaders, we understand this concept of *new essentials* because we are working in a time when the stakes continue to increase expectations about student performance and for the adults working with them. We know that we must thoughtfully and intentionally determine the best tools and skills that will help move us to the next level of our effectiveness. Thus, we offer RESULTS Coaching as the new *essential.* As mentioned earlier in the book, district and school administration is no longer about school leaders who lead only because they supervise others; it's about leaders who lead through the lens of coaching, helping others acquire for themselves their own set of new essentials. It's about helping others move to action based upon their own thinking, doing, and being.

When coach leaders make public their engagement in the difficult processes of change, they become extraordinary teachers. Leaders, who themselves model learning, support a much more powerful learning organization (Kagan & Lahey, 2001).

The focus of this chapter is on the RESULTS coaching skills that committed leaders intentionally use as they coach others to discover and use the brilliance within themselves. This chapter will examine the communication skills of committed listening, paraphrasing, presuming positive intent, reflective feedback, and the cousin to presuming positive intent—powerful questions. For each skill, an opportunity for practice and deepening understanding is provided. To totally integrate these new essentials, continuous ongoing practice is a must!

The intention to focus on these four essential skills does not lessen the importance of a variety of other skills that impact results that will be listed and identified at the end of the chapter and in the Resources.

SKILL 1

Committed Listening

How do we, as coach leaders, begin our journey of identifying, refining, and/or acquiring the essential skills of RESULTS *Coaching?* One important way is to begin with self-assessment. The following self-assessment opportunity provides a structure to look within, to determine where we are now as it relates to where we want to be. Committed listening is so critical and important that it is the most essential of all essential skills. It is the foundational skill for all communication skills.

As Dennis Sparks (2006), former director of Learning Forward (formerly the National Staff Development Council), says, "Committed listening transforms relationships and deepens learning. Its skillful use requires practice and discipline" (p. 52).

When we listen with commitment, we convey, "I care about what you have to say, and I'm listening with all my senses so that I fully understand an issue from your perspective. I am listening for both the content of the words and the emotions that resonate or peek out from behind the words. I am listening to hear the underlying beliefs and thinking that are occurring for the speaker as she or he continues to talk as well as what she or he is creating and learning."

As committed listeners, we listen to

- gain clarity about an issue;
- understand the needs, perceptions, and emotions of the speaker;
- gather data for feedback;
- allow the speaker to refine thinking by speaking to an attentive listener;
- seek patterns of behavior; and
- lay a path for building responses and solutions.

Using the *CFR Committed Listening Reflection Tool* takes a few minutes and identifies where you are, right now, in your use of committed listening. Knowing that your intention is to reside on the right side of the tool as you acquire the skills necessary to do so, where are you now? Identify your current level of consistent use. Where are your strengths, and where are the areas for desired growth?

In completing the self-reflection tool, you may have found some areas that spoke to the need for you to become more intentional in your committed listening behaviors. And if you did, it's safe to say that you are not alone. The inability to use the skills of committed listening in a consistent manner is most likely the reason why people find conversations to be so challenging, unfulfilling, or at the very least, not as productive as they could be.

What keeps us from residing on the right side of the reflection tool? What are all the internal and external distracters that compete for our attention? And how do we, by knowing about these distracters, triumph over them and take control of our listening behaviors?

Cognitive Coaching has identified some unproductive patterns of listening behaviors. Let's examine four patterns that unintentionally lessen our listening effectiveness (Costa & Garmston, 2002). As we listen, any of these patterns have the potential to become "loud" in our head; in other

Figure 5.1 CFR Committed Listening Tool

When I am listening to someone speak, my thoughts drift away instead of listening to what is being said.	Low 1	2	3	4	High 5	I concentrate on what the person speaking is saying and feeling while monitoring my listening behaviors as the conversation evolves.
While I'm listening to someone else, I'm being critical, thinking about my response, or relating to my own experience.	Low 1	2	3	4	High 5	I listen fully to the person speaking and set aside judgment, solution finding, or personal stories.
I'm quick to interrupt to express my own thoughts and opinions.	Low 1	2	3	4	High 5	Before responding, I wait to be sure the other person is finished with his or her thoughts.
I don't ask for clarification when I don't understand what the person means by what he or she is saying, or I interrupt with questions that either hijack or sidetrack the conversation.	Low 1	2	3	4	High 5	I ask questions to better understand what the other person is saying when I'm not clear on what he or she means (I don't interrupt to ask questions or redirect the conversation)
I don't make eye contact or show through my facial expressions, gestures, and posture that I am listening.	Low 1	2	3	4	High 5	I convey nonverbal attention and interest through facial expressions, gestures, and posture.
When I don't agree with what is said, I interrupt and force my ideas into the conversation, or I respond by attacking what the person has said.	Low 1	2	3	4	High 5	I honor others' views, even when they are not my own or when I disagree.
I feel like I need to respond or take action to comments made by others.	Low 1	2	3	4	High 5	I listen without obligation to act and illuminate answers within others.
I don't feel comfortable paraphrasing, and when I do, I tend to "parrot" back what the speaker has said.	Low 1	2	3	4	High 5	I paraphrase for clarity, elaboration, summary, and/or to help shift the thinking for greater meaning.

words, it is like listening to a commentator in our head while we are trying to listen to another person. When we allow judgment, criticism (both positive and negative), autobiographical, inquisitive, or solution listening to overtake our thinking, we unintentionally lessen our ability to be a committed listener. Let's take a closer look at each of these distracters and consider ways we will intentionally set aside any unproductive patterns of listening that may reduce our skill as a listener—we want to "turn down the noise in our head." When we purposefully set aside unproductive patterns of listening and focus on productive patterns of listening, we are literally building new mind maps in our brain that have the potential to become new hardwiring (Rock, 2006). Now, how exciting is that?

UNPRODUCTIVE PATTERNS OF LISTENING

Judgment and Criticism

Judgment takes place when our listening focuses on what we see as flaws or greatness in another person's comments or ideas. Anytime we think or make a judgment statement, something like, "That's a great idea!" or "That won't work!" while another is speaking, we have presented ourselves as the authority, as the "wise one" over the situation. What we want to do, at the very least, is to present the respectful attitude of listening fully to what the speaker has to say. Judgment, as criticism, occurs when we feel a dissonance between what the speaker says and what we think and believe. Use of negative judgment or criticism may be perceived by others as adversarial, and thus, the conversation begins to shut down or take on a totally different tone. Positive judgments given as compliments feel good for a few moments but also can be perceived as if you believe you know best or you are an authority. Through our years of leadership and communication experience, we have seen how criticism or negative judgment is a sure way to reduce or limit thinking, inspiration, and creativity.

Criticism as the first step in a discussion risks halting the discussion and in turn becoming the last step as well. It also holds the potential of impeding the speaker's self-confidence, interfering with her thinking capability, and increasing her dependency upon approval from the listener.

Refraining from listening with an attitude of judgment may present challenges for school leaders because as the leader, you may have been trained or conditioned to appear to know best. Many of us were. It was our old hardwiring of how we thought leaders were supposed to lead. Like the TV series of yesterday, *Father Knows Best*, many thought "Leader Knows Best" was the role we were to assume, even when we were in the role of listener. We now understand that use of criticism or judgment could be viewed as arrogant and could send a message that our thoughts are the only correct thoughts.

The following are examples of judgment or criticism thoughts or statements:

- "How ridiculous!"
- "I tried that three years ago."
- "She's not serious."
- "Your premise is completely flawed."
- "I like what Ann said." (As soon as you approve of one idea, you discredit others.)
- "I tried that once, and it didn't work."
- "Why on earth would you want to do that?"

Autobiographical Listening

Autobiographical listening occurs when our brain exercises its associative powers and the speaker's story stimulates us to think of our personal experiences connected with those being addressed by the speaker. Oh, how we love to tell our own stories when what we want to be doing is listening fully to the thinking of the speaker. As one leader said, "It's hard not to interrupt just long enough to share a personal experience, one that says to the teacher, 'I understand what you mean.'"

As an effective and committed listener, we set autobiographical listening aside as soon as we become aware that our attention has drifted away from the speaker and into our own story. This listening pattern has the potential to lead us to the place of making judgments, forming comparisons, or totally breaking down our ability to attend to the speaker's thoughts. So, we constantly monitor our thinking to make sure we are staying with the speaker. For example, Karen was being consoled by a friend after the death of her mother. What Karen needed from her friend was a space to talk and reflect back on her mother's life and death. Instead, the friend, meaning to be supportive, began to share about her own mother, going into much detail about her mom's illness and subsequent death. What happened? The friend unintentionally hijacked the conversation and went off on her own story, staying there for most of the remaining time of the conversation. The friend thought she was showing compassion by sharing her personal story and most likely left the conversation thinking she had provided much support to Karen, but in fact, Karen left the conversation feeling "unheard" and empty. We are not suggesting that a person never share a personal story or example as they are intentionally listening to another. If the friend had told a brief personal story as an extension of Karen's story or as an illustration of something

Karen had shared, it might have been beneficial, serving as a way of empathizing with Karen's emotions.

We know that personal comments provided while you are listening to another can be beneficial to show your empathy and understanding. The brain is making natural connections to show caring. The committed listener is always monitoring the amount of personal sharing they offer. The committed listener knows sharing a personal example is a way to offer empathy and then quickly return to the other person's story.

One experience Kathy shares is when, as an assistant superintendent, very angry parents arrived at her office demanding the firing of a principal and a teacher. She quickly acknowledged their anger and disappointment in how a situation had been handled and invited them to share how she could partner with them in a solution. The parents shared the details of a situation of how their child, a middle schooler, had been accused of lying. Immediately, the details of their story sent Kathy's brain darting down her dendrites connecting to being a middle school teacher and wondering what made this kid different . . . and then remembering a similar situation with her own daughter. As she listened, she decided to take a chance using autobiographical listening to connect with and show empathy toward these hostile parents. She shared with the parents her similar feelings of a common experience when her daughter was in middle school and asked permission to share what happened to her. The parents eagerly agreed, seeing her genuine caring and interest and obvious similarity to their situation.

Kathy explained that her daughter brought home a letter stating that she had lost her bus privileges for a month for a continued violation on the bus. Her daughter, Jill, vehemently denied that this happened, that she was a victim of false identification, but she knew "her mother would never go to her defense because her mother was a teacher, and teacher parents never go against their fellow teachers." Saddened by her daughter's strong opinion, Kathy assured her daughter that she was her advocate and would go with her the following morning to clear up this false identification. Kathy concluded by asking her daughter one more time, "Are you sure you were not involved in this incident?" to which Jill replied, "Absolutely not, Mom, I am innocent!"

The next morning, they arrived at the assistant principal's office requesting a few moments to clear up the misunderstanding. It was especially uncomfortable because this was the same school where Kathy had taught before becoming an administrator, and these educators were her peers. Very quickly, other players were called into the small office, including her special friend, a prior teaching partner, who was also the bus driver. Kathy began the conversation by stating she knew how busy everyone was and she only desired to advocate for her daughter and a situation that had her mistakenly identified as part of a bus incident. As everyone sat together—the administrator, a teacher, the bus driver, Kathy, and her daughter—Kathy could see the look in the eyes of her friend who drove the bus. He spoke up gingerly offering "Kathy, I am so sorry, but I personally witnessed the incident with Jill."

Kathy slowly turned to look at her daughter, tension building, to hear what she would say. With the innocence of a six year old, Jill replied, "But I only did that one time!" Hearing her daughter's perception of the situation caused an avalanche of emotions within Kathy. She thought first about how sad it was that her daughter would never enjoy the fun of driving, never see her walk across the graduation stage, and so on because her life, as she knew it was over! Then, a second wave of emotions came from being so embarrassed that her daughter would put her in this position with her peers. Kathy was mortified!

At this moment, observing all along the body language cues of the angry parents, she paused, knowing it was time to return to their situation. She could see a change, a softening in their eyes. Almost immediately, the father lifted his hand to stop her. The father spoke by saying, "We have probably overreacted to this situation, but we had to stand up against such a negative accusation about our son." Kathy affirmed all parents' roles as chief advocate for their children and applauded their demonstration of belief to come forward and talk about it. A delightful conversation followed, a new relationship was born, and the parents left with smiles on their faces and a document in their hands that described the developmental characteristics of the seventh and eighth grader.

Autobiographical stories offer the possibility of connecting to others in a way that shows caring and understanding, but without monitoring, they can also highjack another's story and turn the focus away from that person. The committed listener will know exactly when it is time to return to the story and situation of the other. The speaker will feel empathy is when someone is fully listening and attending.

Examples of autobiographical listening include thoughts similar to the following:

- You think Johnny is a challenge? You should have known Sue. Let me tell you about her!
- I remember when I felt like that too. Why let me tell you . . . .
- She thinks she works hard; well, I remember when I first became a teacher. We had no help at all . . . .
- How do you think you would feel if you had four different preps? In my first assignment . . . .

Inquisitive Listening

A third unproductive pattern of listening is inquisitive listening, which occurs when we become curious about something the speaker says that is not relevant to the issue at hand. For example, Mary, one of your third-grade teachers, comes into your office and asks for your help. One of her students, Bill Smith, has just fallen asleep in class for the third time this week. Mary begins to explain why she is so concerned about Bill's change in behavior over the past few weeks. She tells you that she knows she needs to contact Bill's mother, to discuss this with her but knows that Mrs. Smith is leaving tomorrow for an extended trip to Spain. Before you realize it, you are thinking, "I wonder where in Spain she is going? I wonder if she will go to Toledo?" Your inquisitive thoughts have caused you to stop hearing Mary. You might even go from thinking to speaking and provide evidence to Mary that you were not hearing her need. A committed listener knows how distracting inquisitive listening can be, and they intentionally set aside distracting thoughts to stay focused on the words of the speaker, committed to ask questions only for the sake of gaining clarity around the issue at hand and without interrupting the speaker's flow of thinking.

A committed listener needs only to understand the speaker's perspectives, feelings, and goals and how to pose questions that support self-directed thinking and learning. When we speculate, we are trying to figure out what someone is thinking and feeling before they have said it. Speculation is another distraction that does not allow us to pay sufficient attention to what another is saying.

Scrutinizing is also a by-product of inquisitive listening—a curiosity about what is not relevant to the listening moment sinks the conversation into a hole of minutiae that causes us to lose sight of the larger issue. For example, when we become so distracted by the conversation and start focusing on little details that are not essential or are unimportant to the overall purpose, we are demonstrating scrutinizing listening. Or if a teacher brings in a letter to share with me as the leader, and I place my focus on editing the letter instead of the content of the message, I'm scrutinizing while listening.

Kathy witnessed this amusing example between two colleagues:

Excitedly, Anita rushed to her fellow teacher, Sharon, and immediately began to tell her of the weekend encounter she had had with one of their ever-difficult teammates. Anita said, "You will not believe what Lorraine said to me when I saw her this weekend at T.J. Maxx." To which, Sharon replied, "Where is a T.J. Maxx? I love that store."

While pretty funny, the impact to the one desiring to be listened to can be like being stopped by a wall and wanting to yell out, "Did you hear anything I said?"

Examples of inquisitive listening include the following:

- A parent is sharing distractions in their family due to the dad getting a new job. The teacher begins to wonder how much money he will be making and if he might travel.
- A new teacher is talking about the wonderful success she had with her students using a certain strategy. Her teammate wants to know what book she got that idea from and what materials were needed to do it.

Solution Listening

A fourth pattern of unproductive listening occurs when we view ourselves as great problem solvers, ready and eager to help and give suggestions to others. We have probably even been hired for a position because we are such great problem solvers. This ability, this behavior, interferes with our commitment to listen fully because we are searching for the right solution for someone else. In committed listening, however, solution finding interferes with understanding the situation from the colleague's perspective. As we solution listen, we often filter by listening to some things and not to others, paying attention to only those ideas that support the solution approach we see. We filter when we hear what we want to hear or what supports our point of view but not necessarily the point of view of the speaker. As our attention gets focused on preparing the way we are going to present a solution or on rehearsing what we are going to say, we have again stopped listening. Stephen Covey (1989) asks, "Are we listening to understand or to reply?

The following are a few examples of solution listening:

- " Why doesn't she see that will never work . . . . She is going to have to make sure of these things . . . ."
- "I would never write a letter of resignation under those circumstances. He needs to write the personnel director and make sure that he knows about this situation and say . . . ."
- "If she would just stop talking; I need to make her see the need for more student involvement."

Effective listeners monitor and manage their own listening skills by focusing their mental energies to committed listening. To listen with such intensity requires intentionally avoiding these unproductive behaviors that interfere with the ability to hear and fully understand another.

BARRIERS TO COMMITTED LISTENING

Madelyn Burley-Allen (1995), in *Listening: The Forgotten Skill*, speaks to barriers of committed listening we may encounter and how to remain intentional in our committed listening. These barriers naturally organize themselves into two large groups: internal and external distracters.

1. Internal Distractions

Internal distracters are those emotions and thoughts from within us that have the potential to hijack our attention. The list can be endless and includes feeling hungry, sleepy, cold, hot, sad, happy or angry, or thinking about your next appointment. Let's look specifically at four of these areas.

Physical Barriers.

Our body can serve as a barrier to being a committed listener. For example, when we are fatigued, our thought processes slow down as it takes more energy to concentrate on the speaker's meaning. When our energy is low, our concentration declines and our daydreaming capacity increases. Likewise, when our energy is captured by personal problems, we have less energy available for focused listening. To increase the challenge of physical barriers, the human mind is able to hear words at a faster rate than we are able to say them, so if we are not committed listeners, we will find little pockets of time that we can use for our personal daydreaming.

Emotional Reactions.

As we listen, we attend to both the content and emotions of the speaker. As Jill Bolte-Taylor (2006) tells us in *My Stroke of Insight*, although many of us may think of ourselves as thinking creatures that feel, biologically, we are feeling creatures that think. Therefore, we must listen for emotions and content from the speaker, and we must also be aware of our own emotions as we listen. What do we do with these two sources of information that come to us from the speaker? If we are not intentional, we may find ourselves being hijacked from committed listening to emotional or reactive listening. For instance, the speaker uses words that push our "hot button," and before we realize what's happened, we tune out the speaker, rise to our figurative soapbox, and begin to defend our differing point of view, either verbally or internally. Or we may begin to formulate our response to the speaker in the form of either questions or comments. It is critical to remember to keep listening to understand the speaker and to set aside emotional reactions, knowing that you will have a time in the conversation to ask clarifying questions or speak from your point of view. As we have learned from the work of emotional intelligence (Goleman, 1998), we know that the ability to self-monitor and hold our emotions in check until an appropriate time to share is a sign of emotional strength. A RESULTS Coach demonstrates emotional intelligence as he listens to others.

Biases and Judgments.

As discussed earlier, forming judgments while listening is a huge distracter to committed listening. So are personal biases. If we are not intentional in our listening behaviors, previous experiences—whether positive or negative—may influence our ability to listen with intention. For example, Mrs. Billings, an elementary principal committed to overcoming the distraction of listening through the lens of personal biases, speaks about the process she uses to coach Mrs. Garrett, a second-grade teacher on a professional growth plan. Mrs. Billings says, "When Mrs. Garret and I are in conversation about her growth plan, I intentionally set aside thoughts that could move me to forming judgments based on previous years' performance and instead listen intentionally to her descriptions of progress and the steps she is taking to achieve her professional growth plan. I'm setting aside the distracter of where she has been and am listening intently to where she is going. I'll ask clarifying questions or make my comments when it is my time to speak. I find it very helpful to intentionally set aside distracters of biases and judgments."

Here is another example. Mrs. Smith, a third-grade teacher, walks into the principal's office and says, "The influx of all these kids from the new apartments just can't learn like our other kids! It's so frustrating and how on earth are we going to be expected to stay on pace in the curriculum?" Mrs. Smith's statements are in direct opposition to the belief in this school that all students can and will learn at high levels, based on what we do to help and encourage them to learn. While she does not agree with Mrs. Smith's statements, the principal, committed to deep listening, is listening to understand what is behind the teacher's words and emotions so that she can best help her move forward to positive actions based on her concerns.

Bias around poverty, race, religion, lifestyle, and age are other possible examples of internal barriers that may keep us from listening fully to another's point of view. We may encounter big challenges when we, as committed listeners, are faced with issues that confront our own value systems. Instead of trying to change the speaker's point of view, how do we intentionally set aside our bias or judgments to be fully present for the person speaking? As RESULTS coach leaders, we know that we can never influence a new point of view until we first hear and attempt to understand another's point of view.

Semantic misunderstandings may occur as each of us has our own meanings for words that we filter though our personal experiences, beliefs, education, and mindset. While we share words with the people we work with, we still have our personal interpretation of those words. A most important caution for us, as leaders, is to be on guard that what speakers may be saying is not exactly the same as what we think they are saying. Their mind map may be totally different from our mind map. Their words may have different meanings. Remember the quote mentioned earlier in the book, the one that hung for years in Vicky's dentist office? It said, "I know you believe you understand what you think I said, but I am not sure you realize that what you heard is not what I meant." The message for all is to listen for the intent of understanding from the perspective of the speaker and not to let our own words and meanings halt or slow down our understanding. Effective paraphrasing, addressed later, offers a powerful tool to listen and fully understand.

2. External Distractions

In addition to internal distracters, our listening is challenged with external distracters from our environment, competing for our attention. If we are not careful, these distractions can rule us instead of us ruling them. A few that might impact our ability to be a committed listener are as follows:

- You are listening to the speaker when your phone rings, either fully or in the silent mode. What to do? Do you stop and see who is calling, or do you let it go to your voice mail?
- You are listening fully when you hear the sound on your computer that tells you there's new e-mail. Should you take a quick peek? It might be the superintendent or the board president.

- You are listening fully when your secretary opens the door and hands you a paper to sign. Do you sign it as you listen and also make a few comments to your secretary about the paper?
- You notice that the speaker is wearing a beautiful necklace. Do you begin to think about what that necklace might look like on you?

The list could go on and on, but you get the point. Committed listeners strive to be fully present with the conversation. When we cannot, because of external distracters, we have some choices to make to help us stay in the "fully present" mode. We can ask for permission to make an accommodation, like rescheduling the meeting or stopping the conversation for a few minutes to deal with a pressing issue so that we are able to return to the state of being fully present during the conversation. A principal shared with us recently that when she saw the movie, *Up,* she realized she was exactly like the eager dog, who while really wanting to listen, could not resist the distraction of a squirrel running past. She confessed she must look like that dog in her conversations that might sound like the following:

"Yes, how is your class doing?" Squirrel!

"You said Billy was making what grade?" Squirrel!

"Oh, the meeting tonight is about what?" Squirrel!

Squirrel . . . squirrel . . . squirrel . . . They are everywhere!

REFLECTION

RESULTS leaders know that listening is the first step toward helping others move to action. First, we listen, and then, we respond based on what we have heard. To listen with such intensity requires intentionally avoiding unproductive behaviors and overcoming barriers to committed listening that interfere with our ability to hear and understand another.

1. In reflecting back on the unproductive patterns of listening that have been presented in this chapter, what are you learning about what you need to pay attention to in order to intentionally avoid these patterns in your conversations?

2. How do you plan to develop strengths as a committed listener?

3. How do you plan to "be" as a committed listener?

4. Choose one of the barriers from the list above. Create a web with the distracter in the middle of the web. Brainstorm as many options as possible for handling this distraction.

5. What are other barriers that you have discovered that can impede your listening if not addressed and eliminated? What have you learned about the importance of dealing with these barriers or distracters?

SKILL 2

Paraphrasing

Closely connected to the essential skill of listening is the essential skill of paraphrasing. In fact, there is such a strong connection between the two, it's like the song says, "You can't have one without the other!" A skillful paraphrase follows intentional listening and is offered in response to the words spoken and the emotions observed as well, as those hidden or not yet revealed or realized by the speaker. The benefits of paraphrasing are multidimensional both for the listener and the speaker, providing the opportunity for greater clarity and movement of thinking. Paraphrasing is intended to align the people in a conversation and create a safe environment for thinking.

Interestingly, while paraphrasing is an essential skill of RESULTS Coaching, it is typically one of the least used communication skills. Perhaps that is because it requires a commitment to listening more than talking during the conversation. Leaders who develop a consciousness about the power of this skill and commit to using the reflective tool become clearer and more effective in their conversations. In so doing, they are much more likely to help move people to action, action that benefits the individual and the entire organization. Frequently, people ask, "Why paraphrase, I know what he said?" The purpose of the paraphrase is not as much for the listener, as it is for the benefit of the speaker. It reflects the content (and emotions) back to the speaker for consideration and connects the response to the flow of the emerging conversation.

Recently, Vicky observed the value of a paraphrase as she worked with a group of incarcerated women. It was as if a wave of relief came over them when they heard someone say back to them in summarized form what they had expressed in their thinking and feeling. She observed eyes that seemed to say, "Oh yes! You get what I'm saying!" If paraphrasing can positively impact women's thinking in prison, consider the value of paraphrasing within our schools and our personal lives.

A paraphrase has the potential to serve as a gift to the speaker while at the same time creating permission to move forward with more details and elaboration of thought. Without paraphrasing, questioning may seem more like interrogation. With paraphrasing, trustful pathways for thoughtful communication open up, leading towards possibilities of deliberate actions.

THREE MESSAGES OF PARAPHRASING

A paraphrase sends three messages:

1. I am listening.

2. I am interested—I care.

3. I understand you, or I'm trying to understand you.

MOVING FROM I TO YOU

During the 1970s, many people were taught to paraphrase in one particular way that has been very hardwired in our language but is very ineffective. The use of the phrase, "What I hear you saying is . . ." signaled to many speakers that their thoughts became secondary to those of the paraphraser who was inserting his or her own ideas into the conversation. Clearly, that was never the intent of beginning a paraphrase with an "I" statement. By simply moving the paraphrase to a "you" statement, greater benefits are provided to the speaker.

Years ago, Madeline Hunter stressed this point during a UCLA summer institute when she said, "Take the I-Yi-Yi-Yi-Yi out of your paraphrasing and replace it with the you, you, you, you, you!" That point has stuck with us as we help others discover the power potential of paraphrasing!

PRINCIPLES OF PARAPHRASING

Costa and Garmston (2002), Lipton and Wellman (2001), and others have offered some principles of paraphrasing well worth considering. We highlight five that have brought much value to our RESULTS Coaching experiences.

1. **Fully attend**. Set aside all distracters and barriers that compete for your attention and use your committed listening skills. Monitor yourself as you listen to make sure you stay in the moment with the speaker. If you find your thoughts straying to other areas, intentionally bring yourself back to the role of the listener.

2. **Listen with the intent to understand.** Concentrate on both the content and the emotions of the speaker and remember about the words behind the words, or what we have earlier referred to as the river that flows beneath the words. For example, a teacher comes into the principal's office and says, "I've had it with Johnny, and I don't want him in my classroom anymore!" The RESULTS coach leader is hearing her words but is also hearing (and seeing) that she is frustrated and feels she is out of strategies to help Johnny.

3. **Capture the *essence* of the message in a paraphrase that is shorter than the original statement.** It's not about parroting back but rather pulling forward the most important messages contained in the talking. For instance, someone speaks for a full five minutes. You listen and capture the heart of his or her thoughts in a one- or two-sentence paraphrase rather than shifting your thinking over to a space where you tune him or her out, create a response, formulate a solution, or simultaneously attend to another task, clearly moving you from being a committed listener.

4. **Reflect the essence of voice tone and gestures.** Capture or identify emotions you hear or see. Earlier, we talked about listening fully with all of your senses. Much information can be gained through voice tone and gestures. If the speaker is loud, you don't have to respond in kind. Instead, you can name the meaning of the voice tone and gestures and await validation from the speaker. For instance, a paraphrase that deals with voice tone and gestures might be as simple as, "You feel strongly about this issue," rather than, "You don't need to yell!"

5. **Paraphrase before asking a question.** This is frequently overlooked if we are not intentional in our paraphrasing. Cognitive Coaching taught us to "Pause, Paraphrase, Probe" the three Ps that can transform conversations. Pause to truly listen first, paraphrase next to allow the speaker to feel understood and heard, and then ask a question. For example, in talking with a former principal, a first-time administrator expresses her concern about the relationship with her peers in her new role. The former principal could say, "So, what do you want the new relationship to be? How will you do it, and when will you start working on it?" Instead, she begins with a paraphrase that speaks to the value of her new role, reflecting on her relationship with her new staff by saying, "You are wondering how the relationships you value with your peers will change as a result of your new role," pausing for the response. Depending on the speaker's response, you may ask a question such as those asked above.

Recently, Kathy had the opportunity to experience the power of paraphrasing while working with a group of school leaders. After completing a teach piece on paraphrasing, participants moved into small practice groups to try out their new learning. As it happened in one small group, a superintendent was assigned the role of listener for a principal who was asked to speak about an authentic issue she was currently facing, one where she knew she needed to take action. Both the superintendent and the principal voiced feelings of uncertainly as they began the process and both spoke favorably of the experience at the conclusion of the activity.

During the debrief time, the superintendent described feelings of apprehension as he began the activity, unsure of how best to help the principal get what she wanted out of the conversation. He understood that as the listener, his role was to paraphrase but was somewhat hesitant about how to actually do the paraphrasing in the "right" way. The superintendent listened, paused, and then said, "So, you are disappointed in yourself that you have not had a conversation with your teacher." The principal, not feeling judged, continued to speak honestly about the situation. Again, the superintendent listened, paused, and then said, "You have a deep belief that if this teacher's practice was more effective, it would dramatically impact the results of your school." Without judgment, the superintendent paraphrased, and that paraphrase caused insight for the principal that provided the energy for action. The principal resolved to have a conversation with the teacher before the end of the day.

As the two reflected on the conversation, the superintendent spoke of feeling awkward and stiff with his paraphrasing. The principal, however, didn't feel the paraphrases were stiff; in fact, she spoke to the value of his nonjudgmental language in creating clarity, insight, and a sense of support that propelled her to action.

What does this story say to each of us? Perhaps, the message is that a "stiff" paraphrase is better than no paraphrase at all, and the more practice we have with paraphrasing, the better we become at using the skill. The more skilled we become at paraphrasing, the greater the possibility for helping others bring clarity and accuracy to their thinking and doing. The insights created provide energy for action.

One strategy Vicky learned years ago for increasing her paraphrasing skills was to sit in front of the TV, listen to someone talking, and paraphrase what he or she said. It's a great way to flex your paraphrasing skills and to help prepare you to become more proficient in your use of three main types of paraphrases.

THREE TYPES OF PARAPHRASES

We acknowledge again the work of Bob Garmston and Art Costa (2002) in *Cognitive Coaching* and Laura Lipton and Bruce Wellman (2002) in their work on *Mentoring Matters.* We use a scaffold approach for creating paraphrase from three levels:

1. Acknowledging and clarifying

2. Summarizing and organizing

3. Shifting conceptual focus

We paraphrase from two perspectives or arenas: the emotions and the content provided by the speaker.

Level 1: Acknowledge and Clarify

When we acknowledge and clarify, we restate the essence of someone's statement by identifying and calibrating content and emotions. By design, acknowledging and clarifying paraphrases communicate our desire to understand and our value for the person. We intentionally eliminate the word "I" in our paraphrase. Some examples might include the following:

- "So, you're feeling overwhelmed by the new state standards for science."
- "You're noticing that some students are actively involved in the learning and some are not."
- "You're frustrated because your plan is not working as you expected."
- "You're excited about the possibilities of your new approach!"

Kathy offers the concept of "Witness the Struggle" as a powerful acknowledge (emotion) paraphrase. The concept comes from a significant learning that occurred in 1982 while serving as the district gifted and talented coordinator. A psychologist came in to work with the parents of gifted children and with Kathy and her team. As the psychologist listened to Kathy voice concerns over parents who demanded many things of the district, he asked Kathy to remember a very important thing. He said, "People know, rationally, that we cannot always give them everything they want. They know that we can't change policy for them. They understand that there are circumstances or situations that determine our actions in school systems. But they demand that . . . we 'witness their struggle.'" That experience was one of the greatest gifts Kathy received as an educator and fellow human. Those three words became one of the most powerful strategies to really witness the power of paraphrasing.

When a parent would come in upset and say, "My child has got to qualify for the gifted program!" Kathy would remember and say, "You are disappointed and frustrated that our restrictive criteria is not recognizing the talents of your child," or "You are feeling frustrated by the requirements of a program and fearful that without our program your child will miss opportunities."

The significance of " witnessing their struggle" was evident every time. Parents felt heard and understood, which created a pathway to have a conversation, whereas before, there was no real conversation, just a confrontation. Opportunities abound for paraphrasing by "witnessing the struggle." As Assistant Superintendent, Kathy oversaw the district extracurricular activity of cheerleaders. Joyful and thrilling as that responsibility was, it never failed to offer a tearful or angry phone call from mothers whose dreams for their daughters were shattered by not being selected to the squad. One memorable conversation went somewhat like the following:

Cheerleader mom	. . ."I want the district supervisor and the sponsor for cheerleaders fired for having a biased and unfair competition."
Response	. . ."You are extremely disappointed in the district's execution and outcomes with this competition."
The mother continued	. . ."Is there no intelligent person in this district who can organize and run a competition? Did they hire everyone is this district from substandard community colleges?"
Response	. . . Mrs. Cheer, you are convinced that those running our cheerleading competitions need organizational skills."

While the exchange continued for 30 minutes, all Kathy did was patiently listen and "witness her struggle." At the end of her tirade, the mother said, "Well, finally I found someone in the district who listens."

Her final statement was another powerful affirmation that so many times, people simply want to be heard. While this mother had a reputation of being quite troublesome and rude, her future interactions with Kathy were always courteous and respectful.

To acknowledge and clarify are easy and yet powerful ways that language exemplifies listening, caring, and concern.

Level 2: Summarize and Organize

As we move beyond acknowledging and clarifying, we summarize and organize the speaker's comments. By summarizing and organizing, we offer themes and containers that shape the initiating statement or separate jumbled issues. This paraphrase is useful when there has been a great deal said in a long stream of language.

Some examples follow. Notice the inclusion of emotions and content as the paraphrase moves the thinking to a higher level:

- "So, there seems to be two key areas of concern for you with students who have yet to meet the reading standards. First, you are concerned about absences. You are seeing a direct correlation between concept acquisition and consistent attendance. Your second concern is with time. You feel that additional instructional time must be provided to these students for concept development, and you're wondering how best to provide that time."
- "You're describing three big tasks you see for yourself. First, you want to conduct weekly assessment checks with "at risk" students. Second, you want to provide specific instruction twice daily based on the data you have collected from these assessment checks. Third, you want to hold weekly updates with the parents to keep them involved in this concentrated instructional approach."
- "On one hand, you want to talk frankly with the parent, and on the other hand, you are concerned about the receptivity of the parent to a frank conversation."

Level 3: Shifting Conceptual Focus

The third level of paraphrasing is shifting the conceptual focus of the thinking by surfacing assumptions, beliefs, core values, and mental models. Metaphors, analogies, perspective taking, and reframing shift the focus upward or downward. This type of paraphrase helps move thinking to a higher, more conceptual level or to a lower, more logical level, based upon observed need. A shifting-up paraphrase illuminates large ideas or categories, often leading the speaker to new discoveries. A shifting-down paraphrase focuses and clarifies, increasing precision of thinking.

For individuals who think in highly global patterns, the shift down is a way of grounding their thinking in specific examples and details. For individuals who think in highly sequential and concrete patterns, the shift up is a way of helping them explore a bigger picture and provide a wider context for their thoughts. Shifts up tend to grab big ideas about values, beliefs, assumptions, goals, or intentions.

In a conversation years ago with Bob Garmston, Kathy shared her emotional exhaustion from trying to meet demands of the community for the district to be innovative with structures for teaching and learning. With each idea she presented to the district-level committee of parents and community leaders, she felt hammered by their strong allegiance to traditional approaches, contradictory to their requests for innovation. She was feeling defeated and tired of trying. Bob paraphrased, "Kathy, you are feeling like a pioneer, forging a new path and meeting with resistance at every turn of the path." Kathy's tear-filled eyes dried with amazing speed as she heard the word, *pioneer*, . . . wow, yes, that was how she wanted to be, the spirit of a pioneer. Her head immediately went to leadership visionary Joel Barker and the critical importance of pioneers. Her body language went from hunched to straight, from beaten down to strength. One word of a paraphrase had the power to totally transform her attitude and energy to her work . . . a single conversation that reconnected her to her drive and commitment toward the district goal. Within three years, her district became the largest district in the state to achieve the ranking of exemplary.

Another example finds a teacher upset about the consistent tardiness of one of her students. The counselor paraphrased, "So, your frustration from the tardiness is causing you to feel your student doesn't care and preventing you from uncovering the family issues impacting his behavior." After a long pause, it was clear the paraphrase influenced a huge shift in the teacher's thinking. Simply hearing the words of the powerful paraphrase, the teacher's thinking opened to other possibilities around motivation other than simply not caring.

Other examples of shifting up paraphrases include the following:

- "So, a goal that seems to be forming for you this year is to focus on increasing your students' ability to become self-directed learners."
- "You're realizing that one of your strongest beliefs about always maintaining the dignity of every learner is not a belief shared by some of your colleagues."
- "Your view of your work is to build bridges between your content and the real world your students will experience in the future."

We shift down when abstractions and concepts need grounding in details, examples, non-examples, strategies, choices, and actions. A shift-down paraphrase might sound like these examples:

- "Given your deep concern for an engaged, collaborative environment, you think that you need to pay attention to individual discipline procedures you consistently use in your classroom."
- "So one strategy you are considering to address your concern about balance between relationship building and information sharing is to establish a more formal agenda for your parent conferences."
- "Knowing that parent involvement is an important component of successful schools, you are beginning to think about specific steps to increase parent involvement in your classroom."

REFLECTION: PRACTICE PARAPHRASING

The Practice Paraphrasing activity is an opportunity for you to practice your paraphrasing skills, using what you are learning about the two perspectives of paraphrases (emotion and content) and the three levels of powerful paraphrasing (acknowledging and/or clarifying, summarizing and/or organizing, and shifting focus). The following are sample statements made by teachers, organized into the three levels of paraphrasing. Read the teacher comment and create what you consider to be an appropriate paraphrase response. First, look at the example responses provided. Do you agree or disagree with the response? Do you see a need to change the response? If so, how would you change the response? Then, move on to providing your own responses to the other teacher statements.

Figure 5.2   Practice Paraphrasing

Teacher/Parent Comment	Your Paraphrase
Skill: Acknowledge and/or Clarify	
1. **Teacher**: All we seem to do is assessment practice and district benchmarking, and I never have time to teach.	*Example: You are obviously concerned about the students' real learning if all we are doing is assessing tested objectives.*
2. **Teacher**: This student misses school once or twice a week. How can I ever expect to impact her learning?	

(Continued)

Figure 5.2 (Continued)

Teacher/Parent Comment	Your Paraphrase
3. **Parent:** I want my child in Ms. Brown's class next year. I know she is a great teacher and keeps the kids in line.	
4. **Parent:** I can't believe the way the teacher humiliated my son. I want him removed from this class immediately!	
Skill: Summarize and/or Organize	
1. **Teacher:** You want us to meet with our team and differentiate instruction for a half-dozen, different kinds of kids. I never have any time to just plan for the majority of the kids in my class.	*Example: So there are two real areas of concern for you: planning for the majority of your kids and meeting with your team to plan differentiation.*
2. **Teacher:** There are just too many different demands on my time: afterschool meetings, nighttime parent meetings, Saturday tutoring, summer staff development requirements. When do I ever get time for my own life and the life of my family?	
3. **Parent:** I am very concerned about my child's teacher. The work I see is so easy, hardly any homework; my child is not looking forward to going to school anymore; I never know what is upcoming or due. I just am very upset with the quality I am hearing about.	
Skill: Shift Conceptual Focus and/or Mental Model	
Teacher: I have very high standards for my teaching, and some kids just don't meet those standards. I would think you would applaud my efforts for rigor and excellence.	*Example: You are very proud of the rigor and high standards of your teaching and believe that not all of your students have the potential to meet your standards.*
Teacher: I have been teaching a very long time, and my students have been successful. What is the big deal about "best practice" that is so different than what I have been doing for years?	
Teacher: AYP is unrealistic and is another thing to keep our schools from looking like we are making a difference.	

Teacher/Parent Comment Practice—Practice—Practice	Your Paraphrase Response Of Your Choice
"This student is out of control. I don't think I can be expected to teach this curriculum to every child if this student continues to disrupt in my classroom."	
"I believe my twins should be in the same class together. They have been together since kindergarten and just because they are going into the intermediate grades should not make any difference."	
"The parents in this class are in my face all the time. Talk about "helicopter parents!" They question every assignment, every grade, and every test question I ask. I am just sick of it. How am I expected to teach kids with 22 parents thinking they are the teacher?"	
"You keep talking about engaging the students. If I have them work in cooperative groups for every objective I teach, I will finish my curriculum in four years. You don't really mean engage them for everything, do you?"	
"My principal is always in my face. I think she has something in for me and just wants to get rid of me."	
"I have tried to get my team to plan together because I know we could be sharing so many ideas and saving all of us time. The team leader refuses to discuss how we can improve our instruction by team planning."	
"My assistant is very strong in her knowledge and skills about content. She knows hundreds of powerful strategies for teaching and learning, but when she talks with my teachers she is so arrogant and pushy or bossy they don't hear what she says. I am so sad that her knowledge and skills are lost to her poor people skills."	
"My number one priority this year is helping my principals define and measure high quality teaching and learning in their classroom."	

SKILL 3

Presuming Positive Intent and Powerful Questions

At the beginning of this book, our strong belief in the positive was articulated and influences our approach to teaching and supporting others. Our point of view is founded in the belief that people grow from their successes and strengths. Our combined years of life and work experience has shown us that very few people are inspired to greatness with negative and demeaning language. Because our profession is committed to teaching and learning at the highest levels, it must begin with language that aligns with the belief we have—that people want to be their best and do their best. We do believe in the power of positive change and positive psychology. Social psychologists and sociologists all recognize these positive phenomena. Most people want to feel good, do good, have value and worth, and want to make a contribution. Presuming positive intent in others is simply required to walk in any leadership coaching role. So, we begin with the language of presuming positive intent.

Suzette Haden-Elgin (2000, p. 261) teaches us, "A presupposition is anything that a native speaker of a language knows is part of the meaning of a sequence of that language, even if it doesn't appear on the surface."

You know that "he stopped drinking and driving" presupposes "he started drinking and driving" even though "started" in not in the language of the statement. Suzette Elgin says this is why questions like, "Have you stopped cheating on your taxes?" are so dangerous. The sequence, "If you really cared about your health" presupposes, "You don't really care about your health." Language has power and rewiring our language patterns to presume positive rather than negative helps guide our interactions to greater outcomes. Surprisingly, it is harder than anyone can imagine. We have very strong hard wiring when it comes to language patterns in our culture that tend to presume and believe negative as a default.

Communication is almost always troublesome in any relationship, personal or professional. It often stems from the fact that our language is full of embedded presuppositions, subtle and not so subtle meanings that are disguised as overt and covert messages we send to others. By paying attention to our language and the presuppositions within and choosing our words with care, we can more positively influence the thinking and feelings of others.

We say something that may be interpreted at a much deeper level than the surface words we use. At times, our presuppositions may be received by others as negative or demeaning, even when it is not our intent to speak from a negative perspective. Negative presuppositions, both the subtle and not so subtle ones, can be hurtful to others, can move people into a reactive or defensive mode, and can shut down a conversation.

Statements such as the following are rampant in our systems:

- "You look so nice today, are you being evaluated?"
- "That is such a flattering picture of you."
- "Now, can I hear a practical idea?"
- "Did you not have a plan or simply not work your plan?"
- "Have you thought about the message your appearance sends?"
- "Did we do anything important in class today?"

It is no wonder that so few people are joyful, and the field of teaching seems a lesser choice for graduates. Think about it. What meaning do you get from a T-shirt or a coffee cup that reads, "The best thing about teaching is June, July, and August." Or on Monday afternoon, the most common question is, "How much longer until Friday?"

Presuming Positive Intent offers powerful ways to influence by sending messages to the conscious and subconscious that we think the best and find the best in others.

In the work in schools using positive presuppositions presume that others

- have done prior planning,
- have done prior thinking,
- have noble purpose and intent (i.e., others want to be responsible, dependable, competent),
- have articulated standards (we can only expect if we know), and
- have articulated expectations (we can only meet if we know).

Positive presuppositions send out a message that others are acting with positive intentions. As a colleague says, "I want my attitude, words, and actions to reflect positive intent about others' thinking and doing until specific events demonstrate otherwise."

Use of Presuming Positive Intent helps create an environment of trust and respect where people feel safe to think out loud and interact in meaningful conversations. As RESULTS coaches, we pay attention to our use of presuppositions and choose our words with care. It is always our intent to impart messages that convey positive intent on the part of others.

As Costa and Libermann (1997) state in *The Process-Centered School*,

People operate on internal maps of their own reality, and therefore, we assume that they act with positive intentions. This assumption promotes and facilitates meaningful dialogue. Using positive presuppositions assumes and encourages positive actions. (p. 591)

Imagine the influence over time if students heard the following:

- "What was the easiest thing about your homework?" rather than, "Did you do your homework?"
- "When do you expect to finish your report?" rather than, "Did you finish your report?"
- "What other ways can you solve the problem?" rather than, "Do you know any other ways to solve the problem?
- "What character are you finding the most interesting in your novel?" rather than, "Have you started reading your required novel?"
- "Knowing that you want to play with your friends after you've cleaned your room, when do you anticipate being finished?" rather than, "Have you cleaned your room?"
- "What are you looking forward to the most this year in school?" rather than, "Are you looking forward to anything in school?"

Statements framed with positive presuppositions assume that the person has already thought or done what is being asked and embed the standard or the expectation within the statement. Statements framed with positive presuppositions assume that the person has already thought, planned, or done what is being stated or asked by the listener. Embedded in the listener's comment and/or question is the standard or the expectation framed with positive intention on the part of the speaker. This can happen through affirmation of effort, skills, and/or competence.

Imagine the influence over time if educators heard the following:

- "What literacy strategies are having the best results for you?" rather than, "Do you know any literacy strategies?"
- "What best practices are accelerating your students' successful learning the most?" rather than, "Do you know any best practice?"
- "How is the curriculum assisting you in pacing the objectives of the unit?" rather than, "Have you used the curriculum?"
- "What did the superintendent say when you shared your concerns?" rather than, "Have you thought about telling the superintendent?"
- "What learning goals are your students setting this year?" rather than, "Do your student have any learning goals?"
- "Because building trust is a strong commitment for you, what plans have you determined for your new PTA council?" rather than, "Have you thought about how you are going to deal with the distrust on the council?"

Let's look at more examples that demonstrate how our language can send covert messages in Table 5.1. Notice the comment below on the left of the table, all containing presuppositions. Read the comment, and identify the presupposition that has the possibility of being received with negative undertones. Notice the presumption or overt message of the comment. Then, look at the reframing of the comment. Which now speaks from an attitude of positive intent? What do you notice about the change or reframing of the comment? What are the positive presuppositions within the comments on the right side of the table? Why is reframing to reflect positive intention more valuable and helpful to the productivity of the conversation?

Table 5.1		
Comment	Presumption or Overt Message	Positive Presuppositions
"Even Johnny can get an A in this class."	Johnny is not very bright, *and* the class is too easy.	"Knowing that you want your class to be challenging for all students, what is your strategy for accomplishing what you want?"
"Do you use technology in your classroom?"	The teacher is not using technology.	"What technology applications are your students enjoying the most?"
"Have you finished your assignment?"	You have not even started your assignment.	"What in your assignment are you discovering is the easiest to complete?"
"Do you know any discipline strategies?"	Your class looks like you don't know any discipline strategies.	"What discipline strategies are having the best impact on your students?"
"Have you thought about . . . ?"	You have not thought.	"What options are you considering?"

Table 5.1 (Continued)

Comment	Presumption or Overt Message	Positive Presuppositions
"Do you have any goals?"	You don't have any goals and have not thought of any.	"Based on the performance of your students in mathematics, what goals have you set for yourself this year?"
"Did you not have a plan or just not work your plan?"	You did not do anything.	"What are you celebrating the most in your plan for student success?"

Notice the opening phrases of the positive presuppositions above. Other opening phrases used with positive presuppositions might include the following:

- As you . . .
- When you . . .
- While you . . .

Table 5.2 lists other examples of negative presuppositions converted to positive presuppositions. Compare the examples and consider how each might be received.

Table 5.2   Examples of Negative and Positive Presuppositions

Negative Presupposition	Positive Presupposition
"Why did you do that?"	"What factors influenced your choice or decision?"
"Are your students having any success?"	"What are you seeing that indicates you are getting the results you expect on a consistent basis?"
"Why aren't you planning with other teachers?"	"When you are planning with your team, what do you find most valuable?"

Negative Presupposition	Positive Presupposition
"Have you thought about using Cooperative Learning?"	"What additional options for student engagement are you considering?"
"Have you thought of any discipline strategies that will work with Johnny?"	"Knowing how important it is to you that every student is successful, what discipline strategies are getting the best results with Johnny?"
"Don't you think you are wasting important instructional time by taking so long to get started in the morning?"	"What have you found to be your best strategies for managing routine procedures?"
"You seem to be more focused on creating activities for your students than you are on using the district curriculum."	"How has the district curriculum been helpful in planning your instructional activities?"
"Do you use any special process to plan your lessons?"	"As you were planning your lesson, what aspects of the instructional objectives influenced your selection of strategies?"
"Can't you assess student acquisition of skills without giving them so many problems to solve?"	"What criteria do you use to know when students have mastered the required standards?"

Recently, Vicky asked a school leader whom she coached to share which of the coaching skills learned through their coaching relationship he was using regularly in his work as a school leader. He responded,

> Talking with expectations (use of positive presuppositions) and the way I phrase things with individuals so that I am not demanding something. For example, I now say, "How long did it take you to clean the floor last night?" instead of, "Did you clean the floor last night?" Or instead of saying, 'Did you talk to the teacher about that student?' I will say, "What was the outcome of that situation or your discussion with the teacher?" With teachers, instead of firing back with a solution, I now say, for example, "Clearly you are frustrated, and I want to help you move forward." They don't need for me to give them a solution. You don't want to spoon feed your staff, but rather you want them to grow. I'm learning I don't have to solve all the problems.

Instead of figuring it out for them, they figured it out. If you lead with the positive, you set the tone and that makes them feel more empowered to reach their own decision for taking action. And the expectation for taking action is always there.

The longer we use and presume positive intent in our language, the more opportunities for the mirror neurons to be fired. Researches in the fields of cognitive neuroscience and cognitive psychology are learning and speculate that our mirror neuron systems are important for understanding the actions of other people and influencing language abilities. Imagine the possibilities of how leadership language can and will be mirrored in the classrooms.

Another observation has been the numerous opportunities for reinforcing and affirming behaviors in everyday language and conversations. No waiting for a special conference or summative time frame to reinforce and affirm your teachers and students. Consider the language we are beginning to hear in the mailroom, print room, in the halls, and just walking to a car at the end of the day.

Positive Presuppositions offer opportunities to ask powerful questions while affirming

- effort,
- prior knowledge and skills,
- integrity,
- competence,
- caring, and
- commitment.

For example: *Effort*
"Knowing how hard you always work for your students' success, what new strategies are you excited about this year?

For example: *Prior knowledge and skills*
"Because you know the curriculum so well, what areas are you discovering are especially strong or weak?"

For example: *Integrity, competence, commitment, or caring*
"Because building a strong relationship with your students is important to you, what plan have you created for this new student?"

The language of positive intent offers leaders a powerful way to influence and bring forward a student or teacher's best self. Most humans rise to the level of expectation that others see in us.

Practice With Positive Presuppositions

Figure 5.3 provides an opportunity for you to practice presuming positive intent. As you change each of the questions that follow from negative to positive, you will want to frame your revised question in such a way that it encompasses the attributes of positive presuppositions and has opportunities for powerful opening statements.

Figure 5.3

Negative Presupposition	My Positive Presupposition
Have you thought about using cooperative learning to engage your students?	
Do you have any ideas for professional development?	
Are you using any technology with your instruction?	
Have you ever heard of "best practices?"	
Did you check references before you hired her?	
Have you thought about having a classroom management plan in your room?	
Do you know any grouping strategies?	

"Treat a man as he is, he will remain so. Treat a man the way he can be and ought to be, and he will become as he can be and should be."

—Goethe

PRESUMING POSITIVE INTENT SUPPORTS ASKING POWERFUL QUESTIONS

Recently, an event was held in the Dallas area where more than 700 people gathered to hear Ron Hall and Denver Moore (2006), coauthors of *Same Kind of Different as Me,* speak about the development of their extraordinary friendship and their unwavering commitment to carry on the dream of the woman who brought the men together. Vicky was one of the people in attendance, and as she looked around the room, she saw faces of various ages, stages, and walks of life, including some of her personal friends and former principal associates. She felt a sense of eager anticipation in the air as people scurried to find a place to sit and have their lunch before the speakers began. It was as if the audience was preparing to hear a powerful and compelling message that would stay with them long after the meal, which was secondary to the message they'd come to receive. From Vicky's perspective, those in attendance got what they came for, a powerful message.

We use the term "power" in many different ways. We take "power walks" and "power naps." We eat "power bars" and swallow "power drinks," and sometimes, we might even deliver a "power punch," hopefully in figurative terms. Most likely, we all have a similar understanding of the meaning behind the word "power." It's about strength, action, importance, something out of the ordinary. It's as if we know it when we feel it, and as Jill Bolte Taylor (2006) says in *My Stroke of Insight*, the reality is we do feel it before we think it. By the time information reaches our cerebral cortex for higher thinking, we have already placed a feeling upon how we view the information. That same meaning of power holds true when we consider powerful questioning, those important and growth-producing questions we purposefully ask others to help them reach higher levels of understanding and insight as they think in new and different ways.

RESULTS focused coach leaders know that asking powerful questions helps bring maximum benefits to the conversation. Powerful questions follow powerful listening and embed positive presuppositions. First, we listen fully to what the teacher or speaker is expressing through both words and emotions, and we also listen to the messages and emotions behind the words. Then, we determine our best response to help move the teacher's thinking forward. Typically, we provide a short paraphrase to show understanding and caring, and then, when appropriate, we pose a specific and powerful question framed with a positive presupposition to help move the teacher's thinking to a deeper and clearer level so that intentional action is set in motion.

To better understand what powerful questions are, let's first think about what they are not. Powerful questions are not loaded questions asked so that the teacher gives back the answer the leader wants. A loaded question sounds like, "Don't you think calling Johnnie's mother now is the best way to deal with this issue?" In this instance, the leader believes that getting Johnny's mother involved immediately is the best way to deal with a situation that happed earlier in the day and is expecting the teacher to agree with him. So, the question is really not a question asked to help the teacher think about the best action to take but is rather a personal opinion or giving of advice "disguised" as a question. What's so wrong with that? It has the potential of blocking the thinking of the teacher and moving the leader into the role of expert or know it all. That is not the avenue that leads to deep thinking.

Consider the next example. "Would you like my advice on how best to deal with Mrs. Smith?" The leader is not as much focused on helping the teacher think through how she would like to work with Mrs. Smith as he is on solving the problem for the teacher. Advice is a "road block" on the highway of deep thinking.

Powerful questions are open-ended questions with no hidden agendas and are asked for the sole purpose of providing maximum benefit to the receiver of the question. The power of the question comes from the positive impact, somewhat like a human electrical charge, to the thinking of the receiver of the question. Powerful questions have the following characteristics:

- Reflect active and powerful listening and understanding of the teacher's perspective
- Presume positive intent
- Evoke discovery, insight, commitment, or action on behalf of the teacher
- Challenge current assumptions of the teacher
- Create greater clarity, possibility or new learning
- Move the teacher towards what he or she desires
- Move the thinking forward to current and future actions and are not focused on having the teacher justify or look backwards

Consider what happens when someone asks us a powerful question around an issue, situation, or challenge we're dealing with and can't seem to resolve. We have thoughts, feelings, and ideas circulating around within our mind as it relates to the issue, situation, or challenge, but we can't seem to connect them together, to move them along, to clearly understand the implication or to bring about a resolution that leads to appropriate actions. It's as if our thinking is standing still or going in multiple directions at the same time, all within a confined space. And then, someone offers us a powerful question and "Boom!" Thoughts begin to organize, we see things from different perspectives, we get clearer on what we really want, and we begin to move forward without thinking. The powerful question served as a key to unlock the chamber that was holding our thoughts captive. And thanks to what we are learning from the brain research, we have a clearer understanding of what is actually happening in our brains as a result of a powerful question. We are literally making new connections in our brains, new mind maps that are helping us to move forward with our thinking toward clarity of thought, and new insights that lead to action (Rock, 2006).

RESULTS coach leaders understand that powerful questions serve their staff and their school much more than powerful telling. Thus, RESULTS coach leaders ask powerful questions. They hold high expectation of their staff, and they know that results have a much greater probability of reaching extraordinary levels when everyone involved is thinking and focused on achieving greater insights, which in turn moves people toward powerful actions.

Recently, an assistant superintendent of instruction in one of our southern states shared an insight she had gained after spending three days at a leadership retreat with principals from her district. In conversations with the principals, she realized one of their biggest concerns was that they did not know "how to have productive and meaningful conversations with teachers, especially when they attempted to weave positive presuppositions into their conversations." Because the assistant superintendent had completed a number of Coaching For Results seminars, she knew exactly how best to support them and set in motion a series of conversations with principals where they would experience firsthand the positive impact of powerful questions as they prepared to change the way they talked with their staffs.

One of the most important reasons our team of writers so strongly committed to the writing of this book is because we believe that when principals hold powerful conversations with their staff, using our set of research-based coaching skills offered around a clearly articulated set of high expectations for all, teachers will deepen and enhance their own thinking about teaching and learning, and extraordinary results will be a natural result.

RESULTS coach leaders are intentional in their actions and their behaviors. They understand that they don't have to be all knowing to be a great leader. It's about clear expectations, committed listening, powerful paraphrasing and presuppositions, reflective feedback, and asking powerful questions while operating from an attitude of belief that each teacher will produce extraordinary results for each of their students. As principals, it's their responsibility to lead their school based on a set of national, state, and district standards and expectations. They lead their own staffs to indentify clarity about their school's vision, mission, and core values, and they ask the powerful questions around those clearly articulated set of performance expectations to help and encourage teachers to achieve great results.

Reflection: As you review some powerful questions from *Fierce Conversations* (Scott, 2002) below, what patterns are you seeing in the questions, and how would you best articulate the attributes of powerful questions?

- Knowing how committed you are to strong results for all of your students, what has become clear since we last met?
- What is the area that, if you made an improvement, would give you and others the greatest return on time, energy, and dollars invested?
- What is currently impossible to do that, if it were possible, would change everything?
- What topics are you hoping that I won't bring up?
- Who are your strongest employees, and what are you doing to ensure that they are happy and motivated? Who are your weakest employees, and what is your plan for them?
- What conversations are you avoiding right now?
- What things are you doing that you would like to stop doing or delegate to someone else?

"The scientific mind does not so much provide the right answers as ask the right questions."

—Claude Lévi-Strauss

SKILL 4

Reflective Feedback

Giving and receiving feedback is an important part of everyone's life and is a vital skill for RESULTS Coaching. After all, when we create, invite, and support an environment of dialogue, feedback is a natural component of our dialogue. It's as if a dance is going on between the participants in the conversation, and it's helpful when we all dance to the same beat. As a RESULTS coach, we listen and speak with intention, and that includes the intentional way in which we give feedback to others.

Improvements in performance depend on effective language, "feedback loops," with one speaker at the end of each loop. An air conditioning system set on 72 degrees will periodically sample the air for temperature, either coming on or turning off—a one-way feedback loop. In conversations, each utterance must be based in some way on what is said before it. The difference between the feedback loop in cooling systems and conversation feedback loops is that language flows in both directions.

Remember a time when you were talking with someone with a strong southern accent or to someone who said "like" or "okay" or "I mean" every few words. Soon, you picked up on those same sounds or habits. Or consider a time when you were in an argument that you knew was ridiculous, but everything the other person said to you was so infuriating that you just could not let it pass—only to have what you said provoke one more outrageous statement. Experiences like these demonstrate how communication, our language, is one big feedback loop. The most basic skill underlying successful communication is establishing and maintaining an interactive feedback loop through speaking and listening and by reading and interpreting body language. This is the key work of leaders and effective communicators! (Hattie & Timperley, 2007)

To use Oprah's idea of "what we know for sure," we know for sure that feedback is one of the most powerful influences on learning and achievement. Feedback is fundamental to performance and learning in individual, community, and organizational situations. Numerous psychological studies in both behaviorist and cognitive traditions have demonstrated repeatedly that improvement in performance depends on feedback loops. Several Gallop surveys have reported that people who receive regular recognition and praise show increased productivity, increased engagement with colleagues, and were more likely to stay in the organization. Sadly, surveys also show that more than 60% of workers receive no recognition at all. While feedback is a major influence, the type of feedback and the way it is offered will greatly determine its effectiveness.

Through the decades, we have learned that feedback is usually given in the following forms (Costa & Garmston, 2002):

- **Judgment**—(e.g., "Important information was missing." "Great tool." "Poor job.")
- **A type of personal observation**—(e.g., "I like . . . ." "I was moved by the story." "I loved it.")
- **Inference**—(e.g., "It sounds as if there are many hidden agendas." "Her failure to respond is diminishing your enthusiasm.")
- **Some type of data**—(e.g., "You called on nine students." "You paraphrased four times.")
- **Questions**—(e.g., "Have you thought about using?" "Are you planning to . . . ?")

At one time or another, we have all been the recipient of unwanted, uninvited, and unappreciative feedback that comes with all kinds of negative presuppositions and intonations that cause our emotions to either shut down or elevate! David Perkins (2003) offers that possibly; it was the reason behind the hit song of the 50's, *"Yakety Yak! Don't Talk Back!"* In the song the parents nagging talk (Yakety Yak!) at the teenager and the teen's response are received by the parents as inappropriate (Don't talk back!"). When we fast forward to television's *Charlie Brown* specials, everyone remembers the language of the scolding teacher. "Wau wau wau," the students were hearing. David Perkins believes that just might be the sound of most feedback! Words matter and so do relationships when it comes to feedback.

David Perkins (2003), in *King Arthur's Roundtable: How Collaborative Conversations Create Smart Organizations*, offers new ideas about feedback as well as possibilities of new responses for long standing habits. The good news about feedback is that it is essential for individuals and community reflection and growth, and the bad news is that it often flops, yielding no meaningful exchange of information and driving people apart.

How people give feedback to each other exemplifies organizational intelligence. Organizational intelligence includes maintaining relationships that are crucial for positive outcomes and results. As we consider giving feedback, it is important to simultaneously hold two things in our mind: the content of the message and the potential impact on the relationship. Our goal becomes: How do we say what needs to be said (the content) in a way that supports another's growth and maintains a positive relationship?

Perkins' research offers more effective responses that align with Coaching For Results' belief of supporting another person's thoughtful reflection and decision making. David Rock (2006) reinforces that if our commitment is to promote another's learning, feedback is essential. The reality is that feedback is usually done poorly, and we are rarely prepared for the emotional charge that comes with it. One goal as Coach Leaders is to use language that shows positive intent in another's actions, thoughts, and behaviors. Reflective feedback is the vehicle that will support and mediate another person's thinking and reflection.

Consider feedback as a two-arm approach. One of the arms contains the content of the feedback (the information to be shared), and the other carries the importance and value of the relationship. When the feedback is productive, open, and reflective, it's as if both arms are open, inviting to the listener. But when the feedback is received negatively or painfully, it's as if the arms have closed up, especially the one holding the relationship. Whether at work or in our personal lives, maintaining relationships is crucial to positive results. We want that open-armed approach when giving and receiving feedback.

Perkins (2003) has categorized feedback into three distinct groups: negative, conciliatory, and communicative, which we have renamed reflective. Let's take a look at each in the following three tables (Table 5.3, 5.4, and 5.5) and decide for ourselves within which group we choose to reside.

Table 5.3 Negative Feedback: The Yakety Yak Type: "Just Tell People What's Wrong!"

Reason For Giving This Type of Feedback	Example of Negative Feedback
Lay-it-on-the-line critical feedback	"That was not worth the time or energy!"
The most painful type of feedback because it tells people straight out what's wrong	"No, you are wrong about your plan! That will not help raise student performance!"
The most obvious to give and usually follows a natural avalanche of impulse	"Oh, good grief! Don't say that to the parent! Once again, what are you thinking? Do you ever think about the reaction you will receive?"
People need to know what's wrong, so why not tell them?	"Your presentation is way too long and will not hold the interest of the parents. It's putting me to sleep right now!"
The information can be alienating and over time can provoke defensiveness and negative attitudes.	"How many times and in how many ways do I have to tell you this! There you go again, doing it your usual wrong way."
Negative feedback is worsened when it focuses on a person's core identity rather than a product or an idea.	"Are you stupid or what? Where is your back bone? How could such a worthless person be in this group?"

Table 5.4 Conciliatory Feedback: Focuses on Being Encouraging and Vague

Positive and vague. Avoids criticizing to be supportive and avoid conflict; comes from belief that negative feedback will be rejected and relationship harmed	"Well, uh, it is okay. Sure, it could be interesting."
Often called "social stroking"	"You always know what needs to be done."
Usually read as pleasant, encouraging, and nonthreatening. Not feedback at all: it's encouragement and conflict avoidance in the guise of feedback.	"Great idea!" "Keep working hard!" "You are the man!"

The rationale for conciliatory feedback is that relationships are so important and feedback is so difficult; therefore, the person chooses relationships over information and to play it safe and nice. Sadly, the receiver learns over multiple occasions that the feedback is empty and reads it as evasive or pandering.

Reflective Feedback is the vehicle that will support and mediate another person's thinking and reflection. David Perkins (2003) offers communicative feedback (Reflective Feedback) as a better habit and response. Reflective Feedback requires more time to consider—it truly requires thought and effort. But as with any new learning, with practice, the language patterns emerge, and somehow, it does not sound different or unusual and—the benefits—wow! The benefits are realized in the way people hear and respond to what they feel as respectful, honest, and thoughtful. Let's examine the options for Reflective Feedback:

Table 5.5 Reflective Feedback: Clarifies Ideas or Actions Under Consideration and Offers Values, Concerns, and Suggestions	
CLARIFY: One option provides the opportunity to clarify an idea or behavior under consideration (to be sure talking about the same thing)	"How much time does the district require that principals are in classrooms each week?"
VALUE POTENTIAL: Communicates positive features of actions and moves toward preserving and building upon them	"Your commitment to being in classrooms 70% of the time has the potential for dramatically impacting high levels of learning for all students in your school."
REFLECTIVE QUESTIONS FOR POSSIBILITIES: Vehicle for communicating concerns, considerations, or options toward improvement	"In addition to yourself, what other leadership team members are being utilized to support your goal of being in classrooms?"

Perkins (2003) offers these three as steps, but as we have worked with the practice and application of this language, the most useful application of them in steps is when teachers or leadership teams are using them in a protocol structure—a structure that offers a formalized sequence of speaking, responding, and offering feedback. An example of a protocol structure is provided at the end of the chapter and in Resource G of the book.

Today, with the gift of this new thinking on Reflective Feedback, we may offer or give feedback in a way that will dramatically increase the thinking, consideration, and reflection of others. Let's review the three options for reflective feedback.

1. Clarifying questions or statements for better understanding

2. Feedback statements that identify *value* or value potential

3. Feedback to mediate thinking through the use of reflective questions for possibilities

Used as a frame for conversations, reflective feedback generally evolves during the flow of conversation so that the three options become integrated, moving both the message and the relationship forward. For example, early in the conversation, there is frequently a need for *clarity*. As the conversation progresses, expressing *value* for the thought or action may present itself. Then, it may be a *reflective question of possibility* that mediates the thinking of the other person allowing him or her to go to a new place or discover a different point of view. The thinking behind options is that most typical conversation in schools using feedback are informal and not in the setting using a structured protocol. A structure and protocol can be enormously helpful when teams are learning to interact together and use new language.

A CRITICAL ATTRIBUTE OF REFLECTIVE QUESTIONS

All reflective questions presume positive intent. To not presume reflective thinking on the part of educators is a huge trust withdrawal and incongruent with the work of teaching and learning. Once the language of positive presuppositions is a part of one's natural way of speaking and thinking, the use of reflective questions is as natural and easy as finding a word in a dictionary.

Some Examples of Reflective Feedback

Clarifying Questions for Understanding

- "How do you see this objective different from . . . ?"
- "How did your students respond to the process?"
- "What costs were calculated to put this in place?"
- "Which groups provided useful input to the plan?"
- "When you checked state assessment alignment, what did you find as strengths or gaps?"

- "What input did the parents give and how was it helpful?"
- "What information from central office assisted you?"

Expressing the Value or Value Potential

- "This could offer value to students with time issues."
- "The strength of the idea is long-term retention."
- "The scaffolding of your design will help teachers understand and gradually embed practice."
- "You have really thought deeply about this concept."
- "There is clear evidence that students learned at high levels and were continually engaged."
- "As a parent and teacher, the idea is very exciting because it supports learning."
- "Your plan provides high engagement for students."

Reflective Questions or Possibilities

- "What goals have your students set for individual mastery?"
- "What are you considering in regard to differentiation?"
- "I wonder what would happen if . . ."
- "What gaps have you noticed, if any, in student understanding?"
- "What other considerations for student engagement are you thinking about?"
- "To align more closely with high stakes assessment, what if . . . ?"
- "What connections have you made to . . . (other subjects, real world, assessments)?"
- "What resources—people or things—have been the most useful, helpful, and so on?"
- "What 'next step' for you could be evolutionary?"
- "As you consider best practice, what strategies will you use to achieve your goal?"

REFLECTIVE FEEDBACK

Important Issues to Keep in Mind

Be specific.

Numerous studies have shown the minimal impact of general praise. The use of "I like" is not very important, but consideration of the reason "why I like it" makes the most powerful influence. Replacing "I like" with "when you did . . . there was evidence of . . . ." Before giving reflective feedback, consider questions like the following: What made this great? What effort was put into this work? What challenge was faced to get the result? What is the impact on others? What did they do to make the difference? Examples of how it might sound include the following:

- "Your opening statement hooked my attention and interest throughout."
- "Your idea has the potential to strongly increase our achievement goals."
- "Your long hours of study and preparation are evident in this valuable work."

Be generous.

Many people are not comfortable receiving positive feedback. Speak in a way that will open the person to learning. Choose words that are very sincere and authentic. Prepare reflectively so others will seriously consider your words of reflective feedback. One principal, in realizing that her campus leadership team almost always identified why something would not work or what was wrong with an idea first, created a norm that required everyone to identify first the value potential of any idea brought to this leadership team. She was amazed with the difference it made in discussion and consideration of many ideas that would have otherwise been tossed aside.

Ask permission.

When people think about receiving feedback, they often fear the worst. It is very useful to ask permission to give feedback before beginning, letting them know what to expect. For example,

- "You asked for some reflective feedback, is this a good time to share it with you?"
- "Your actions in the parent conference are worthy of reflective feedback. Is this a good time?"

Be prepared and know that there is almost always a physical reaction to feedback even with our most trusted colleagues. It is very natural because our brains have been wired for this language and hears the feedback as a threat to status. In time and with language that is reflective, new wiring of safety and autonomy will emerge.

Remember the goal is self-directed learning.

Allowing people to give themselves feedback will make powerful connections in their own mind. Before giving your feedback, you might ask the following questions:

- "What three things went really well?"
- "What two things are you learning about yourself?"
- "What two big challenges did you face and overcome?"
- "What resources did you utilize, internally and externally, to make this happen?"

Even with below par or poor performance, negative feedback has little impact.

Understanding the cause of failure is very helpful for managing processes but not very effective in managing people. Be prepared for the emotional charge with weaker performance. Questions that focus on solutions rather than blame or problems offer potential for the most effective feedback loop and improved behavior.

- "How can I best support you in fulfilling your potential for this role?"
- "How can I be most helpful in assisting you to meet the conditions of your contract?"
- "What would be the most helpful to you in meeting the expectations and/or goals of your campus?"
- "What insights have you had from this situation?"
- "What have you learned from this experience?"
- "What skills have you identified to focus on for the results you desire?"
- "In order to meet the requirements of the district, what three things are you planning to put in place?"

Giving effective reflective feedback requires thought and practice.

Taking a few moments to consider data and the language of reflective feedback hits the 80/20 rule. Your investment in planning and rehearsal will dramatically reduce time in the conversation and increase impact from the conversation. With each conversation, your wiring for reflective feedback language becomes stronger and more hard wired.

Feedback is not the answer,
rather, it is but one powerful answer.

While leaders have much knowledge, skill, and experience, there are many ways to accomplish the goals in our work. Few things carry with them the need for the words "always" or "never." There are many ways to "skin a cat." We know that with adults, learning is voluntary—reflective feedback is offered for consideration. Given the parameters of job expectations, feedback will be most helpful when its intentions support the achievement of goals and the hard work of the thinking of the person doing the work.

Growth and change are very difficult because of internal "hard-wiring" impacting behaviors, attitudes, and habits. The good news is that change is possible and likely when we focus on what is desired—the goal, the outcome, and the impact for success. Time, attention, repetition, and Reflective Feedback are all that is required:

- *Time* for conversation, practice, and reflection
- *Attention* or focus aimed toward the goal
- *Repetition* via practice to build confidence and sustained success
- *Reflective Feedback* to offer self-direction, self-mediation, and self-assurance as new pathways of wiring are created and supported

Reflective Feedback is a tool and a skill that holds the potential for dramatically supporting the growth of educators. It is a model of a new way of giving feedback within our educational system. This new knowledge gives us the important information and opportunity to teach more effective ways to give feedback to leaders, to teachers, and to students.

"To tell denies or negates another's intelligence. To ask honors it."

—Sir John Whitmore

REFLECTION

- What are you teaching yourself about feedback?
- What benefits do you predict from the use of reflective feedback?
- What practice opportunities are you considering in the coming weeks?
- Where are you thinking you would like to begin internalizing reflective feedback?

- How will you share your new learning goals with others around reflective feedback?
- Who will you select as a fun partner to practice reflective feedback?

AUTHORS' NOTE

Although the skills we have targeted in this chapter are not inclusive of the numerous skills required in coaching. The four mentioned in the chapter are essential to being a powerful coach leader.

Other critical skills for coaching are specified in the ICF Competencies that include or embed the following:

- The skillful use of silence and pausing
- Mindful attention to body language—verbals and nonverbals sent and received
- Attention to the emotional intelligence of self and others
- Building and maintaining trust and rapport

The Resources will offer short insights into a variety of coaching essential skills.

> *"Reexamine all that you have been told in school or in church or in any book. Dismiss whatever insults your soul."*

> —Walt Whitman

The Leader's GPS

6

GUIDED PATHWAYS FOR SUCCESS

"The greatest thing in this world is not so much where we are, but in what direction we are moving."

—Oliver Wendell Holmes, Jr.

Figure 6.1

The GPS (Global Positioning System) has become a godsend to consumers who incorporate this space-age technology into their day-to-day lives. Not so many years ago, consulting Mapsco or MapQuest for directions prior to starting out for a new destination was an essential. Today, the digital-mapping technology of the GPS is quickly emerging as the newest essential. The GPS assists those who are directionally challenged with verbal and visual support required for finding a final destination. What was once only possible through the special effects of a Tom Clancy movie is now possible in our everyday lives. Today's GPS helps us get from point A to point B with audible driving directions, color maps, and points of interest from shopping centers to restaurants. In addition, the audio component will redirect us if we get off track, indicating that a "recalculation" is being made to assist us to return to the destination path. Amazing!

Today's school leader can find the same support and assurance when they utilize the coaching GPS, Guided Pathways for Success, as they navigate the range of conversations that are *essential* to leadership and leading. Whether the leader is leading a faculty meeting, a five-year strategic planning summit, or a formative instructional conversation with a new teacher, the coaching GPS will support and ensure one's successful arrival at the desired destination.

Every productive conversation is guided by important principles and skills. First and foremost are the communication skills we learned in Chapter 5. Committed listening, powerful paraphrasing, presuming positive intent, and reflective feedback are the cornerstones of effective and life-changing conversations. As educators, we have been exposed to many conversation formats, maps, or outlines. We have engaged in hundreds of structured protocols, dozens of configurations for professional learning communities, and even more supervisory conference formats. Regardless of the format or sequence, nothing will replace the importance of committed listening—being truly present with another person to hear his or her point of view and perspective. One of the greatest barriers observed in schools is the constant demand on a leader's time that heightens his sense of urgency to act. This results in a cycle of never really listening to another without simultaneously doing numerous other tasks. It is not unusual for the school leader to be signing purchase orders, responding to the administrative assistant about a fire drill, checking an e-mail from the superintendent, knowing that an angry parent is waiting in the outer office—all while attempting to talk with a teacher about differentiating instruction. Our urgent and rapid paced world has begun to crush the meaning from the critically important conversations in our lives.

The focus of this chapter is a set of tools that offer pathways for at least four types of conversations that are prevalent in our schools. These four come from our experience over a 10-year span of time with numerous models and have repeatedly been the most useful and helpful in effective conversations impacting school success. The four tools of our coaching GPS—Guided Pathways for Success include the following:

- Solution-Focused Conversation
- Goal-Focused Conversation
- Planning-Focused Conversation
- Reflection-Focused Conversation

Once the standards and expectations are articulated, the GPS of the Coaching Navigation System will guide conversations as they move to solutions, goals, planning, or reflecting on how outcomes are being achieved. Let's examine each of the pathways and explore the possibilities of each.

CONVERSATION TOOL 1

Solution-Focused Conversation

> "Be careful what you water your dreams with. Water them with worry and fear, and you will produce weeds that choke the life from your dream. Water them with optimism and solutions, and you will cultivate success. Dream."
>
> —Lao Tzu

The first tool in the coaching GPS is one that can be used when the conversation centers around the need for solutions to a topic, issue, or concern. David Rock's (2006) findings in *Quiet Leadership* have had a significant influence on our work, reframing our mindset to that of helping educators focus on solutions rather than problems. *Appreciative Coaching* (Orem, Binkert, & Clancy, 2007) reinforced the importance of moving from the weight of focusing on problems to the energy of seeking solutions. So often, we solve the wrong problems or solve one problem only to find another. Because school leaders are faced with an overload of priorities and deadlines, it is very difficult to change behaviors and habits. With every good intention, the school leader easily slips into old habits and actions because there is so little time to focus on the new way of being. This is why leadership coaching makes such a difference for school leaders. A coach is the constant, the reminder, the focus, the energy that comes from knowing someone supports our thinking, our new habits, and our new goals. It makes a tremendous difference to school leaders when

Figure 6.2 GPS: Guided Pathways for Success

Coaching School Results - GPS (Guided Pathways for Success)© 2009

Solution Focused

- "Witness the struggle"
- Listen for words, phrases, metaphors that guide thinking
- Reframe from problem to solution focus
- Language of discovery and appreciation
- Ask questions to evoke talents, successes discovery, dreams, and desires
- Ask powerful questions to make solutions possible
- Support thinking to create clear image of attributes of the solution

Goal Focused

- What do you want? Clarify and articulate goals—be explicit; what does it look like, feel like when achieved?
- Prioritize your goals
- Generate multiple pathways for achieving your goal; identify the top 10 strategies
- Create an action plan
- Identify resources (people & things) needed to facilitate your achievement
- Reflect and celebrate!

Planning Focused

- Clarify goals
- Determine success indicators
- Anticipate approaches, strategies, decisions
- Identify the data for self-assessment
- Determine the plan for action
- Reflect on benefits of conversation

Reflection Focused

- Summarize impressions
- Recall supporting information
- Compare, analyze, infer cause and effect relationships
- Construct new learnings and applications
- Reflect on benefits of conversation and any refinements

Coaching School Results, ©2009

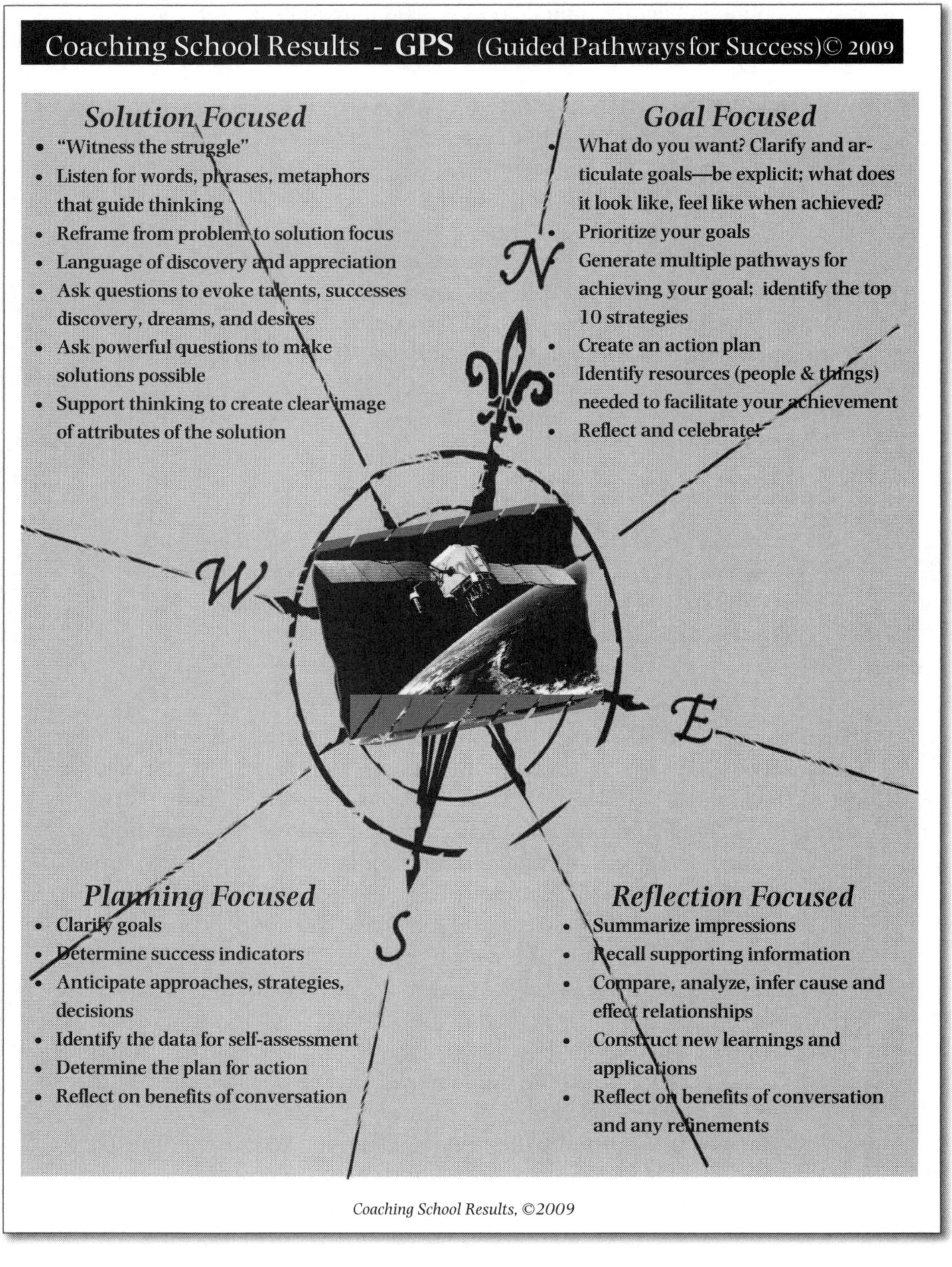

Coaching School Results - GPS (Guided Pathways for Success)© 2009
Sample Language

Solution Focused
- You are really hurting from this.
- The broken trust has emptied your bank account.
- (Miracle ?) What would have happened to achieve the most positive outcome?
- You are seeking your most successful strategies to apply to this situation.
- What actions and strategies have given you success in the past that could be "re-gifted" in this situation?
- What compels you to ensure the solution you desire?
- Your courage and commitment to your students have created a clear vision of your goal.

Goal Focused
- What do you want?
- What will it look like when you have achieved this goal?
- Of the four goals you want, rank them in priority and time commitment for yourself.
- What five strategies are you thinking you want to put in place to achieve your goals?
- What are three more ways you can do it? Two more?
- Of your 10 strategies, which three offer the most powerful steps to achieving your goal?
- What is your timeline for accomplishing your goal?
  - Who will you utilize to assist you in realizing your goal?
  - As you reflect on this conversation and your upcoming goal achievement, what will you be celebrating in two months?

Planning Focused
- What are you wanting to achieve?
- How will you know when you have achieved it?
- What strategies have you determined will support your success?
- How will you know when you have achieved your mission? What data will affirm your accomplishment?
- What will be your first steps in your plan for action?
- How has this conversation been helpful?

Reflection Focused
- How do you feel about your performance?
  What data supports your feelings?
- What did you do to get the results you achieved? What specifically impacted your results?
- If you were to do this again, what would you want to repeat? Refine? Eliminate?
- How has this conversation supported your reflective practice?

Coaching School Results, ©2009

they clearly identify the insights they want to hardwire and are reminded over time of their intentions.

If we want to improve performance, the coach leader helps others find new ways to approach situations that leave their existing wiring where it is, allowing for the development and ultimately hardwiring of new actions and behaviors. *Coach leaders help others focus on solutions rather than problems.* We need to give up the desire to find and fix behaviors and become energized and amazed by the potential of identifying and growing people's strengths. *Appreciative Coaching* teaches us that positive energy is created from solution seeking. Focusing on positive connections and successes allows people's thinking to be unleashed and open to innovation and creativity for the challenges of work.

This pathway offers the busy leader with a time-efficient way to have conversations that focus on the goals or solutions that have been communicated. In observing thousands of conversations, David Rock (2006) noticed that they tend to go "north," being very philosophical, or "south," being very detailed, or maybe to the "west," focusing on the problem. He offers that the most effective conversation can go "east" and focus on solutions. Figure 6.3 illustrates the visual Rock uses.

Figure 6.3   David Rock, *Quiet Leadership*

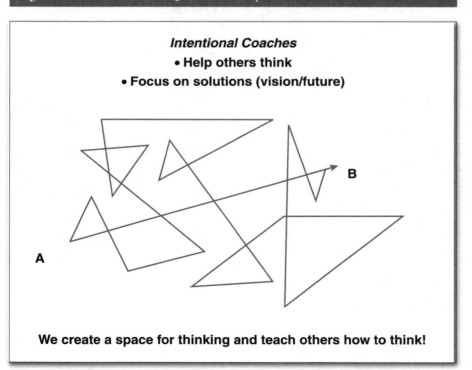

Intentional Coaches
- **Help others think**
- **Focus on solutions (vision/future)**

B

A

We create a space for thinking and teach others how to think!

When leaders focus on solutions, they also realize new energy that comes from leaving a conversation with a sense of direction and action. The components of this type of conversation might be as follows:

Witness the struggle.

In Chapter 5, this concept was shared as an attribute of paraphrasing. To acknowledge the emotion the other individual is feeling can convey understanding and open the door for greater trust in the relationship. Simply recognizing the feelings of others sends the message that you are listening and that you care. This recognition is shown by a comment such as, "You're really disappointed in the motivation of your students to accomplish the results you expected."

Listen for words, phrases, and metaphors that guide thinking.

Listening carefully to the language of the other person offers many opportunities for using key words that actually increase clarity of thought. Words like the following suggest a metaphor that describes the thinking of the other person: "Clearly, you are *building bridges* between your content and a successful classroom through the meaningful relationships you create with your students."

Reframe from problem to solution focus.

When we reframe, we immediately offer the option of hope and possibility. When people complain to us, they are simultaneously telling us what they care deeply about. Our job as coach leader is to listen for what the other people are passionate about and "hold" it up for them to see. In response to, "My students don't care about this class," a reframe might sound like, "You care deeply about the learning of each student in your class."

Use language of discovery and appreciation.

When language is affirming and nonjudgmental, it results in positive change in others. "Your passion and commitment to your content have produced amazing results for your students every year. Your kids leave your classes content zealots. Given your committed passion for student success, what have you celebrated the most as you fired them up to your content and watched their motivation increase?"

**Ask questions to evoke talents,
successes discovery, dreams, and desires.**

Reconnecting people to their strengths, their passions, and their past successes brings energy into the conversation, refreshing and reigniting them to believe they can do it—whatever "it" is. Sample language could be, "When you were so excited last year because Henry won the interscholastic league competition, how did you describe how far he had come? What was the word you used to describe how you felt? A miracle worker. Hummm . . . . What is inspiring our 'miracle worker' this year?"

Ask powerful questions to make solutions possible.

Most people have the answers to their own questions, *and* the best answers usually come from within us. The role of coach leader is to connect to prior knowledge, prior experience, prior success, and inner confidence. "Given your experience and knowledge of the developmental stages of kids when they encounter your content, and given the magic you work with their self-confidence, what high yield strategies are you planning for this special group of reluctant students?"

**Support thinking to create a
clear image of attributes of the solution.**

A quote from the movie *Field of Dreams* represents this idea well, "If you build it, they will come." Knowing the details of what your solution looks like and sounds like works like a magnet to draw you toward it. The language might sound like, "Your courage and commitment to knowing the needs of each student creates a clear pathway to your goals. What are your next steps for achieving your student goals?"

Additional language for the Solution-Focused Conversation includes statements such as the following:

- "You are really hurting from this."
- "The broken trust has emptied your bank account."
- (Appreciative Coaching's Miracle Question—a question that presumes a miracle has happened overnight) "What would have happened to achieve the most positive outcome?"
- "You are seeking your most successful strategies to apply to this situation."
- "What actions and strategies have given you success in the past that could be "re-gifted" in this situation?"

- "What compels you to ensure the solution you desire?"
- "Your courage and commitment to your students has created a clear vision of your goal."

The following coaching conversation demonstrates the GPS for a solution-focused conversation.

Principal: This year, our district has been pushing for a more "balanced literacy" approach in reading in every classroom. My teachers have been to training, and I have tried to provide time for focus on balanced literacy at many faculty meetings. Yet when I walk through classrooms, I still see many of the old practices rather than the strategies we have been focusing on. I am getting pretty upset about the "hold out" and refusal to teach in a way that has more potential for student learning. I guess I need to have a difficult conversation with a few of my teachers who just don't get it.

Coach: Linda, you are truly committed to the use of balanced literacy as the way to maximize reading and writing success for your students, and you are disappointed at not seeing the application in your classrooms at the level you expected by now.

Principal: Yes, we have brought in consultants, we have taught so many strategies, and I thought everyone was on board. It is time for some teachers to just get on with it.

Coach: In the morning, you wake up and go to school. A miracle has happened. As you walk through your school, every classroom is a model of balanced literacy. You are so thrilled and excited for your teachers and students. What are you seeing that thrills you?

Principal: Oh, wow, I see all the components of balanced literacy . . . . I see the teacher reading aloud to students, being a model of a fluent reader while students are being active listeners. I see teachers and students reading text together, practicing fluency and phrasing, which increases comprehension. I see my teachers using guided reading that builds on their reading strategies, which is increasing student motivation to read. I see students reading independently because they are confident and feel good about reading. And everywhere, students are working together on writing, expressing themselves, becoming good spellers, and enjoying the fun of writing and reading to others. Oh, my gosh. I am a happy principal!

Coach: What a fabulous image of learning you have for your campus. You want to see not only the skill but also the joyful motivation of the balanced literacy process.

Principal: Oh, yes . . . so what do I do to get there?

Coach: Knowing that transfer is one of the most powerful strategies required in order for the brain to make connections to new learning, what balanced literacy strategies are you currently seeing in your classrooms that your teachers are doing that you can build upon—that would reinforce their confidence and competence as implementers of a balanced literacy program?

Principal: Well, hmmmm, they are doing some things . . . they are using guided reading, they are focusing on building vocabulary, and . . . (silence . . .) they are doing several things I can connect to . . . oh, my gosh (silence . . .). I am not pointing out what I am seeing. I am only focused on what I am not. Oh, oh, . . . I know exactly what I need to do.

Coach: Wow, from your face, it seems the pathway to your vision is clearer.

Principal: I need to start all over. I need to build on what they are doing, the results they are getting, and celebrate the small ways they are implementing balanced literacy.

Coach: So, what are your next three steps that will provide support and scaffolding in order for your teachers to have higher levels of success with balanced literacy?

Principal: I am having a faculty meeting tomorrow. I want to celebrate the strong strategies my teachers are using, and I want to label connections to balanced literacy.

Coach: How exciting to see the joy and excitement on your face. Congratulations! You have a clear plan and are ready to get started creating that vision for your school.

"Focus 90% of your time on solutions and only 10% of your time on problems."

—Anthony J. D'Angelo

CONVERSATION TOOL 2

Goal-Focused Conversation

"Goals are dreams with deadlines."

—Diana Scharf Hunt

A second tool in the GPS: Guided Pathways for Success system is the one for a goal-focused conversation. Often, this kind of conversation naturally flows from the solution-focused conversation as the person gains clarity about what they want. Much of our work in schools is about setting goals, monitoring and assessing our goals, and getting things successfully completed. After reflecting on our goal attainment, we begin again. As our leaders have these important conversations with teachers, the model is in place for teachers to do the same with students. Schools hold the potential to model for adults and students a lifelong habit of the goal-setting process. Billy Mitchell (1986) in the *Power of Positive Students* speaks to the power of setting goals. He offers these statistics:

- 87% of people do not have goals.
- 10% of people have goals and do not write them down.
- 3% of people have written goals.
- The 3% accomplish 50 to 100 times more than others.

What we know about goal setting is that we can have varying levels of goals. There are the big "macro" goals like achievement and career goals as well as "micro" goals around daily and weekly aspirations. Regardless, a goal-focused conversation might include the following components:

What do you want? Clarify and articulate goals—be explicit; what does it look like and feel like when achieved?

One of the most important questions for a coach leader to ask of self or others is, "What do you really want for your school, your district, and your students?" There are so many times when it is the only question needed to begin the journey of achievement. It is critical that one can articulate how things will look and sound when they are successful. In Chapter 2, you experienced the physical timeline that had you step into the future to envision goal accomplishment. It's extremely powerful to listen and watch as leaders describe how their schools look and sound after achieving a significant goal. The words and emotions describing the transformation can motivate even the most skeptical to believe.

Prioritize your goals.

Often, we have so many goals they begin to compete with each other for time and energy. A coach leader assists the other person to prioritize during the decision-making process when demands begin to pull time and attention away from goals. The RESULTS Coaching Model in Chapter 7, Step 5 Leverage Options speaks more about the process of prioritizing based on impact potential. An example of an actual coaching conversation follows:

> While coaching a principal about her goals for a professional development day, Kathy asked the principal, "When the day is over what will your teachers know and be able to do that will support the goals of the campus?" The principal responded that she wanted the teachers to know about the new guidelines about autism; she wanted them to review the new procedures for team budgets; she also wanted them to share strategies for engaging students in lessons; she wanted them to review the curriculum for the upcoming six weeks together; and she wanted them to review test and classroom walk through data and set goals for the next six weeks.
>
> Kathy paraphrased a summary of her lofty and aligned goals. Then, she asked, "As you consider these six important goals, how are you prioritizing them in sequence and time?" As the principal begin to order the goals and put time to them, she easily realized she had way too many things to bring to her staff on a single day and setting. The insightful principal prioritized, knowing which things were urgent and which were ongoing issues. She then determined three areas of focus for this important day. Her insightful thinking and decision making ensured a powerful day of learning as well as meeting a district requirement.

Generate multiple pathways for achieving your goal; identify the top 10 strategies.

One of the most significant things we have learned is the value of bringing multiple options to our work. As described above, the fast paced world of the educator has created a number of unintended results. We noted poor listening above and will add a tendency to jump to action too quickly here. Give educators a good idea, and they are off and running! We are proposing new hardwiring around the notion of creating possibilities—lots of them.

As mentioned earlier, the old Chinese fortune cookie teaches the idea well, "The best way to have a good idea is to have many ideas." Chapters 2 and 7 emphasize the details of this component.

Consider the following conversation:

Principal speaking with a department head who wants to build a stronger team.

Principal:	Jim, I know you have been working on building a stronger team with your department. What are you seeing and hearing that is providing strong data for you?
Department Head:	Well, it seems we are always rushed, and every meeting is so full of business items we don't ever have time to talk about team building. It is still a goal, maybe our next meeting will be better.
Principal:	Would it be helpful to do some thinking together? I know this is an important goal for you.
Department Head:	Sure, that would be very helpful.
Principal:	So, as you have been planning team strategies for opening your meetings, what has been working the best for you?
Department Head:	Well, I often ask them to share their challenges for the week in the hopes of supporting each other.
Principal:	That does offer a way to hear what other team members are doing and support one other. What strategies are you using to build personal regard for each other?
Department Head:	Well, really I don't think I do any that just builds on personal regard. I am always focused on our department goals. What ideas do you recommend?
Principal:	Well, let's just think about the trust research we have studied. Personal regard is knowing someone, their interests, their strengths, their passions— all the kinds of things we use to differentiate for kids. Let's see if together we can generate a dozen ideas you can select from. One idea we did last week at our faculty meeting was for each person

to share the most exciting news for him or her, outside of school. Wow, did we learn a lot about the lives of our faculty!

Department Head: Yes, that was fun and interesting. Would another idea be to identify some things we share in common outside of education?

Principal: Absolutely. Let's keep going.

After a few minutes, Jim and his principal generated the following 12 ideas:

1. This week's most exciting news about you or your family is . . . .

2. Three things our team shares in common outside of education are . . .

3. If you could choose another name, what name would you choose to be called and why?

4. What book best defines you and your beliefs about life?

5. What movie best exemplifies your personal values or characteristics?

6. What song epitomizes you or your personal beliefs about life?

7. What famous or infamous person would we invite to a dinner with our team? What would we talk about?

8. What 10 values do we all hold in common?

9. What educator had the greatest influence on our lives? Why? How?

10. What holiday is the most special? Why?

11. What little known fact about you would surprise people?

12. If not an educator, what profession would you choose? Why?

Principal: Jim, that was fun for both of us. Now, knowing your team better than anyone, which of these would you want to begin with?

Department Head: They will all be fun, but I think I will start with the book, movie, and song. I think as an English department, they will love sharing those, and it will support our planning for the next three weeks.

Principal: Sounds as if you are already looking forward to building your team. Keep me posted on your success.

Creating multiple options might relate to teaching strategies or discipline strategies. The lists and possibilities are endless and offer a strong support for the least experienced to the most experienced. The only thing certain about our work is that every day holds new challenges and opportunities because we work with people. People are all different, and no one way will be a certainty for success; however, identifying many options will give a person the confidence and energy to confront the daily challenges of his work.

Create an action plan.

Without a doubt, educators have a great deal of experience creating action plans. In fact, we have so much experience in this area, a degree of numbness can be associated with the process of action planning. What we know is that having a plan with steps and strategies, timelines, and resource considerations is critical to making things happen. Previously, Chapter 2 spoke about the importance of clarity of intention with regard to planning for action, and the upcoming Chapter 7 will detail this idea in the RESULTS Coaching model. In the most simple of conversations, it might sound like, "So, what are your next three steps?" or "What are the five major actions of your plan, and what is your timeline for those actions?"

A major learning from neuroscience is that when people face insight and push beyond it with the question, "Now what?" it ensures deeper learning from the insight (Rock, 2006). Leaders want action plans to be real and relevant, not just paper work. Powerful conversations offer the potential for action plans that exceed expectations.

**Identify resources (people and things)
needed to facilitate your achievement.**

Facilitating planning and thinking helps to identify the stepping-stones for success. Many of us have created hardwiring around assuming the responsibility for implementation of all of our plans. A coach leader knows that when this question, "Who can be your partner in the accomplishment of this plan?" is met with silence, they have opened up the possibility for new wiring. A major factor for success in schools today is collaboration and teams working together to tackle tough issues around the achievement of their students. Identifying important resources, both material and human, needed for successful implementation of a plan offers greater energy for task accomplishment.

Reflect and celebrate!

Because there is always the next goal or task to be accomplished, we often fail to engage in the opportunity to reflect and celebrate. This is a missed opportunity for building trust, instilling confidence, and recognizing effort for the hard work of being an educator. Celebrations of success lift us up and energize us for what is to come. Many books have been written about the important of celebrating the journey, not just arrival at the destination. Some of the ways coach leaders reflect and celebrate are to do the following:

- Ask others to identify and celebrate small steps to goal achievement— "What accomplishments are you celebrating?"
- Demonstrate personal regard through individual comments that offer value for work done—"Your organization of our parent night (campus goal) ensured time for each parent to have quality time with their child's teacher."
- Tell success stories about the progress of specific children with details of the intentional difference the teacher has made.
- Make a big deal out of small gains—five points, 10 points.
- Set goals with kids and join in their celebrations.
- Honor collaboration and team effort.
- Listen and smile a lot—the work is hard and needs a lot of support.
- Structure time so that everyone can thank someone else for his or her part of the group success.

Additional language for the Goal-Focused Conversation includes the following:

- What do you want?
- What will it look like when you have achieved this goal?
- Of the four goals you want, rank them in priority order and assign time commitments for yourself.
- What five strategies are you thinking you want to put in place to achieve your goals?
- What are three ways you can do it? Name two more.
- Of your 10 strategies, which three offer the most powerful steps to achieving your goal?

- What is your timeline for accomplishing your goal?
- Who will assist you in realizing your goal?
- As you reflect on this conversation and your upcoming goal achievement, what will you be celebrating in two months?

"If we are facing in the right direction, all we have to do is keep on walking."

—Buddhist Proverb

CONVERSATION TOOL 3

Planning-Focused Conversation

"He who fails to plan, plans to fail."

—Old Proverb

Connected to the goal-focused conversation is the third tool in the GPS: the frame for a planning-focused conversation. The idea of creating an action plan discussed above actually segues into the possibility of a planning-focused conversation. The world of education offers a magnitude of opportunities for planning. Planning for instruction, planning for meetings, planning for activities, planning for presentations, and the list goes on. Garmston and Wellman (1992) tell us that "all presentations are made twice—first in the presenter's mind, during the design stage, and second, during the actual presentation. Eighty-five percent of the quality of the second presentation is a product of the first. The remaining 15% comes from personal energy, charisma, and our openness to serendipitous relationships with our audience. In planning presentations we must remember the carpenter's adage, 'Measure twice and cut once'" (p.15).

Planning is the thoughtful consideration of what it will take to achieve a goal. In our lives, it shows up personally and professionally as in planning for one's financial future, planning for a special event, or planning for an outstanding lesson. The planned activity will always produce more effective and purposeful results. No magician ever pulled a rabbit out of a hat without carefully putting the rabbit there in the first place. No man hopes to arrive at his destination if he does not know where he is going. He will be like a ship without a rudder, adrift at the mercy of the wind and tide. Worthwhile accomplishments are seldom, if ever, accidental. They are the end result of planned efforts towards concrete goals. The secret of success in any endeavor lies in six magic words: *Plan your work, work your plan.*

The GPS offers some options for supporting others as they create a plan for successful achievement. Components include the following:

Clarify goals.

Just as the goal-focused conversation began with goal clarity, so does the planning-focused conversation. Gaining crystal clarity on our goals is the greatest factor in achieving a goal. Educators have many goals, and they are often complex. Supporting another's thinking to be very clear on the goal will dramatically impact the accomplishment of the goal. If, for example, a teacher has a goal of having a safe and caring learning environment, the coach leader will ask important questions to clarify this goal. "What does a safe and caring learning environment mean?" "What are students saying and doing in this environment?" "What specific skills will they be demonstrating?" As clarifying questions are asked, the teacher may discover what she really wants are students who work together well. The clarification dramatically influences the plan to achieve the goal.

Determine indicators of success.

Once goals are clarified, it is important to identify the indicators of success. If our goal is to have students successfully writing a descriptive paragraph, it is extremely important to identify the criteria or measures that indicate success. One of the gifts from our colleague, Shirley Hord, Scholar Emerita, NSDC, is always asking the question, "How will you know?"

- How will you know when your students are enthusiastic readers?
- How will you know when teachers are collaborative?
- How will you know when your campus is exceptional at meeting the needs of all students?
- How will you know that teachers are using the curriculum?
- How will you know when your campus exemplifies best practice?
- How will you know when you are a *coach leader*?

Anticipate approaches, strategies, and decisions.

Once your goal is clear and you know how you will measure your success, the fun begins. In today's classroom, the curriculum is prescribed tightly, but the approaches and strategies offer many options. When we think about the science and art of teaching, art abounds. Today, we are fortunate to have research that has identified which strategies have the greatest potential to impact student success. Robert Marzano (2003) has given us numerous "What Works" titles to help us select strategies that will increase our potential for success, whether it is teaching a lesson or leading a campus or district. The coach leader holds up those best practice strategies to remind, connect, and narrow the choices that scaffold the process so the student, the teacher, or the leader is successful. Powerful questions might include the following:

- What best practice strategies have you determined will support students mastering the objective?
- As you have considered your options for engaging your students at high levels, what strategies have you determined are best for your students?
- In your quest for an exemplary campus, what high yield strategies have you determined will ensure your success?
- As a superintendent who has led numerous districts to high levels of student success, what have you determined are your most critical, high leverage strategies to replicate in this district?

Identify the data for self-assessment.

Returning to the indicators of success, it is important to attach the powerful data question to achievement of the goal. What data will inform your progress and ultimately your results? So, using the questions above, we will add, "What data will verify your progress?"

- How will you know when your students are enthusiastic readers? *What data will be used to measure your goal?*
- How will you know when teachers are collaborative? *What data will serve as indicators of success for this goal?*
- How will you know when your campus is exceptional for meeting the needs of all students? *What data will provide evidence of your success?*
- How will you know that teachers are using the curriculum? *What data will document that this requirement is being met?*
- How will you know when your campus exemplifies best practice? *What data from your walkthroughs will align with your achievement benchmarks?*
- How will you know when you are a *coach leader*? *What data will inform you that you have achieved the characteristics of a coach leader?*

Determine the plan for action.

With a clear goal and specific indicators for knowing when we have reached the goal, we have added powerful strategies to make it happen plus data that will inform others and us that we have achieved our goal. The coach leader will now add energy and motivation to the goal by intentionally asking about steps in the plan for success. Without this component, a person may have crafted the greatest goal and measures for success, but when he walks away, distractions abound interfering with accomplishment of the goal. Coaching supports the movement of planning into action that begins with very simple, turbo questions.

- In achieving your goal, what are your five major steps?
- What will be your first steps to achieving your goal?
- As you think about your plan of action, what steps will catapult you to success?
- In designing your plan of action for your goal, what will be the major components during the first month, the second month, and the third month?

Chapters 2 and 7 offer additional information to support the development of a plan for action.

Reflect on benefits of conversation.

The simple, yet important question that informs the coach leader of the impact of the conversation is, "How has our conversation been helpful to you?"

In closing a conversation, the question provides data for the coach leader about the value of the time spent in the conversation. It also offers feedback to the coach on the use of her skills of listening, paraphrasing, and presuming positive intent. While supporting others in their planning and thinking, it provides the opportunity for the speakers to identify what they will take away from the conversation. It reinforces the concepts of "closure" and "checking for understanding," two very essential components of teaching and learning and continuous improvement.

Additional language for the Planning-Focused Conversation includes the following:

- What do you want to achieve?
- How will you know when you have achieved it?
- What strategies have you determined will support your success?

- How will you know when you have achieved your mission? What data will affirm your accomplishment?
- What will be the first steps in your plan for action?
- How has this conversation been helpful?

"If you don't have a plan for yourself, you'll be part of someone else's."

—American Proverb

CONVERSATION TOOL 4

Reflection-Focused Conversation

"Only by reflecting on our actions can we increase our capacity and the likelihood that we will enhance our decisions and actions in the future.

—Donald Schon

Finally, we come to the fourth tool in the GPS—Reflection-Focused Conversation. What happens when you pick up a mirror? Are you checking for how you look? Are you modifying your hair or glasses or checking your teeth? The reflection we see offers the opportunity to change or modify and adapt for improvements. Reflection is the intellectual work of teaching and learning and is key to deeper understanding, greater meaning, and continuous improvement. "Reflection is the process of making meaning of the learning experience before, during, or after the experience has occurred. It is a conscious and intentional process for allowing time for the brain to make meaning" (Schon, 1987).

Educators know intellectually that reflection is important, and we work hard to include it in our practice. With deadlines and timelines always pushing against us, reflection is frequently overlooked or relegated to the last few minutes of a conversation, a meeting, or a training session. We have known for years the value and importance of reflection to the process of learning, "Adults do not learn from experience; they learn from reflecting on experience" (Judy-Arin Krupp, 1982).

The coach leader knows and values the importance of reflection and provides opportunities for reflection to occur in conversations, in meetings, and in trainings. The reflection-focused conversation on our GPS offers another pathway to structure conversations that will value, embrace, and celebrate the opportunity to pause and reflect on our practice.

During reflection conversations, the following components offer a sequence that will assist the brain in making new and insightful connections.

Summarize impressions of an event.

To summarize one's impressions is to honor what was witnessed and observed. It provides the person most closely involved in an event to stop and reflect on what he or she saw and how he or she felt about it. Simple questions from the coach leader can offer opportunities to recall feelings and observations.

- How did you feel the lesson went?
- When you left the meeting, what impressions were speaking to you?
- At the close of the conversation, how were you feeling about your success?

Recall supporting information.

When the brain is asked to provide support or evidence to a feeling or an impression, it searches for data to substantiate the impression. It begins the important connection and process of using specific information to quantify perceptions and ideas.

- What caused you to feel that way?
- What did you see and hear to form those impressions?
- What did the parent do or say to support your feeling about the conversation?

Compare, analyze, and infer cause and effect relationships.

As we continually work to support others in thinking about how they do their work and what they do that is making a difference, assisting others to consider their direct relationship to a success event aligns with our belief of operating from successes and strengths. Asking the brain to compare, analyze, and infer strengthens the hardwiring for new behaviors and actions. The language of the coach leader would be as follows:

- As you reflect on the lesson, what did you intentionally do to produce the results?
- As you view your outcomes before and after the meeting, how are they comparing?

- As you reflect on the conversation, what two things did you do or pay attention to that impacted the response of your parent?
- Compare your intentions for how you wanted to show up for this meeting with what actually happened. What do you notice?

Construct new learnings and applications.

The brain is always making connections, and reflection strengthens new ways of thinking and being—it is making new wiring around new or more successful actions and behaviors. Supporting another's thinking from consideration of impact to implications for applying the learning in the future creates stronger pathways and connections to new behaviors and actions. The coach leader's language would sound like the following:

- As you consider the decisions and choices you made in the lesson, what new possibilities are you seeing for future lessons?
- As you have reflected on this meeting, what are you learning about your staff and your role in meetings?
- You have reflected upon and identified specific thoughts and language that produced a hoped for result in the attitude and support of a parent. What insights are you having about other conversations?

Reflect on benefits of conversation and any refinements.

Again, the simple yet important question that informs the coach leader of the impact of the conversation is:

- How has our conversation been helpful?

Additional questions may include:

- What questions, if any, might I have asked that would have supported your reflection even more?
- What was the most significant benefit of today's conversation?
- What was of greatest value in the time we spent together today?

The following is a Reflection-Focused Conversation.

Coach Leader: John, it is always great to get into your classroom and watch the magic you work with students in math. Your passion for math is evident. I am thrilled to reflect with you about your teaching this week.

Teacher:	Thanks. I wish I was as excited about every student I have.
Coach Leader:	So, John, as you are reflecting on the success of your students, how are you feeling? What is behind this worried face I see?
Teacher:	Well, I do work hard to make instruction interesting and meaningful, and I think most of my students are progressing very well. It is always just five or six kids who have so many challenges. I struggle to keep them engaged and connected to the work.
Coach Leader:	As you reflect on your observations, what are you doing when all of your students are engaged and learning at your expected levels?
Teacher:	I have planned for different levels of learning. I have either grouped kids for learning or grouped them by areas for practice. It is just so time consuming to prepare, and so sometimes, I have them all together.
Coach Leader:	So, your frustration is really about time for planning activities that meet your students' needs.
Teacher:	Yes.
Principal:	When you are planning with your team, what are you noticing about how your colleagues are grouping for activities and for special needs?
Teacher:	Well, you know in the limited time we have, we have just been planning content and whole-class activities. I don't think we have shared how we differentiate. I should bring that up.
Coach Leader:	What might you find when you do?
Teacher:	Well, that my colleagues are struggling just like me, and maybe we could stay 30 minutes longer and share ideas for all our student groupings.
Coach Leader:	As you reflect on your successful instruction, you are thinking that working with your teammates and sharing the planning load might give you the time you need to work with students who need you most.
Teacher:	Yes, and you know, it is not the regular instruction that is troublesome; it is always the planning needed for the

kids who are struggling. By simply modifying our time and focus, my hunch is that all members of the team would benefit.

Coach Leader: So what next steps are you thinking you want to take?

Teacher: I am going to talk with our team leader today.

Coach Leader: John, in our 30 minutes, how has this time to reflect been helpful to you?

Teacher: Well, I thought I would dissect my lesson but really, I have revealed something that has been bothering me, and I think I've uncovered a way that will help me improve how I serve some kids and maybe even a way that will save time.

Coach Leader: Your willingness to always explore new possibilities for yourself and your students is an inspiration. I look forward to next week to hear about the whole team's collaboration and insights. Let's talk this time next week.

Teacher: Yes, thanks again. I look forward to sharing the results.

Additional language for a Reflection-Focused Conversation includes the following:

- How do you feel about your performance? What strikes you about this lesson?
- What data supports your feelings?
- What did you do to get the results you achieved? What specifically impacted your results?
- If you were to do this again, what would you want to repeat? Refine? Eliminate?
- How has this conversation supported your reflective practice?

SUMMARY

The coach leader's GPS is as easy as entering the destination on the equipment in our cars or iPhones. It offers a guided pathway to what will best support the other person whether he is seeking solutions, goal setting, planning for action, or reflecting on something that has occurred. The course may be changed along the way. The time and distance may vary. The direction may change. What stays constant is the coach. The coach leader promises committed listening, powerful paraphrasing, presuming positive intent, and reflective feedback resulting in a conversation that has

- great clarity,
- new insights,
- a plan for action,
- multiple options,
- knowledge and skill,
- a sense of status, and
- evidence of trust.

REFLECTION

1. Which GPS pathway are you discovering is a frequent path for you and your conversations?

2. Which GPS pathway do you want to use more often in your conversations?

3. How will holding the "A-to-B" solution focused visual in your head aid in time demands while supporting others with challenges?

4. What opportunities for reflection do you want to structure to support and refine teaching and learning?

"There are three methods to gaining wisdom. The first is reflection, which is the highest. The second is limitation, which is the easiest. The third is experience, which is the bitterest."

—Confucius

RESULTS
Coaching Plan
for Action

7

ESSENTIAL FOR UNLEASHING
PROMISE AND POSSIBILITY

"Vision without action is merely a dream. Action without vision just passes the time. Vision with action can change the world."

—Joel A. Barker

Because Frances loves to travel to new and unfamiliar surroundings, she frequently finds herself lost. This prompted her decision to purchase a portable GPS (Global Positioning System) device that could easily be carried along and used in a rental car. It's great! She just puts in the address or name of a site she wants to visit and voila! She is guided directly to her destination with a friendly voice that anticipates every turn in plenty of time for her to steer the car to the correct lane for turning. Yet even with this advance warning, she sometimes finds herself unable to make the required traffic move in a timely manner, missing the turn. When that happens, the "friendly" voice becomes "mechanical," and she hears, "Recalculating. Please make a legal u-turn at your next available opportunity." That is followed by a new set of directions from the friendly voice that continues directing her to her desired destination.

Frances notes that even when she has the GPS with her, she doesn't automatically think to use it and has pulled out a map or stopped to ask directions from someone more familiar with the territory than herself.

She has not yet developed complete reliability or faith in her ability to use a newer, more sophisticated system than the ones she has come to rely on. She's noticed the same tendency to be true when she attempts to add a new leadership behavior to her set of skills. While realizing the new skills will improve her efficiency and effectiveness as a leader, she also knows it is hard to integrate the new patterns into her actions.

Just like using a GPS that offers direction and focus, RESULTS Coaching leaders carry coaching tools and models in their heads as scaffolds for framing interactions. When a school leader is not seeing the desired connections or results in herself or himself or in staff members, the leader as coach is able to assist the person to "recalculate" and make a u-turn that has greater potential for transporting the person to his or her desired destination.

There are many ways to reach a destination, whether it's a geographic one or a goal to be attained. When a leader is navigating in new territory, she often defaults to a more familiar or comfortable process, even though it may not be as effective as the new technology. Until we add the new technology or the new process to our repertoire, our habits will not change, and we will continue to get the same results we have always gotten. It takes time and intention to adjust to new ways of being and doing.

We all have goals or results we want to achieve in our work environments. In order to obtain these outcomes, we create plans. Traditional planning is often linear and involves one-track thinking. The RESULTS approach to planning action is more cyclical and will unleash some of the creative potential within, promoting out-of-the-box thinking that creates energy for accomplishment of the goal.

This chapter arms the school leader with a mental model for designing actions that bring desired results. The RESULTS Coaching model builds the leader's internal resourcefulness and capacity to impact change. The planning framework allows for integration and application of the skills learned in previous chapters.

RESULTS COACHING MODEL

Work in schools is transformed when school leaders use the RESULTS Coaching Model to frame their conversations. It causes conversations to focus on the most important outcomes in a way that brings clarity, insight, and energy to action. Leaders using the model get improved results with teachers and parents, and teachers get greater results with students. The RESULTS

Coaching Model helps all school personnel get clearer about the goals they want to obtain by "beginning with the end in mind" (Covey, 1989).

The acronym R-E-S-U-L-T-S assists us with the exploration of the steps in this planning process and serves as a way to help us remember the steps. Each of the letters represents one step in this planning process.

- ***Resolve . . . to change results***
- ***Establish . . . goal clarity***
- ***Seek . . . integrity***
- ***Unveil . . . multiple pathways***
- ***Leverage . . . options***
- ***Take . . . action***
- ***Seize . . . success***

As we explore the steps in the RESULTS Coaching Model, the Intention Pyramid discussed in Chapter 2 (see Figure 7.1) becomes an inherent part of this model. You will recall that this tool allowed the leader to focus on his intentions and explored what the leader wanted to "have," to "do," and to "be."

Figure 7.1   Intention Pyramid

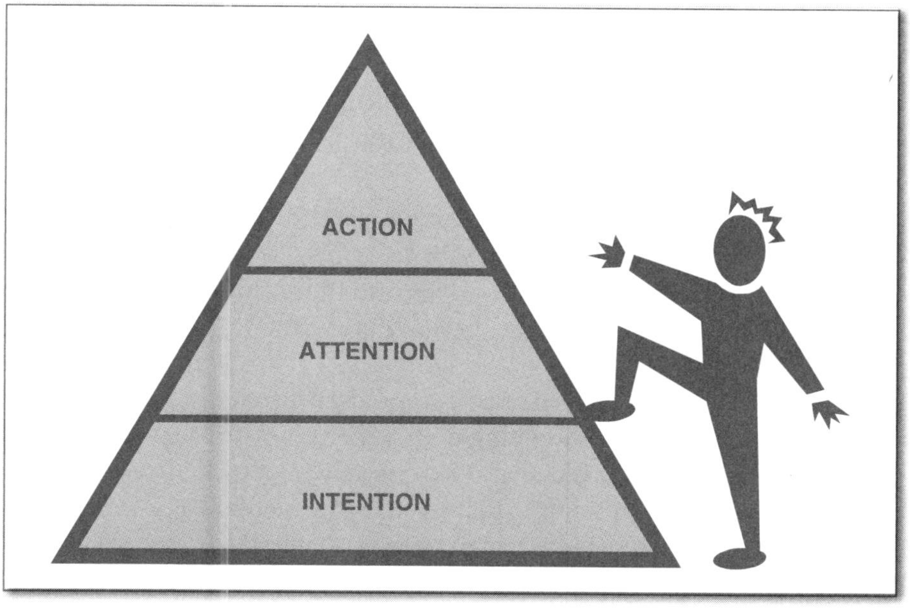

Source: Garmston & Wellman, 1999

By embedding the intention pyramid, we create the powerful, essential RESULTS Coaching Model illustrated by Figure 7.2.

Figure 7.2

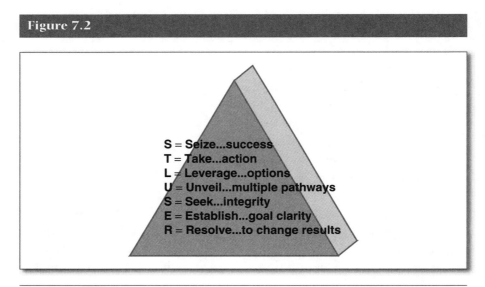

S = Seize...success
T = Take...action
L = Leverage...options
U = Unveil...multiple pathways
S = Seek...integrity
E = Establish...goal clarity
R = Resolve...to change results

Source: Coaching School Results, *RESULTS Coaching Model,* 2009

INTRODUCTION

The RESULTS Coaching Model can be used in at least three ways. The first two approaches focus on the leader as she works on her own behaviors to enhance what she is doing, what she wants to have, or how she wants to be. The third approach addresses how the leader can assist others in reaching the results they desire.

First, the school leader can develop a plan for action around a goal such as a particular behavior or skill he wants to incorporate into his repertoire. It might be around the skills taught in Chapters 4 and 5. The leader will state the goal using the language of intention described in Chapter 2.

Examples include, "I want to be a committed listener," and "I expect to use paraphrasing when interacting with others at least twice a day." Plans developed to promote professional skill development often relate to the school leader's state of being. "Being" plans for action have a profound impact on the life of the leader and indirectly (covertly) influence organizational change.

The second way the school leader can use the RESULTS Coaching Model is to design actions to complete new or routine tasks inherent in job performance. These actions may revolve around any goal the school leader would like to meet, such as conducting a faculty meeting that focuses on professional development, having a meeting with an unhappy parent, holding a difficult conversation with a teacher, or adding a new instructional program to the curriculum. These plans generally deal with the "doing" (overt) aspects of the school leader's responsibilities and have a direct impact on organizational change.

The third way the RESULTS Coaching Model can be used is to coach others in the organization in order to build capacity. For this process to be successful, the leader must examine his mindset regarding people and approach each interaction with the belief that every person has the desire to impact students' success even when they have been exhibiting behaviors that do not seem to support that belief. When implemented with authenticity, the strategies presented in Chapter 5—committed listening, paraphrasing, presuming positive intent, and reflective feedback—assist the leader to model this mindset. When the tool is used to support the growth of others, the thinking and solution finding abilities of each staff member are enhanced. Thinking is reinforced, individuals feel valued for what they contribute to the organization, and morale increases. As staff members feel more empowered, they interact with students differently and student success is maximized.

A leader may elect to use the RESULTS Coaching Model several ways when working with others. First, she may use the model when teachers and parents present issues or challenges they are trying to resolve and need assistance to reach a solution. This strategy moves the leader out of the role of advice giving or problem solving and into the role of coaching others to increase their own solution-finding abilities. A second strategy would be to teach the model to the staff and assist them in the development of their own RESULTS plans. It is possible that the leader could do both. As staff members see the leader using the model, they gain greater understanding of how to use the model and see the impact it has for achieving stated goals or intentions.

To illustrate the power of the RESULTS Coaching Model, an actual story of a school leader will be embedded in the model as we address each step. Her story can be found in its entirety in the Resources. Two additional stories are also included in the Resources to illustrate examples of how school leaders have used the RESULTS model to achieve the outcomes they wanted for themselves and for their schools.

Meet Camille

Let's meet Camille. She is the second-year principal of a large high school. Her administrative team is comprised of capable individuals, each fulfilling their own areas of responsibility. Her concern is that the team is territorial and divisive. She often has to handle disagreements between team members. She would like the team to function more cohesively, to share in the visioning for the campus, and to develop plans and solutions that everyone can support. She is disappointed that she has been unable to get this team to function as one voice, and she worries that this divisiveness is causing dissention among staff and has the potential to cause morale problems. With the help of her coach, Camille developed and implemented a plan for action.

STEP 1: RESOLVE . . . TO CHANGE RESULTS

Resolve is the first step in the RESULTS Coaching Model. Resolve defined means "to make up your mind," "to decide," "to determine." It begins with an intention to change or a shift in one's mindset. Resolve presupposes that the leader is already aware of a behavior he would like to change, has identified his change goal, examined his competing commitments, and is ready to develop a plan for action to implement this change for accomplishment of a new result.

Resolve is not synonymous with willpower. Blumenthal (2007) reminds us that willpower might be great, but it doesn't hold the key to success. Changing a behavior is not simply a matter of replacing an old one with a new one. In his book, *Quiet Leadership,* David Rock (2006) states that the behaviors and experiences we have had are hardwired into our brain and that it is almost impossible to deconstruct our wiring. If change were simply a matter of willpower, every individual in America would be a nonsmoker and skinny. Obviously, that is not true. People don't change their behavior due to a lack of willpower; they change when they have a specific plan for action and then exhibit the courage to implement that plan. Rock describes it as creating new wiring or a new pathway for achieving what we want.

Resolve does, however, involve effort. Leaders have passion about their work, and they want to turn that passion into actions that promote student success. Change fosters creativity, suggests new possibilities and brings new energy. Dweck (2006) reminds us, ". . . effort is what ignites [a leader's] ability and turns it [their passion] into accomplishment" (p. 41). Insight alone is not enough. Leaders are more willing to expend the effort and energy needed to design and promote change when they stay focused on the goal and when the plans they implement are getting the desired results for children.

Camille Resolves to Change

Camille shares the following:

> As I thought about this situation with my assistants and discussed this situation with my coach, I realized that I have contributed to the lack of unity among teammembers. I have allowed my competing commitment to be liked and seen as part of the team to keep me from taking the leadership role that will get me the results I want. I've allowed other meetings and situations to take precedence over my meetings with them; consequently, our regularly scheduled meetings are often cancelled. When we do meet, it is in my office. I sit behind my desk, and they haul in chairs. They hold their materials and reports in their laps. I am also aware that I provide solutions to issues and often tell them how I want things handled. I serve as the referee and/or mediator when disputes arise between them. I know that I must change my behaviors if I expect to get different results.

Reflection

What am I passionate about?

1. How do I want to "be" different as a leader? What behavior(s) do I resolve to change and/or add to my skill set?

_____

_____

_____

_____

2. As a leader, what do I want for my organization? Where am I willing to put my time, energy and effort?

_____

_____

_____

_____

STEP 2: ESTABLISH . . . GOAL CLARITY

The second step in the RESULTS Coaching Model is to *establish* goal clarity. Whether the school leader is designing a goal for himself or for his school, it is important that the goal be specific and clear.

There is a compelling tendency to move from this step in the process too quickly. If the goal is unclear, the results will not support the desired change. When this happens, people become disappointed, and their commitment and energy around the change decreases. Without goal clarity, we often find ourselves working on the wrong thing. We are busy "doing"; however, it is like throwing freshly cut grass into the air. We can predict with little certainty where our action might land or the impact it might have. Covey (2006, p.172) reinforces this idea when he defines our constant "doing" as *counterfeit behaviors*—those that keep us busy in activities rather than busy clarifying goals that get results.

Chapter 2's focus on the Intention Pyramid offers several strategies for establishing goal clarity around our intentions. Those include the following:

- Beginning with the end in mind
- Using the notion of hypertext as a strategy for elaborating on a word or concept
- Eliciting input from others about the specificity and clarity of our goal

You practiced using those strategies as you got clearer about the goal you described around stating your intention. The first level of the Intention Pyramid—intention—correlates to this step, Establish Goal Clarity in the RESULTS Coaching Model.

Helping others get clear about what they want ensures a greater likelihood that the goal they have set will get the intended results. When leaders assist teachers by setting outcomes for children based upon the state and district goals and expectations, there is a greater likelihood that results for students will be realized.

Camille Establishes Goal Clarity

As Camille continued her interaction with her coach, she realized she wanted to get clearer about her expectations for her administrative staff. She made the commitment to share these expectations openly. She will share data—specific incidents where administrators disagreed inappropriately—and she will talk about how this arguing and divisiveness has had a negative impact among the staff and the students. She will state how she has contributed to this disunity and the changes in her behavior they can expect. Camille realized that there was a lot at stake if things continued as they were. She knew she would have to be courageous in order to deal with this issue. She elected to use strong language to reflect her resolve.

Her goal:

> I want to use powerful, speak-the-truth language to bring unity to my administrative team and encourage solution-finding behaviors.

Through the coaching interaction, Camille was able to think at a deeper level and generate a goal that had greater clarity and specificity. She left the coaching session feeling energized, confident in her ability to accomplish the goal, and committed to making the necessary, courageous changes.

Reflection

Go back to the thoughts you recorded in the Resolve section. Write goals around both your thoughts. Select new intentions or goals from the one you selected in Chapter 2 when you created your first Intention Pyramid.

1. How will you gain clarity about this goal? Who can you ask to critique this goal for understanding?

_____

_____

_____

_____

2. If this goal is met in your school, what will the students say or do differently? What will teachers have said or done to bring about this change?

_____

_____

_____

_____

Once the goal has been clearly stated, move to the Intention Pyramid and write that goal in the intention box. You will remember that this box is broader and serves as the foundation of the pyramid. The second box is labeled "attention," and the top section deals with actions. For the next several steps of the RESULTS Coaching Model, we will be moving back and forth between these two planning processes—the RESULTS acronym and the Intention Pyramid.

STEP 3: SEEK . . . INTEGRITY

The third part of the RESULTS Coaching Model is to *seek* integrity. In this step, the school leader is ensuring that he is being honest, sincere, and upright. A leader shows integrity when his actions match his purpose, values, and beliefs; there is alignment between who the leader is (or is becoming) and the behaviors or actions he is taking. The leader's expectation for his behavior is to be "real" and to be authentically present in all interactions. His integrity underlies and supports the intentions he has for himself and for those he leads or coaches.

Since a significant part of integrity addresses who the leader wants to "be," this step in the RESULTS coaching model is a direct overlay to the Attention section of the Intention Pyramid. The two questions posed around Attention are as follows:

- "How do I want to be (as the leader)?"
- "What do I want to pay attention to as I accomplish my intention and/or goal?"

Leaders can respond to these questions whether they are designing an action plan around self improvement or helping others develop plans for themselves.

When leaders assist others, it is important to remember that relationships are built upon trust and belief in people. We are reminded again of Tschannen-Moran's (2004) definition, "Trust is one's willingness to be vulnerable to another based on the confidence that the other is benevolent, honest, open, reliable and competent."

People follow leaders who make honest commitments to change their own behaviors and who provide opportunities for others to realize their own potential. Leaders use RESULTS coaching strategies and language to coach their staff to higher levels of performance so that student success goals are achieved.

The RESULTS Coaching Model pushes integrity and trust to a deeper level because it asks leaders to be bold and speak their truth and to make and keep their promises—two Essential Language Connectors presented in Chapter 4.

Seek . . . integrity addresses what the school leader wants to pay attention to—those "being" behaviors that will help the leader reach the desired goal. The leader matches her intention or goal with the mindset she has adopted about the professional change she has resolved to accomplish.

Let's see how Camille addressed the Seeking Integrity step by answering the two questions from the Intention Pyramid.

- "How do I want to be (as the leader)?
- "What do I want to pay attention to as I accomplish my intention and/or goal?"

Camille Seeks Integrity

Camille *wants to be* in control, using language that is definite but not directive or overbearing. She wants to share her observations, concerns, and expectations using a firm, even, nonaccusatorial tone of voice. (She wants to tell the truth without blame or judgment.)

Camille *wants to create* a no-nonsense collegial working environment. She decides to move the meetings out of her office and into a conference room that has a large rectangular table. She plans to position herself at the head of the table and to be seated with the teammembers.

Reflection

1. How do I want to "be" as I accomplish my intention or goal? What, if anything, will help me do this?

_____

_____

_____

_____

2. What do I want to pay attention to as I accomplish my intention or goal?

_____

_____

_____

_____

This step completes the second section of our Intention Pyramid called Attention. Before you add these statements to the pyramid, check to see how what you wrote in Seek integrity aligns with your intention or goal. How are they compatible? Do you want to make any adjustments? Keep modifying your responses until you can answer yes to, "Is this how I would best accomplish my intention?" Then, record that information in the Attention box of the pyramid.

Notice that the steps in the RESULTS Coaching Model allow the leader to move back and forth as needed in this planning process. In this case, the leader moved from his intention to attention and back again to make sure there was alignment. Although the steps in the RESULTS Coaching Model are linear in their construction, they provide the leader with the ability to move between the components, thereby assuring that all the steps in the process remain aligned. This illustrates how this planning tool becomes cyclical in design.

STEP 4: UNVEIL . . . MULTIPLE PATHWAYS

The fourth step in the RESULTS Coaching Model is to *unveil* multiple pathways. This step and the two that follow—Leverage Options and Take Action—mirror the Action section of the Intention Pyramid. Unveiling multiple pathways is a process that promotes multiple options—all possibilities to the attainment of the stated goal or intention. Generating many possibilities for goal achievement ensures that a person has several viable options for success. If, for example, a leader only selects one applicant from the hiring pool and that person accepts a job at another school, the leader is disappointed and has to repeat the entire hiring process. There is no Plan B or a fallback strategy for ensuring forward movement.

You will recall from Chapter 2 that this action section of the Intention Pyramid asks the leader to record as many ideas as he can think of to accomplish the stated goal or intention. We will use that same process to think of as many ideas as you can that would help you reach your goal. Remember, our purpose is to generate as many great ideas as possible rather than trying to figure out which idea is the best one. At this point, you are brainstorming without judging any of your possibilities. When you hear your mind saying, "That's impossible!" or "How in the world would we accomplish that?" write down that idea anyway. List things you would never do and wish you had the courage to do. Think outside the box; come up with some really bizarre ideas. At this point, the goal is not quality of ideas but quantity. Just write the first things that come to your mind.

Reflection

Use the same process you used in Chapter 2 when you brainstormed options in response to the Action section of the Intention Pyramid. The steps are repeated here for your convenience.

You have one minute. Think of at least five options that would lead you toward the attainment of your intention.

1.

2.

3.

4.

5.

You have one more minute. Now, think of five more.

6.

7.

8.

9.

10.

You have a minute and a half. Now, add some really wild and crazy ideas.

11.

12.

13.

14.

15.

You have two minutes. Push yourself to come up with even five more.

16.

17.

18.

19.

20.

If possible, do this activity with a partner. Each of you will write your goal on one side of an index card. When it is your turn to generate options, pass your index card to your partner so that she can capture your brilliant ideas. When it is your partner's turn, you write down all her ideas. When you have both had a turn, the card is returned to its owner.

Remember this is not the time to give advice or offer suggestions to your partner. Your partner is very capable of generating her own ideas. You can assist by offering encouragement or asking the following questions:

- What ideas have you come up with to achieve your goal?
- Come up with one more.
- What else?
- These are great. Give me two more.
- Give me something wild and crazy.
- If you could give me one more, what would it be?
- Give me something really fun.

This can be a time to borrow and adapt. If your partner has an idea that you like, add it to your list. This activity can also be done with a group. Each participant shares his or her card with two or three additional partners.

Reflection

1. What did you notice about your ability to generate possibilities?

2. What did you notice about the ideas you generated?

3. What did you learn about yourself?

4. What happened when you worked with a partner?

5. How would you apply this process?

Camille Unveils Multiple Pathways

1. Seek input from administrators regarding their solutions.

2. Share my expectations regarding working together as a team.

3. Explain how this disunity makes me feel and how I intend to change my behavior by showing up differently.

4. Describe data by giving examples of behaviors that are unacceptable.

5. Express my concerns regarding the impact divisiveness is having.

6. Be clear about what I see as the problem.

7. State how I would like to see the problem resolved.

8. Share how I have contributed to disunity.

9. Write out my conversation—making it no more than two minutes in length.

10. Practice speaking my truth out loud.

STEP 5: LEVERAGE . . . OPTIONS

The fifth step in the RESULTS Coaching Model is to *leverage* options. Before the leader finalizes his plan for action, he will want to examine all the options generated in Unveil Multiple Pathways and select those that have the greatest potential for accomplishing the stated intention. This often involves prioritizing and categorizing. The leader is now taking all of his options and making some value judgments regarding their potential impact, thereby narrowing his list so he can create a targeted plan. The leader is narrowing the list of options to include those ideas he is really serious about trying. He may be "weeding out" or deleting some options at this time. The advantage for Unveiling Multiple Pathways is the leader has some additional strategies if the current plan he is developing is unsuccessful or if the plan needs to be modified in the future.

Camille Leverages Her Options

When Camille reviewed her list, she categorized two items that involved preplanning—items nine and 10. She realized the remaining options were steps to help her reach her goal, so she wanted to include all the items on her list in her conversation with her administrative team.

STEP 6: TAKE . . . ACTION

The next step in the RESULTS Coaching Model is to *take* action. The leader organizes all his selected options to create his best plan of action. In this step, the leader creates the sequence or order for taking action given the strategic options previously generated.

Camille Takes Action

Camille decided to use the following order to organize her conversation

1. 6: Be clear about what I see as the problem.

2. 4: Describe data by giving examples of behaviors that are unacceptable.

3. 5: Express my concern regarding the impact divisiveness is having on staff.

4. 3: Explain how this disunity makes me feel and how I intend to change my behavior by showing up differently.

5. 8: Share how I have contributed to disunity.

6. 2: Share my expectations regarding working together as a team.

7. 7: State how I would like to see the problem resolved.

8. 1: Seek input from administrators regarding their solutions.

This step completes the third section of our Intention Pyramid called Action. Before you add these ideas to the pyramid, check to see how your proposed actions align with your intention or goal and what you have written in the Attention area of the pyramid. How are they compatible? In what ways do they support achievement of your goal? What, if any adjustments, will you make? Keep modifying your responses until you can say, "yes" to, "This is how I can best accomplish my intention." Then, record that information in the Action area at the apex of the pyramid.

The plan you develop will be customized to meet your own needs. Notice that "doing" plans for action tend to be more sequential and linear in nature; "being" plans, more random. In both cases, however, the leader can use this cyclical model—moving back and forth between the steps— to align his or her thinking (doing—action steps) with his or her being (integrity). Modifications to your plan can be made and "re-made" at any step in the planning process.

In summary, the leader is taking all the data generated in the last five steps of the RESULTS coaching model (Establish goal clarity, Seek integrity, Unveil multiple pathways, Leverage options, and Take action) and finalizing his plan of action. His list of options has been narrowed and reordered. His initial plan of action has now been developed.

As leaders explore the implementation of their plan, other factors may emerge for consideration. Those might include some of the following factors:

- "What resources will I need in order to accomplish this goal?
- "What is the timeline for completion of this goal?"
- "If I am involving other people in this action plan, who are they? How will I request their assistance?"
- "How will I know that the plan I developed is successful? What will have changed, and how will I see and hear these changes in my work environment?"

Some leaders find it helpful to use an additional planning tool such as a chart or table that moves these action steps into a refined action plan that specifies resources, timelines, who's responsible, and indicators of success. There are many templates of planning tools that exist in education and have been used particularly in the area of developing campus and/or district improvement plans.

A sample is included here for consideration. Leaders are encouraged to use any additional planning tools that yield successful implementation of their goals.

Action Step	Resources Needed	When Completed	Who's Responsible or Partners	Indicator(s) of Success

Reflection

1. How did the written RESULTS coaching plan or model shift you from "intention to act" to "commitment to act?"

_____

_____

_____

_____

2. As you think about implementing your plan for action, what barriers do you foresee? What are ways to reduce or eliminate these barriers?

_____

_____

_____

_____

3. What emotions do you anticipate as you implement your plan? How will you handle these feelings?

_____

_____

_____

_____

STEP 7: SEIZE . . . SUCCESS

The last step in the RESULTS Coaching Model is _Seize_ success. When people reach goals they have set, it is important to celebrate. If, as the leader, you have set some professional goals for yourself, monitor your progress and celebrate steps along the way. Set up your own rewards customized to your desires. You might post a note on your computer saying, "I did it!" You might invite a friend to lunch and share your accomplishment. You might throw a party—you get the idea. Have fun and go for it. Life is short.

When teachers and students meet goals, celebrate. It is always nice if you can celebrate each individual in a very specific way. Build celebration into the fabric of your school. Celebrate little things. Celebrate big things. Celebrate everything in between. People feel valued and appreciated when they are recognized for who they are and for what they have contributed to the success of the organization.

Reflection

1. How did your intentions and actions lead to the results you are celebrating?

_____

_____

_____

_____

2. How do you plan to celebrate the accomplishment of your goal?

_____

_____

_____

_____

In summary, the cyclical nature of the RESULTS Coaching Model maintains focus on the intention or goal. It ensures alignment of action with one's core values. It encourages us to move from reactive (Ready-Fire-Aim) to proactive (Ready-Aim-Fire) behaviors. As school leaders evaluate the plan they have developed, they can continually check for alignment between intention, attention, and actions. They can modify their action steps or even select a new option from the list they generated. The cycle continues when plans are revised or there are new challenges to the organization.

You know that implementing a plan of action involves energy, effort, and plain hard work. Developing a plan to change a behavior, to create a new way of being, or to employ new actions is no simple matter. It requires more than willpower. It demands that we set up new situations that facilitate the practice of our desired behavior.

For example, if it is my intention to have collaborative conversations with people in my work environment, I will want to select an upcoming event, such as a meeting where I can purposefully apply this new plan or skill. I will be conscious of my behaviors—what questions I ask, how I respond to input from others. Or perhaps I am monitoring a behavior that interferes with collaboration like "interrupting when others are speaking." My new behavior is "to wait until the other person has completed speaking." Taking action involves a combination of awareness, preparation, and practice. The RESULTS Coaching Model is a process designed to get RESULTS for both the individual and the organization, and it takes a leader who is courageous and committed to that action.

WHEN A LEADER GETS STUCK

As leaders develop actions to deal with the continuous demands of their jobs, they often get stuck in their thinking and resort to old behaviors— "the way we have always done things around here." When this occurs, leaders continue to get the same results. Often, it is an interaction with a coach that helps leaders clarify their thinking.

Recall the example of Sara discussed in Chapter 2. She is the principal who was able to move from old patterns of thinking to a new plan for action. This came from her own out-of-the-box thinking that was stimulated by a conversation with her coach.

Sara is the principal of a low-income middle school. She was planning a back-to-school night and wanted to explore ideas about how to get the parents involved. As she brainstormed (*Establish* goal clarity), she thought of many of the usual things she had done in the past—notices posted around the community, an ad in the community newspaper, letters sent home to parents, a notice on the school billboard, and so on. Then she laughed as she said she could pay parents to come, but of course that was against district policy, and she didn't have the funds anyway. But that crazy out-of-the-box idea caused her to think about holding a clothing drive in conjunction with the meeting. The school had lost and found items left over from the previous year. Teachers would contribute to the drive. Perhaps she could even get businesses to contribute prizes for drawings. Her creative juices were flowing. She left the coaching call with a renewed vision and spark. She worked with her coach to develop the plan and then with her staff to refine and develop the implementation steps. The event was a huge success. Parents visited classrooms and talked with teachers before they selected clothing. The principal had over 50% of the families in attendance, up from under 10% the previous year. Not only did interactions with her coach help her develop a more comprehensive plan of action, it also gave her the courage to make the identified changes.

SUMMARY

Just like a GPS, the school leader carries the RESULTS Coaching Model in his head as a roadmap for ensuring success for his school. He sets the direction (intention) and like the GPS, chooses the most direct path to help each teacher achieve student success (results). He uses the tools presented in Chapters 4 and 5 and the model in this chapter as guides for reaching the destination of results for students. When the results are not what are desired, he "recalculates" choosing a different route. Results for students in no longer an option; it is a necessity. A skilled leader uses his plan for action to maximize RESULTS.

CONCLUSION

In the Introduction to our book, we stated our intention to provide a guide that will inspire and motivate school leaders to commit to the use of new *essential* coaching behaviors for greater results for their schools and relationships.

Our passion for coaching is rewarded by watching people bloom and expand into incredible leaders and educators. And nothing is greater evidence or more revealing than the words that come from those we coach when it comes to the impact that has been made on both their personal and professional lives. Our work has inspired so many and offered provocative reflections in many forms. Here are two we would like to share.

My Coach and Me

by Rachel Nance (2004)

3:15 my time

I wait for the phone to ring

Anticipating that she will help me decide

What I've already

Decided

Or make sense of it

Not making sense

Someone new and unknown

But not

I open

She helps me

Into, through, out of and away

I can say what I want, fear, and dream

I talk and am heard

I'm clear and understood

I'm risking and safe

Thank you for letting me

Slow down

Think

Feel

Decide

And then believe.

Growing Pains

by Melissa True (2009)

Today I grew—and it hurt.

Dealing inside my own head, my own heart.

Allowing thoughts to swirl, doubts to run amok.

Chastising myself for wrongs I must right.

Realizing my first step has already begun.

The lump in my throat makes this experience too real to forget.

Forgiving myself—there is power in that.

Starting today, I make things right.

Guilt-free, I give myself freedom to try and maybe even fail.

Leading is about taking the risk and being transparent, while helping others realize the value within themselves.

Today I grew—and it feels great.

Our continuing work in the field has allowed us to write about lessons we have learned from our work with school leaders. Seeing the profound impact of learning the knowledge and skills of coaching continues to inspire and motivate us to recommit to our purpose of helping school leaders achieve extraordinary results. Our work is to support and foster confident, competent, courageous school leaders who lead their schools to high performance.

We believe coaching holds the greatest possibility for building and creating environments that support and build capacity in others in a way that will influence more effective and transformative teaching and learning for our students. With each new *coach leader* who is committed to leading schools in this way, the mission is advanced.

RESULTS Coaching is the new *essential* for today's school leaders. Being a "coach-leader" is a key competency, a new identity, for anyone in the business of building capacity of teachers, staff, and students. Because coaching language and skills require alignment of the integrity of one's attitudes and behaviors, coaching continually strengthens emotional intelligence for self-awareness, self-control, motivation, social awareness, and skill enhancement. On a daily basis, coaching challenges the leader to walk the talk—to continuously grow and improve before modeling and leading others. Being the coach leader offers the opportunity to create school communities that inspire and motivate for excellence and results!

Resources

Resource A

RESULTS COACHING—
GPS—VISUAL

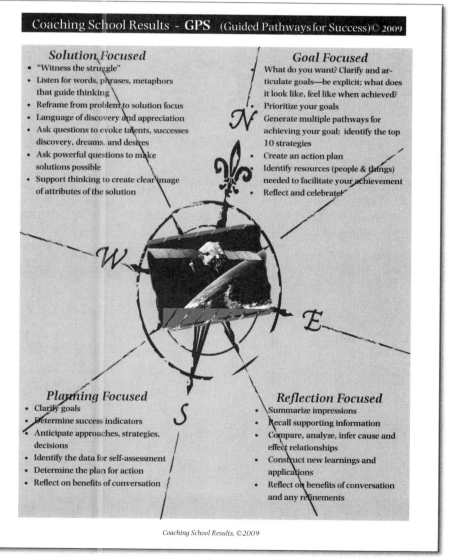

Coaching School Results - GPS (Guided Pathways for Success)© 2009

Solution Focused
- "Witness the struggle"
- Listen for words, phrases, metaphors that guide thinking
- Reframe from problem to solution focus
- Language of discovery and appreciation
- Ask questions to evoke talents, successes discovery, dreams, and desires
- Ask powerful questions to make solutions possible
- Support thinking to create clear image of attributes of the solution

Goal Focused
What do you want? Clarify and articulate goals—be explicit; what does it look like, feel like when achieved?
- Prioritize your goals
- Generate multiple pathways for achieving your goal; identify the top 10 strategies
- Create an action plan
- Identify resources (people & things) needed to facilitate your achievement
- Reflect and celebrate!

Planning Focused
- Clarify goals
- Determine success indicators
- Anticipate approaches, strategies, decisions
- Identify the data for self-assessment
- Determine the plan for action
- Reflect on benefits of conversation

Reflection Focused
- Summarize impressions
- Recall supporting information
- Compare, analyze, infer cause and effect relationships
- Construct new learnings and applications
- Reflect on benefits of conversation and any refinements

Coaching School Results, ©2009

Coaching School Results - GPS (Guided Pathways for Success) © 2009

Sample Language

Solution Focused

- You are really hurting from this.
- The broken trust has emptied your bank account.
- (Miracle ?) What would have happened to achieve the most positive outcome?
- You are seeking your most successful strategies to apply to this situation.
- What actions and strategies have given you success in the past that could be "re-gifted" in this situation?
- What compels you to ensure the solution you desire?
- Your courage and commitment to your students have created a clear vision of your goal.

Goal Focused

- What do you want?
- What will it look like when you have achieved this goal?
- Of the four goals you want, rank them in priority and time commitment for yourself.
- What five strategies are you thinking you want to put in place to achieve your goals?
- What are three more ways you can do it? Two more?
- Of your 10 strategies, which three offer the most powerful steps to achieving your goal?
- What is your timeline for accomplishing your goal?
  - Who will you utilize to assist you in realizing your goal?
  - As you reflect on this conversation and your upcoming goal achievement, what will you be celebrating in two months?

Planning Focused

- What are you wanting to achieve?
- How will you know when you have achieved it?
- What strategies have you determined will support your success?
- How will you know when you have achieved your mission? What data will affirm your accomplishment?
- What will be your first steps in your plan for action?
- How has this conversation been helpful?

Reflection Focused

- How do you feel about your performance?
- What data supports your feelings?
- What did you do to get the results you achieved? What specifically impacted your results?
- If you were to do this again, what would you want to repeat? Refine? Eliminate?
- How has this conversation supported your reflective practice?

Coaching School Results, ©2009

Resource B

RESULTS COACHING—
MODEL—VISUAL

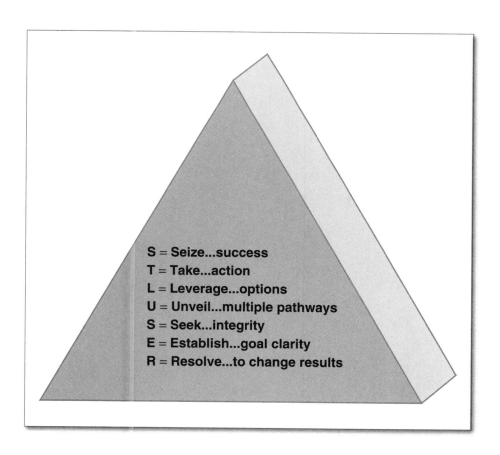

S = Seize...success
T = Take...action
L = Leverage...options
U = Unveil...multiple pathways
S = Seek...integrity
E = Establish...goal clarity
R = Resolve...to change results

Resource C

ASSESSMENTS

Resource C1: CFR Communication Assessment

Below are five concepts associated with "being" intentional as a communicator. Assess your personal strengths and areas where you want to grow stronger.

Powerful Listening
(Listening fully)

I am intentional about listening to what others have to say. I am aware of the amount of airspace available and am purposeful about how I choose to use it. I monitor or set aside distracters that interfere with being fully present.

Low			High	
1	2	3	4	5

Powerful Speaking
(Choosing words of power)

I am intentional about my choice of words because I know that words inspire or deflate, encourage involvement or cause retreat, invite action or inaction, lead to solutions or failures, and offer hope or despair.

Low			High	
1	2	3	4	5

(Continued)

(Continued)

Speaking the Truth
(Being "real" with self and others)

I speak my truth in a genuine and respectful manner while also listening to the truth from other perspectives. Before I speak, I honor silence to gain my own clarity, choose words carefully, and I deliver my message with personal regard.

Low				**High**
1	2	3	4	5

Making and Keeping Promises
(Displaying honesty and integrity)

I am intentional about making and keeping promises to myself and others. Before making a promise that commits my time, energy, and resources, I thoughtfully weigh the implications based upon priorities and values. My promises reflect my intention to follow through. When I cannot keep a promise, I take responsibility for speaking the truth to myself and others.

Low				**High**
1	2	3	4	5

Requests Versus Requirements
(Inducing desirable responses with adeptness)

I know the difference between a request and a requirement and am clear when I use each. I lead from the viewpoint of making requests that offer options and hold requirements for those areas that are nonnegotiable.

Low				**High**
1	2	3	4	5

Resource C2: Intention Self Assessment

I assume that everyone knows how we do things around here.	1	2	3	4	5	I set clear expectations about desired results and make overt agreements about ways we work together.
I frequently make decisions or take action impulsively and then deal with what happens.	1	2	3	4	5	I seek and attain clarity about intended outcomes and communicate my intentions to others.
I hold my thoughts and feelings closely, only sharing with a few close colleagues.	1	2	3	4	5	I share intentions and feelings openly, which frees up energy and expands possibilities.
I tolerate mediocrity by couching my language in vagueness and niceness and by skirting issues regarding less-than-desired performance of staff.	1	2	3	4	5	I intentionally and effectively address attitudinal, performance or behavioral issues and create multiple pathways for positive change.
I focus on activities and reasons why it is not possible to achieve desired results.	1	2	3	4	5	I purposefully focus on results and accountability at every level in the organization.
I micromanage instead of leading. There's no leadership development.	1	2	3	4	5	I intentionally coach and delegate to develop high quality future leaders.
As a leader, my job is to dispense advice.	1	2	3	4	5	I routinely seek input and involve people in goal setting and solution finding.
It's important that I convince others that my point of view and course of action are correct.	1	2	3	4	5	I explore multiple points of view and multiple options for action that leads to better results.
I protect my staff from many of my leadership decisions, enabling them to do their jobs.	1	2	3	4	5	I share challenging situations with my staff, empowering them to contribute to the process of goal attainment.

Resource C3: Committed Listening Tool

	Low High	
When I am listening to someone speak, my thoughts drift away instead of listening to what is being said.	Low High 1 2 3 4 5	I concentrate on what the person speaking is saying and feeling while monitoring my listening behaviors as the conversation evolves.
While I'm listening to someone else, I'm being critical, thinking about my response or relating to my own experience.	Low High 1 2 3 4 5	I listen fully to the person speaking and set aside judgment, solution finding, or personal stories.
I'm quick to interrupt to express my own thoughts and opinions.	Low High 1 2 3 4 5	Before responding, I wait to be sure the other person is finished with his or her thoughts.
I don't ask for clarification when I don't understand what the person means by what he or she is saying, or I interrupt with questions that either hijack or sidetrack the conversation.	Low High 1 2 3 4 5	I ask questions to better understand what the other person is saying when I'm not clear on what he or she means (I don't interrupt to ask questions or redirect the conversation)
I don't make eye contact or show through my facial expressions, gestures, and posture that I am listening.	Low High 1 2 3 4 5	I convey nonverbal attention and interest through facial expressions, gestures, and posture.
When I don't agree with what is said, I interrupt and force my ideas into the conversation, or I respond by attacking what the person has said.	Low High 1 2 3 4 5	I honor other's views, even when they are not my own or when I disagree.
I feel as if I need to respond or take action to comments made by others.	Low High 1 2 3 4 5	I listen without obligation to act and illuminate answers within others.
I don't feel comfortable paraphrasing, and when I do, I tend to "parrot" back what the speaker has said.	Low High 1 2 3 4 5	I paraphrase for clarity, elaboration, summary, and/or to help shift the thinking for greater meaning.

Resource D

ICF Code Of Ethics

INTERNATIONAL COACH FEDERATION

http://www.coachfederation.org/ethics

PART ONE: DEFINITION OF COACHING

Section 1: Definitions

- **Coaching:** Coaching is partnering with clients in a thought-provoking and creative process that inspires them to maximize their personal and professional potential.
- **A professional coaching relationship:** A professional coaching relationship exists when coaching includes a business agreement or contract that defines the responsibilities of each party.
- **An ICF Professional Coach:** An ICF Professional Coach also agrees to practice the ICF Professional Core Competencies and pledges accountability to the ICF Code of Ethics.

In order to clarify roles in the coaching relationship, it is often necessary to distinguish between the client and the sponsor. In most cases, the client and sponsor are the same person and therefore jointly referred to as the client. For purposes of identification, however, the International Coach Federation defines these roles as follows:

- **Client:** The "client" is the person(s) being coached.
- **Sponsor:** The "sponsor" is the entity (including its representatives) paying for and/or arranging for coaching services to be provided.

In all cases, coaching engagement contracts or agreements should clearly establish the rights, roles, and responsibilities for both the client and sponsor if they are not the same persons.

PART TWO: THE ICF STANDARDS OF ETHICAL CONDUCT

Preamble: ICF Professional Coaches aspire to conduct themselves in a manner that reflects positively upon the coaching profession; are respectful of different approaches to coaching; and recognize that they are also bound by applicable laws and regulations.

SECTION 1: PROFESSIONAL CONDUCT AT LARGE

As a coach:

1) I will not knowingly make any public statement that is untrue or misleading about what I offer as a coach, or make false claims in any written documents relating to the coaching profession or my credentials or the ICF.

2) I will accurately identify my coaching qualifications, expertise, experience, certifications and ICF Credentials.

3) I will recognize and honor the efforts and contributions of others and not misrepresent them as my own. I understand that violating this standard may leave me subject to legal remedy by a third party.

4) I will, at all times, strive to recognize personal issues that may impair, conflict, or interfere with my coaching performance or my professional coaching relationships. Whenever the facts and circumstances necessitate, I will promptly seek professional assistance and determine the action to be taken, including whether it is appropriate to suspend or terminate my coaching relationship(s).

5) I will conduct myself in accordance with the ICF Code of Ethics in all coach training, coach mentoring, and coach supervisory activities.

6) I will conduct and report research with competence, honesty, and within recognized scientific standards and applicable subject guidelines. My research will be carried out with the necessary consent

and approval of those involved, and with an approach that will protect participants from any potential harm. All research efforts will be performed in a manner that complies with all the applicable laws of the country in which the research is conducted.

7) I will maintain, store, and dispose of any records created during my coaching business in a manner that promotes confidentiality, security, and privacy, and complies with any applicable laws and agreements.

8) I will use ICF member contact information (e-mail addresses, telephone numbers, etc.) only in the manner and to the extent authorized by the ICF.

SECTION 2: CONFLICTS OF INTEREST

As a coach:

9) I will seek to avoid conflicts of interest and potential conflicts of interest and openly disclose any such conflicts. I will offer to remove myself when such a conflict arises.

10) I will disclose to my client and his or her sponsor all anticipated compensation from third parties that I may pay or receive for referrals of that client.

11) I will only barter for services, goods or other non-monetary remuneration when it will not impair the coaching relationship.

12) I will not knowingly take any personal, professional, or monetary advantage or benefit of the coach-client relationship, except by a form of compensation as agreed in the agreement or contract.

SECTION 3: PROFESSIONAL CONDUCT WITH CLIENTS

As a coach:

13) I will not knowingly mislead or make false claims about what my client or sponsor will receive from the coaching process or from me as the coach.

14) I will not give my prospective clients or sponsors information or advice I know or believe to be misleading or false.

15) I will have clear agreements or contracts with my clients and sponsor(s). I will honor all agreements or contracts made in the context of professional coaching relationships.

16) I will carefully explain and strive to ensure that, prior to or at the initial meeting, my coaching client and sponsor(s) understand the nature of coaching, the nature and limits of confidentiality, financial arrangements, and any other terms of the coaching agreement or contract.

17) I will be responsible for setting clear, appropriate, and culturally sensitive boundaries that govern any physical contact I may have with my clients or sponsors.

18) I will not become sexually intimate with any of my current clients or sponsors.

19) I will respect the client's right to terminate the coaching relationship at any point during the process, subject to the provisions of the agreement or contract. I will be alert to indications that the client is no longer benefiting from our coaching relationship.

20) I will encourage the client or sponsor to make a change if I believe the client or sponsor would be better served by another coach or by another resource.

21) I will suggest my client seek the services of other professionals when deemed necessary or appropriate.

SECTION 4: CONFIDENTIALITY/PRIVACY

As a coach:

22) I will maintain the strictest levels of confidentiality with all client and sponsor information. I will have a clear agreement or contract before releasing information to another person, unless required by law.

23) I will have a clear agreement upon how coaching information will be exchanged among coach, client, and sponsor.

24) When acting as a trainer of student coaches, I will clarify confidentiality policies with the students.

25) I will have associated coaches and other persons whom I manage in service of my clients and their sponsors in a paid or volunteer

capacity make clear agreements or contracts to adhere to the ICF Code of Ethics Part 2, Section 4: Confidentiality/Privacy standards and the entire ICF Code of Ethics to the extent applicable.

PART THREE: THE ICF PLEDGE OF ETHICS

As an ICF Professional Coach, I acknowledge and agree to honor my ethical and legal obligations to my coaching clients and sponsors, colleagues, and to the public at large. I pledge to comply with the ICF Code of Ethics, and to practice these standards with those whom I coach.

If I breach this Pledge of Ethics or any part of the ICF Code of Ethics, I agree that the ICF in its sole discretion may hold me accountable for so doing. I further agree that my accountability to the ICF for any breach may include sanctions, such as loss of my ICF membership and/or my ICF Credentials.

Approved by the Ethics and Standards Committee on October 30, 2008.

Approved by the ICF Board of Directors on December 18, 2008.

Resource E

ICF Professional Coaching Core Competencies

INTERNATIONAL COACH FEDERATION

http://www.coachfederation.org/research-education/
icf-credentials/core-competencies/

A. SETTING THE FOUNDATION

1. Meeting Ethical Guidelines and Professional Standards
2. Establishing the Coaching Agreement

B. CO-CREATING THE RELATIONSHIP

1. Establishing Trust and Intimacy With the Client
2. Coaching Presence

C. COMMUNICATING EFFECTIVELY

1. Active Listening
2. Powerful Questioning
3. Direct Communication

D. FACILITATING LEARNING AND RESULTS

1. Creating Awareness
2. Designing Actions

3. Planning and Goal Setting

4. Managing Progress and Accountability

A. SETTING THE FOUNDATION

1. **Meeting Ethical Guidelines and Professional Standards** - Understanding of coaching ethics and standards and ability to apply them appropriately in all coaching situations

   a. Understands and exhibits in own behaviors the ICF Standards of Conduct (see list, Part III of ICF Code of Ethics);

   b. Understands and follows all ICF Ethical Guidelines (see list);

   c. Clearly communicates the distinctions between coaching, consulting, psychotherapy and other support professions;

   d. Refers client to another support professional as needed, knowing when this is needed and the available resources.

2. **Establishing the Coaching Agreement** - Ability to understand what is required in the specific coaching interaction and to come to agreement with the prospective and new client about the coaching process and relationship

   a. Understands and effectively discusses with the client the guidelines and specific parameters of the coaching relationship (e.g., logistics, fees, scheduling, inclusion of others if appropriate);

   b. Reaches agreement about what is appropriate in the relationship and what is not, what is and is not being offered, and about the client's and coach's responsibilities;

   c. Determines whether there is an effective match between his/her coaching method and the needs of the prospective client.

B. CO-CREATING THE RELATIONSHIP

3. **Establishing Trust and Intimacy With the Client** - Ability to create a safe, supportive environment that produces ongoing mutual respect and trust

   a. Shows genuine concern for the client's welfare and future;

   b. Continuously demonstrates personal integrity, honesty and sincerity;

   c. Establishes clear agreements and keeps promises;

d. Demonstrates respect for client's perceptions, learning style, personal being;

e. Provides ongoing support for and champions new behaviors and actions, including those involving risk taking and fear of failure;

f. Asks permission to coach client in sensitive, new areas.

4. **Coaching Presence** - Ability to be fully conscious and create spontaneous relationship with the client, employing a style that is open, flexible and confident

a. Is present and flexible during the coaching process, dancing in the moment;

b. Accesses own intuition and trusts one's inner knowing - "goes with the gut";

c. Is open to not knowing and takes risks;

d. Sees many ways to work with the client, and chooses in the moment what is most effective;

e. Uses humor effectively to create lightness and energy;

f. Confidently shifts perspectives and experiments with new possibilities for own action;

g. Demonstrates confidence in working with strong emotions, and can self-manage and not be overpowered or enmeshed by client's emotions.

C. COMMUNICATING EFFECTIVELY

5. **Active Listening** - Ability to focus completely on what the client is saying and is not saying, to understand the meaning of what is said in the context of the client's desires, and to support client self-expression

a. Attends to the client and the client's agenda, and not to the coach's agenda for the client;

b. Hears the client's concerns, goals, values and beliefs about what is and is not possible;

c. Distinguishes between the words, the tone of voice, and the body language;

d. Summarizes, paraphrases, reiterates, mirrors back what client has said to ensure clarity and understanding;

e. Encourages, accepts, explores and reinforces the client's expression of feelings, perceptions, concerns, beliefs, suggestions, and so on;

    f. Integrates and builds on client's ideas and suggestions;

    g. "Bottom-lines" or understands the essence of the client's communication and helps the client get there rather than engaging in long descriptive stories;

    h. Allows the client to vent or "clear" the situation without judgment or attachment in order to move on to next steps.

6. **Powerful Questioning** - Ability to ask questions that reveal the information needed for maximum benefit to the coaching relationship and the client

    a. Asks questions that reflect active listening and an understanding of the client's perspective;

    b. Asks questions that evoke discovery, insight, commitment or action (e.g., those that challenge the client's assumptions);

    c. Asks open-ended questions that create greater clarity, possibility, or new learning;

    d. Asks questions that move the client towards what they desire, not questions that ask for the client to justify or look backwards.

7. **Direct Communication** - Ability to communicate effectively during coaching sessions and to use language that has the greatest positive impact on the client

    a. Is clear, articulate, and direct in sharing and providing feedback;

    b. Reframes and articulates to help the client understand from another perspective what he or she wants or is uncertain about;

    c. Clearly states coaching objectives, meeting agenda, purpose of techniques or exercises;

    d. Uses language appropriate and respectful to the client (e.g., nonsexist, nonracist, nontechnical, nonjargon);

    e. Uses metaphor and analogy to help to illustrate a point or paint a verbal picture.

D. FACILITATING LEARNING AND RESULTS

8. **Creating Awareness** - Ability to integrate and accurately evaluate multiple sources of information and to make interpretations that help the client to gain awareness and thereby achieve agreed-upon results

    a. Goes beyond what is said in assessing client's concerns, not getting hooked by the client's description;

b. Invokes inquiry for greater understanding, awareness, and clarity;

c. Identifies for the client his or her underlying concerns, typical and fixed ways of perceiving himself or herself and the world, differences between the facts and the interpretation, disparities between thoughts, feelings and action;

d. Helps clients to discover for themselves the new thoughts, beliefs, perceptions, emotions, moods, and so on that strengthen their ability to take action and achieve what is important to them;

e. Communicates broader perspectives to clients and inspires commitment to shift their viewpoints and find new possibilities for action;

f. Helps clients to see the different, interrelated factors that affect them and their behaviors (e.g., thoughts, emotions, body, background);

g. Expresses insights to clients in ways that are useful and meaningful for the client;

h. Identifies major strengths versus major areas for learning and growth and what is most important to address during coaching;

i. Asks the client to distinguish between trivial and significant issues, situational versus recurring behaviors, when detecting a separation between what is being stated and what is being done.

9. **Designing Actions** - Ability to create with the client opportunities for ongoing learning, during coaching and in work and/or life situations, and for taking new actions that will most effectively lead to agreed-upon coaching results

a. Brainstorms and assists the client to define actions that will enable the client to demonstrate, practice, and deepen new learning;

b. Helps the client to focus on and systematically explore specific concerns and opportunities that are central to agreed-upon coaching goals;

c. Engages the client to explore alternative ideas and solutions, to evaluate options, and to make related decisions;

d. Promotes active experimentation and self-discovery, where the client applies what has been discussed and learned during sessions immediately afterwards in his or her work or life setting;

   e. Celebrates client successes and capabilities for future growth;

   f. Challenges client's assumptions and perspectives to provoke new ideas and find new possibilities for action;

   g. Advocates or brings forward points of view that are aligned with client goals and, without attachment, engages the client to consider them;

   h. Helps the client "Do It Now" during the coaching session, providing immediate support;

   i. Encourages stretches and challenges but also a comfortable pace of learning.

10. **Planning and Goal Setting** - Ability to develop and maintain an effective coaching plan with the client

   a. Consolidates collected information and establishes a coaching plan and development goals with the client that address concerns and major areas for learning and development;

   b. Creates a plan with results that are attainable, measurable, specific and have target dates;

   c. Makes plan adjustments as warranted by the coaching process and by changes in the situation;

   d. Helps the client identify and access different resources for learning (e.g., books, other professionals);

   e. Identifies and targets early successes that are important to the client.

11. **Managing Progress and Accountability** - Ability to hold attention on what is important for the client and to leave responsibility with the client to take action

   a. Clearly requests of the client actions that will move the client toward their stated goals;

   b. Demonstrates follow through by asking the client about those actions that the client committed to during the previous session(s);

   c. Acknowledges the client for what they have done, not done, learned, or become aware of since the previous coaching session(s);

   d. Effectively prepares, organizes, and reviews with client information obtained during sessions;

   e. Keeps the client on track between sessions by holding attention on the coaching plan and outcomes, agreed-upon courses of action, and topics for future session(s);

f. Focuses on the coaching plan but is also open to adjusting behaviors and actions based on the coaching process and shifts in direction during sessions;

g. Is able to move back and forth between the big picture of where the client is heading, setting a context for what is being discussed and where the client wishes to go;

h. Promotes client's self-discipline and holds the client accountable for what they say they are going to do, for the results of an intended action, or for a specific plan with related time frames;

i. Develops the client's ability to make decisions, address key concerns, and develop himself or herself (to get feedback, to determine priorities and set the pace of learning, to reflect on and learn from experiences);

j. Positively confronts the client with the fact that he or she did not take agreed-upon actions.

Resource F

Resource F1: Evaluation of Coaching Services

HOW WE HAVE EVALUATED OUR WORK

Coaching for Results has endeavored to evaluate the professional development programs and coaching services that are offered. The evaluation consists of two strands: (1) There is a standardized evaluation administered after each event, and (2) We seek to understand the impact of our services and make meaning of what is reported through periodic qualitative phenomenological studies. The data on file with Coaching For Results, Inc. from 2003–2009 represents involvement with over 800 educators. We continually strive for greater accountability, greater clarity of our purpose, and greater understanding of impact.

The following summary shows key findings of phenomenological studies undertaken since 2003.

Name of study:	Researcher:	Key findings:
Coaching for Results: A Study of Outcomes, 2003	Shirley M. Hord, PhD Scholar Emerita, Southwest Educational Development Laboratory, Austin, Texas	• Respondents felt that as a result of coaching, they had sharpened their focus or better identified the direction to take with their work. This made it possible to prioritize and delegate activities to others. • Respondents noted tools or processes that they had learned from the coaching that they now use in their everyday work. • Respondents expressed a newfound confidence in them and in their leadership capacity.

(Continued)

(Continued)

Name of study:	Researcher:	Key findings:
Coaching for Results: A study of Impact, 2007	Shirley M. Hord, PhD and William A. Sommers	• Key Question: What were the results of the training and coaching, and what differences did it make for you? • Coaching is not for making poor employees better but for taking the best and making them better. • Biggest change in behavior is goal setting and writing them (goals) down. Respondent feels more "leveled" and balanced. • Respondent felt that coaching kept her passion going. She has become a better listener and clearer speaker. The training was confidence building. • Helped clarify my role. "It is a powerful program. It has made a big difference in the way I operate."
Report to the Board: A Qualitative Analysis of Interview Data From Coaching Clients 2009	Diana Williams,PhD Chief of Evaluation Services, Coaching for Results (Sandee Crowther and Essie Richardson, interviewers)	• The variable that most frequently emerged from the data was "confidence gained" from being coached. • While respondents relied on recommendations from their supervisors to engage in coaching, once they were coached, they reported that they would engage in coaching with or without a supervisor's recommendation. • In the initial phase of coaching, clients reported most often that they valued the trust and co-creation of the relationship with their coach. In later phases of coaching, they reported that they valued their ability to get results and communicate more effectively in their work as a result of coaching.

The following data represent standardized evaluation reports collected by CFR from coaching workshops across the country. The workshop evaluation forms are based on a five-point Likert Scale with five (5) being the highest value.

Data Collected From July, 2008–January, 2009

Questions:	1	2	3	4	5	a	b	c	d	e	f
Instructional Coaching: An Essential for School Success N=9	5.0	5.0	5.0	5.0	5.0						
Leadership Coaching for High Performance Montclair Univ., NJ N=17	5.00	5.00	4.94	4.94	5.00						
Leadership Coaching for High Performance Level Howard Co., MD N=15	4.87	5.00	4.73	4.67	5.00	4.87	4.73	4.93	4.87	5.00	
Leadership Coaching for High Performance Level I Winton Woods, OH N=20	4.75	4.90	4.80	4.78	4.95	4.45	4.85	4.40	4.26	4.42	4.68
Leadership Coaching for High Performance Level Howard Co., MD N=40	4.74	4.97	4.89	4.82	4.74	4.55	4.89	4.71	4.68	4.84	4.81

Data Collected From February 2009–June 2009

Questions:	1	2	3	4	5a	5b	5c	5d	5e	5f	6
Leadership Coaching for High Performance Howard Co. N=39	4.92	4.95	4.82	4.92	4.82	4.51	4.90	4.79	4.69	4.77	4.82
Leadership Coaching for High Performance Michigan N=12	5.00	5.00	4.92	4.92	4.67	4.83	4.92	4.75	4.64	4.92	
Leadership Coaching for High Performance Little Rock, AK N=21	4.90	4.95	4.90	4.95	4.86	4.81	4.76	4.90	4.76	4.81	4.90
Leadership Coaching for High Performance Kansas N=7	4.86	5.0	5.0	4.86	4.86	4.86	5.0	5.0	4.86	5.0	5.0
Instructional Coaching June 22, 2009 Carrollton-Farmers Branch ISD N=17	5.0	5.0	5.0	5.0	5.0	5.00	4.94	5.00	4.94	4.88	4.94
Questions:	1	2	3	4	5a	5b	5c	5d	5e	5f	6
Strategies for Powerful Coaching II Howard Co. N=23	4.61	4.91	4.65	4.52	4.61	4.52	4.57	4.78	4.59		

Resource F2: Rave Reviews
For Coaching for Results Seminars

Coaching School Results consistently receives outstanding feedback from seminar participants. Here are just a few comments by recent participants:

"Imagine having the skills for listening, reframing of questions, believing in others, and open communication that supports the success of all on your campus daily. The power of coaching will build on these skills and many more to ensure your students and campus family will grow and continue to be successful."

Jerry Miracle, Campus Instructional Coordinator, Clements/Parsons Elementary; Copperas Cove ISD

"This course is essential to effectively communicate in all aspects of your life. The skills gained through this training are going to help me become a powerful coach and person. I feel that it will impact me in every aspect of my life."

Erica Reyes, Instructional Development Coordinator, Salesmanship Club, Dallas, TX

"Regardless of whatever experience or background you bring with you, opportunities to grow are abundant. The information shared is applicable in both professional and personal areas and can enrich relationships across the board. Coaching empowers us to make a difference."

Zelene Lovitt, At-Risk Facilitator, Carrollton-Farmers Branch ISD

"This experience inspires me to make some very positive changes in both my personal and professional life. I feel that every education leader would benefit from this phenomenal professional development."

Marsha Watson, Director of Curriculum and Instruction, White Oak ISD

"This seminar is a gift that is life changing for me, both professionally and personally. I believe that the principles of coaching have the power to change the way we relate to others which will greatly increase results."

Beth Crisp, District Reading Specialist, Richardson ISD

Resource G

REFLECTIVE FEEDBACK, SKILL ESSAYS, AND COACHING SCRIPTS

RESOURCE G1

REFLECTIVE FEEDBACK

Relationship

Information

- Clarifies an idea or behavior under consideration (to be sure talking about the same thing)
- Communicates positive features toward preserving and building upon them
- Communicates concerns and considerations toward improvement
- Requires more time, thought, and effort, and it reads as careful, respectful, and honest

OPTIONS FOR GIVING REFLECTIVE FEEDBACK

1. **Clarify questions for understanding**

    "How do you see this program different from. . . .?"

    "How did your students respond to the process?"

    "What costs have been calculated to put this in place?"

    "Which resources most supported your planning and provided the foundation for this work?"

    "Which groups provided useful input to the plan?"

    "When you checked state assessment alignment, what data supported moving forward?"

    "What input did the parents give and how was it helpful?"

(Continued)

(Continued)

2. Express the Value Potential specifically

"This could offer value to students with time issues."

"The strength of the idea is. . . ."

"The scaffolding of your design will help teachers understand. . ."

"You have really thought deeply about...building relationships
with your students."

"There is evidence of...thoughtful planning
and preparation."

"As a parent and teacher, the idea is very exciting because
it supports learning."

"This instructional project provides high engagement for
every level of student need."

3. Reflective Questions or Possibilities

"What goals have (did) your students set for individual mastery?"

"I wonder what would happen if. . ." or "What might happen if. . ."

"What learning gaps, if any, did you notice in student understanding?"

"What differentiation strategies are you considering to support your
students' success?"

"What other considerations are you thinking about?"

"What connections have you made to. . . (other subjects,
real world, other assessments)?"

"What aspects are you thinking may be a barrier for
parents or critical groups?"

"As you consider 'best practice' – what strategies will
you use to achieve your goal?"

Kee, 2008

Resource G2: Reflective Feedback Practice

PRACTICE 1

The purpose of this practice is to help learners wrap their mind around the three options for Reflective Feedback—Clarify, Value or value potential, or Reflective questions for possibilities.

- Divide the room into thirds with each group having one type of reflective feedback.
- Offer a scenario appropriate for the audience (e.g., a principal who wants to do more walkthroughs, a teacher who wants to incorporate more active learning strategies, etc.)
- Ask each third of the room to offer the type of feedback assigned.
- After sharing, change the type of feedback the group has and repeat the practice.

Modeling Feedback Protocol

- The Feedback Practice Protocol follows below.
- Review the Protocol prior to modeling. This step is important for creating the Big Picture of expected behaviors, norms, and process steps that support successful use of the protocol.
- Leaders may want to model it first and then staff will repeat the process at their tables. One of the trainers gives an issue and others offer feedback following the steps in the protocol.
- Large Group Debrief, the whole group will debrief of benefits of using this protocol.

PRACTICE 2—USING A STRUCTURED PROTOCOL FOR REFLECTIVE FEEDBACK

In small groups, learners will practice using the feedback protocol. It may be helpful for trainers to help the groups determine roles—a facilitator of the process, the person sharing the issue, and a timekeeper prior to beginning the protocol.

Provide the following instructions:

1. One member of your group will share a puzzling or worrisome issue from the past year. He or she will share some of his or her experiences and actions. That member will have five minutes to share. The conversation will be confidential.

2. After the person has shared, members of the group will write down as many questions or statements as they like from the Reflective Feedback guide. They will have three minutes to think and write.

3. Beginning with the person to the left of the speaker, each person will offer only one type of reflective feedback—either a question or statement for Clarifying, for Value Potential, or for Reflective Question or Possibility.

4. Each person will offer only *one* question or statement going around the group. There is *no cross talk,* and the speaker only listens, considers, or possibly takes notes.

5. Once each group member offers one question or statement, the group will go around again until all statements or questions are exhausted. Once completed, the speaker has a few moments to think and then respond to the group.

6. The speaker needs to know that he or she is not required to respond to all individual questions or statements; the speaker is only required to share new thoughts, ideas, or considerations he or she now has as a result of the sharing.

7. The members agree and understand that their feelings will not be hurt if the speaker does not comment on their statement or question.

8. Once all ideas are shared and the speaker has responded to the whole group, Cross Talk is allowed as the members share the benefit of this experience.

9. Whole Group Reflection
   o What worked for you in this conversation protocol?
   o What was difficult?
   o What was easier than expected?
   o How did the language of reflective feedback positively impact the sharing?
   o What refinements would you make? (Using Reflective Feedback)

Facilitator Note: Ask the group permission to gently nudge them to refine their questions or statements. Remind everyone that we are learning new language and patterns of language. Gently offer a question if the feedback does not represent the attributes of the type of reflective feedback. Because it is important not to practice incorrectly, interrupt politely. We might say something like, "She has thought about it; now, talk with her as if she has thought about it."

Elementary people tend to use judgmental language because they praise all the time. Positive judgment is still judgment. Move them, from "I like" to feedback that shows value such as, "The strength of your . . . was," or "There is evidence of . . . ."

Resource G3

SOUNDS OF SILENCE

By Jane Bidlack

We all live in a fast-paced, noise-filled world that seems to become louder each day. Even when we try to escape and relax, we continue to stay attached to cell phones, computers, iPods, and many other forms of technology that interrupt any possibility to experience total quiet. We are so accustomed to having noise around us that we are often very uncomfortable with silence, and yet we know that silence is a critical attribute of skillful listening. We can all plead guilty to being distracted while trying to listen or formulating what we are going to say next before the other person even completes his or her thought.

In coaching, each of us is eager to use the variety of skills that we have learned to encourage our clients to see themselves as capable of self-discovery, problem solving, reflection, and change. Our training and practical experience as coaches may lead to a tendency to be very busy, focusing our attention when we are with a client. We all know the value of active listening in the coaching process, and silence is an effective and essential tool in listening. How does silence factor into our coaching skills?

Gandhi says, "In the attitude of silence, the soul finds the path in a clearer light, and what is elusive and deceptive resolves itself into crystal clearness."

Silence, when used in conversation, may empower another person and help build a relationship as well. This is a challenge—to be comfortable with just being quiet is an acquired art. Silence can produce some of the best results of reflection and insight because we give a client the gift of time to work things out in his or her own brain. When we hold back and remain silent, we allow clients to discover more about what they are thinking and feeling and what they really want and also how we can best help them. It helps clients slow down their minds to discover more effective solutions to areas of concern. We give them a time and place to dig deeper and deal with an issue. Silence can lead clients to a break through or catharsis—that great leap to new understanding.

An added benefit of silence occurs because we send a strong message that the client's words and insights are important. This can help a person feel a sense of increased capacity. Silence is active attention and can be fully effective in coaching when the client accepts trust and support from the coach. Silence, when used correctly, is not abandonment—it is heightened presence. What happens on the other side of silence is often an exercise of problem solving, innovation, thinking, and brilliant ahas!

Silence can be uncomfortable. We must learn to become comfortable with the uncomfortable. We need to give clients assurance that we are listening and interested and that they are cared for while the silence settles in. It can be a powerful tool for those who use it well. Silence works wonders in letting clients know that we see them as capable. Silence also allows us to listen better to ourselves.

Utilizing the sounds of silence is truly a tool in the masterful coach's art of communication.

Jane Bidlack serves as a leadership coach with Coaching For Results, Inc. She has been a school administrator for seventeen years and delights in offering individual support for current school leaders to realize their full potential through the coaching process. For more information about Jane and our other coaches, go to *www.coachingschoolresults.com* and click on "coaches."

Coaching School Results, 2009

Resource G4

PRINCIPAL AND COACH CONVERSATION

(1) Coach: Good Morning, Linda. How are you today? And . . . how are those beautiful and brilliant grandkids you were seeing this past month?

(2) Principal: Oh, I am fine, just behind as usual (sense of frantic in tone) . . . but seeing those kids was so special. They were in town for a long weekend and wow, how they have grown. It was great to be with them. Thanks so much for asking.

(3) Coach: Was that stress that I heard in your voice. What's going on?

(4) Principal: Well, I am feeling a lot of pressure, probably self-imposed, but I can't seem to focus on the right things at the right time. Walking through classes has brought to light literacy issues, math issues, science issues, and even management issues. I feel like I am racing, but I don't know which way to go. Ha!

(5) Coach: Linda, sounds like you have several curricular and instructional areas needing your attention. To be the most helpful to you in our time together, which area would you like to focus on first? Literacy, math, science, management, or another area?

(6) Principal: Oh, without a doubt, literacy.

(7) Coach: So, what's going on?

(8) Principal: This year, our district has been pushing for a more "balanced literacy" approach in reading in every classroom. My teachers have been to training, and I have tried to provide time for focus on balanced literacy at many faculty meetings. Yet when I walk through classrooms, I still see many of the old practices rather than the strategies we have been focusing on or taught in professional development. I am getting pretty upset about the "hold out" and refusal to teach in a way that has more potential for student learning. I guess I need to have a difficult conversation with a few of my teachers who just don't get it.

(9) Coach: Linda, you are truly committed to the use of balanced literacy as the way to maximize reading and writing success for you kids, and you are disappointed at not seeing the application in your classrooms at the level you expected by now.

(10) Principal: Yes, we have brought in consultants, we have taught so many strategies, and I thought everyone was on board. It is time for several teachers to just get on with it.

(11) Coach: Let's play a little and pretend. In the morning, you wake up and go to school. A miracle has happened. As you walk through your school, every classroom is a model of balanced literacy. You are so thrilled and excited for your teachers and students! What are you seeing that thrills you?

(12) Principal: Oh, wow, I see all the components of balanced literacy. . . . I see the teachers reading aloud to students, being a model of a fluent reader while students are being active listeners. I see teachers and students reading text together, practicing fluency and phrasing, which increases comprehension. I see my teachers using guided reading that builds on their reading strategies, which is increasing student motivation to read. I see students reading independently because they are confident and feel good about reading. And everywhere, students are working together on writing, expressing themselves, becoming good spellers, and enjoying the fun of writing and reading with others. Oh, my gosh. I am a happy principal!

(13) Coach: What a fabulous image of learning you have for your campus! You want to see not only the skill but also the joyful motivation of the balanced literacy process.

(14) Principal: Oh, yes . . . so what do I do to get there?

(15) Coach: Knowing that transfer is one of the most powerful strategies required in order for the brain to make connections to new learning, what balanced literacy strategies are you currently seeing in your classrooms that your teachers are doing that you can build upon—that would reinforce their confidence and competence as implementers of a stronger balanced literacy program?

(16) Principal: Well, hmmmm, they are doing some things . . . (silence) . . . they are using guided reading, they are focusing on building vocabulary, and . . . (silence) . . . they are doing several things I can connect to . . . oh, my gosh, (silence) . . . I am not pointing out what I am seeing. I am only focused on what I am not. Oh, oh, . . . I know exactly what I need to do.

(17) Coach: Wow, from your face and BMIRS*, it seems the pathway to your vision has gotten clearer. What has become clearer for you?

(18) Principal: I need to start all over. . . . Well, maybe not start all over, but I do need to build on what they are doing, the results they are getting, and celebrate the small ways they are implementing balanced literacy.

(19) Coach: Wow; so you are realizing they are doing some things to affirm and that those things will be the bridge to the next level.

(20) Principal: Yes! I can affirm what they are doing, even if it is not as much as I would want to see, and hopefully my acknowledgement will provide some positive motivation to do more . . . and you know, I really think they will want to. (silence)

(21) Coach: So, what are you thinking will be the next three things you want to do that will provide motivation, support, and scaffolding to your teachers in order for them to have higher levels of success with balanced literacy?

(22) Principal: Well, hmmmm . . . I am having a faculty meeting tomorrow. I think I want to celebrate the strong strategies my teachers are using, and I want to label connections to balanced literacy.

(23) Coach: So, who are you thinking can best support you in making this happen at the faculty meeting?

---

*BMIRS=Behavioral Manifestations of Internal Response States

(24) Principal: Oh, I must enlist my assistant principal so we can together lift the staff up and guide them to next steps.

(25) Coach: So, your first step, with your assistant, is to have a faculty meeting focused on literacy strategies that are being used and then label them so you can celebrate the many ways your teachers are implementing balanced literacy. What else?

(26) Principal: Yes, and then, I want to talk with the reading coordinator and share what we are doing and determine the most important aspects of balanced literacy to target for focus and highlighting next.

(27) Coach: Hot dog, enlisting the central office reading coordinator to support and advocate your process. Genius! What else?

(28) Principal: I want to meet with my leadership team that includes my team leaders and enlist their ideas and energy to support and label things in their team meetings. They have the pulse of the campus, and feedback from them will help guide me and my assistant principal in knowing what will be needed to continue this journey.

(29) Coach: Wow, look at the powerful steps you are going to take: first, a general faculty meeting to celebrate, connect, and label; second, enlisting support from the reading coordinator, and third, working strategically with each grade-level leader and team. Your insight to affirm efforts now and enlist others collaboratively will reap many benefits. How exciting to see and hear the joy and excitement on your face and in your voice!

(30) Principal: Can't believe when we started this conversation I was so frustrated, and now I am excited about what is up coming. Thank you so much.

(31) Coach: Hey, you did the great thinking! Congratulations! You have a clear plan and are ready to get started creating that vision for your school. Can't wait until we talk again to hear about the things you are celebrating.

Resource G5

TEACHER COACH COACHING
CONVERSATION 1 (FIRST WEEK OF SCHOOL)

(1) Teacher: Hi Brad, I hear you are moving into a role of coach this year. When did you decide to do that?

(2) Coach: Hi, Cindy, yes, I am very excited about the opportunity to support teachers in this new role.

(3) Teacher: Does this mean you will be in class evaluating how I teach?

(4) Coach: Oh, no, my role as coach is to support you in your instruction in the way you want. It might be planning or teaching or simply designing your lessons for differentiation. My role is to give you a safe place to think and reflect. I also want you to know that our relationship is confidential. I do not report back to the principal on our conversations. Just like your role as teacher is to support your students to their best learning, my role as coach is to support your best work in teaching. And please know that this doesn't mean I think I know everything about teaching and learning; it just means I offer you a place to think and reflect out loud on your instruction. I will also not show up and tell you what you should be doing. I will support you in the goals you set for your class and campus and your work in meeting the campus expectations. My role is to bring your goals in focus each time we visit.

(5) Teacher: Well, I haven't been teaching very long, and I hope you will offer suggestions and ideas.

(6) Coach: I know in the years you have been teaching you have worked very hard going to professional development and learning many strategies for high levels of student engagement. I will bring those successful ideas back for you to use and refine. And of course, I will offer some great strategies we have had in trainings or that I continue to see in classrooms like yours.

(7) Teacher: Well, I will tell you right now I really get nervous when the principal and others do those learning walks. I am very concerned about academic rigor since most of my students seem to be working at a very low level.

(8) Coach: Cindy, your concern for your students is evident. You want to begin with students at the appropriate level and at the same time ensure rigor for their learning which sounds like a contradiction.

(9) Teacher: Exactly, how can instruction be rigorous and also be below level instruction?

(10) Coach: Cindy, I know you are heading back to class right now, but this will be a great focus for our next conversation. Would it be helpful, when we meet again to review your objectives for the upcoming three weeks, if we take the curriculum and carefully identify the core concepts that your students will master?

(11) Teacher: Sure, but how will I know from that I will be providing rigor?

(12) Coach: Cindy, my hunch is that you are already building in rigor with the high engaging strategies and accountable talk you use with your kids. So, when are you available to meet next week?

(13) Teacher: Well, next Tuesday at this time works for me.

(14) Coach: Great. So next Tuesday, we will review together the upcoming learning objectives and your tools for evaluating mastery . . . this will give us an opportunity to consider best practice strategies to ensure rigor.

(15) Teacher: Wow, thanks. I think I was thinking I had to create lessons at very high levels to be rigorous; I think I am beginning to understand that rigorous learning can be on level learning.

(16) Coach: You are right. Rigor is about the level of thinking of the student throughout the instruction.

(17) Teacher: Hey, I think I might get this after all. Looking forward to next week. Thanks again, Brad. Have a great week.

COACHING CONVERSATIONS 2 (A WEEK LATER)

(18) Coach: Hi Cindy. How are you today? I heard your child was sick last week, is he better?

(19) Teacher: Oh yes, just a 24-hour thing, I guess. Thanks for asking. You know when kids are toddlers, every little fever or cold is scary. But he seems to be back to normal.

(20) Coach: That is wonderful. So what content for the next three weeks or so do you want to focus on today?

(21) Teacher: I am thinking I would like our focus to be on math. It is not my most confident content, and I would like to talk out loud about it.

(22) Coach: So you want to target math instruction and have the same confidence in math as you do other subjects.

(23) Teacher: Yes. I work hard at planning, but I am never really sure if what I am doing is really rigorous.

(24) Coach: So, when you plan with your team, what content areas are the focus?

(25) Teacher: Well, we really spend the most time on language arts . . . you know, writing and reading is so important, and it consumes a lot of time.

(26) Coach: Wow, your team planning is targeting another foundation learning that all subjects will reap benefit from.

(27) Teacher: Yes.

(28) Coach: So, given our 30 minutes today, how would you like to tackle your math content?

(29) Teacher: Well, how do I know I am building instruction for academic rigor?

(30) Coach: So, Cindy, when you describe "academic rigor" to another new teacher . . . how do you define it?

(31) Teacher: Well, I think it means that the learning is challenging for students . . . it's hard.

(32) Coach: Well, let's pull out the definition to be sure we are working with a clear definition. (Brad pulls out his definitions of the Principles of Learning that he keeps in a plastic sleeve, along with best practice strategies. Together, Brad and Cindy read the attributes of academic rigor.)

(33) Coach: So as you read this, what insights are you having about academic rigor?

(34) Teacher: Well, a couple of things . . . my students must under-stand the content they are learning and second, they must do the work on making connections about the content. I think, as I read this, that the most important thing I do, as I plan my lessons, is to have very clear learning goals and active strategies for my students.

(35) Coach: All right, two things you know that will be crucial to rigor. So, having those two things in you mind, let's get into the curriculum, and consider what your content journey may be for the next few weeks.

(36) Teacher: Cool.

(37) Coach: Looking at the math instruction for the next three weeks, what will be your specific math goals?

(38) Teacher: The kids will be deepening their use and understanding of fractions.

(39) Coach: So, what specifically will the students have to know and do to deepen that understanding and use of fractions?

(In the next 20 minutes, Coach and Teacher reviewed the curriculum for the next three weeks.)

References

Blumenthal, N. (2007). *You're addicted to you: So hard to change—and what you can do about it.* San Francisco, CA: Berrett-Koehler.

Bolte-Taylor, J. (2008). *My stroke of insight.* New York: Viking Penguin Press.

BrainyQuote. (2010). *BrainyQuote-Galileo Galilei.* Retrieved April 14, 2010, from http://www.brainyquote.com/quotes/quotes/g/galileogal381318.html

Bryk, A., & Schneider, B. (2002). *Trust in schools: A core resource for improvement.* New York: Russell Sage Foundation Pub.

Burley-Allen, M. (1995). *Listening: The forgotten skill.* Hoboken, NJ: Wiley, John & Sons.

Coaching School Results. (2009). *RESULTS plan for action.* Powerful coaching: level II, training materials.

Coaching School Results. (2010). *Coaching navigation system.* Advanced coaching: level III, training materials.

Costa A., & Garmston B. (2002). *Cognitive coaching: A foundation for renaissance schools.* Norwood, MA: Christopher-Gordon Pub.

Costa, A., & Libermann, A. (1997). *The process-centered school.* Thousand Oaks, CA: Corwin.

Covey, S. (1989). *The seven habits of highly effective people.* New York: Simon and Schuster.

Covey, S. (2006). *The speed of trust.* New York: Simon and Schuster.

Dweck, C. (2006). *Mindset: The new psychology of success.* New York: Random House.

Ellis, D. (2002). *Falling awake.* Rapid City, SD: Breakthrough Enterprises.

Ellis, D. (2006). *Life coaching: A manual for helping professionals.* Norwalk, CT: Crown House Pub.

Fay, C. (2010). Effects of the 9 essential skills for the love and logic classroom® training program on teachers perceptions of their students behavior and their own teaching competence: A preliminary investigation. Retrieved April 14, 2010, from http://www.loveandlogic.com/pdfs/research_data_9e.pdf

Fay, J., & Foster C. (2006). *Parenting with love and logic.* Colorado Springs, CO: Pinon Press.

Fullan, M. (2001). *Leading in a culture of change.* San Francisco, CA: Jossey-Bass.

Gardner, H. (2006). *Five minds for the future.* Boston, MA: Harvard Business School Pub.

Garmston, R., & Wellman, B. (1992). *How to make presentations that teach and transform.* Alexandria, VA: ASCD.

Garmston, R., & Wellman, B. (1999). *The adaptive school: A sourcebook for developing collaborative groups.* Norwood, MA: Christopher-Gordon.

Glasser, W. (1965). *Reality therapy.* New York: Harper & Row Pub.

Glasser, W. (1990). *The quality school: Managing students without coercion.* New York: HarperCollins.

Glasser, W. (1998). *Choice theory: A new psychology of personal freedom.* New York: HarperCollins.

Goleman, D. (1998). *Working with emotional intelligence.* New York: Bantam Dell, Random House.

Greenleaf, R. K. (2002). *Servant leadership: A journey into the nature of legitimate power and greatness.* Mahwah, NJ: Paulist Press.

Haden-Elgin, S. (2000). *The gentle art of verbal self-defense at work.* Paramus, NJ: Prentice Hall.

Hall, R., & Moore, D. (2006). *Same kind of different as me.* Colorado Springs, CO: Thomas Nelson.

Hattie, J., & Timperley, H. (2007). *The power of feedback.* University of Auckland: Review of Educational Research.

Henry, R. (2003). *Leadership at every level: Appreciative Inquiry in Education.* New Horizons for Learning.

Hord, S., Rutherford, W., Huling-Austin, L. & Hall, G. (1998). *Taking charge of change.* Austin, TX: Southwest Educational Development Lavatories.

International Coach Federation. (2009). Core coaching competencies, ethics and standards. Retrieved April, 2010, from http://www.coachfederation.org/research-education/icf-credentials.

Kagan. R., & Lahey, L. (2001) *How the way we talk can change the way we work.* San Francisco, CA: Jossey-Bass.

Krupp, J-A. (1982). *Adult learner: A unique entity.* Manchester, CT: Adult Development & Learning.

Leider, R. (2004). *The power of purpose: Creating meaning in your life.* San Francisco, CA: Berrett-Koehler.

Leonard, T., & Larson, B. (1998) *The portable coach: 28 sure-fire strategies for business and personal success.* New York: Simon & Schuster.

Lipton, L., & Wellman, B., with Humbard, C. (2001) *Mentoring matters: A practical guide to learning-focused relationships.* Sherman, CT: MiraVia.

Marzano, R. (2003). *What works in schools: Translating research into action.* Alexandria, VA: Association for Supervision and Development.

Miedaner, T. (2000) *Coach yourself to success: 101 tips from a personal coach for reaching your goals for work and in life.* Chicago, IL: Contemporary Books.

Mitchell, W. (1986). *Power of positive students.* New York: Bantam.

Obama, B. (2009, January 18). What I want for you—and for every child in America. *Parade Magazine,* p. 2.

Olsen, W., & Sommers, W. (1999). *Trainer's companion—Stories for reflection and action.* Highland, TX: Aha! Process.

Orem, S., Binkert, J., & Clancy, A. (2007). *Appreciative coaching: A positive process for change.* San Francisco, CA: Jossey-Bass.

Perkins, D. (2003). *King Arthur's round table: How collaborative conversations create smart organizations,* Hoboken, NJ: John Wiley & Sons.

Prensky, M. (2001, Oct.). Digital natives, digital immigrants. *On The Horizon. 9*(5) 1–6.

Rock, D. (2006). *Quiet leadership.* New York: Harper Collins.

Schon, D. (1987). *Educating the reflective practitioner,* San Francisco, CA: Jossey-Bass.

Scott, S. (2002). *Fierce conversations: Achieving success at work and in life—one conversation at a time.* New York: The Berkley Publishing Group.

Smalley, G. (1993) *Gift of the blessing.* Nashville, TN: Thomas Nelson.

Sparks, D. (2006). *Leading for results: Transforming teaching, learning, and relationships in schools.* Thousand Oaks, CA: Corwin.

Tschannen-Moran, M. (2004). *Trust matters: Leadership for successful schools.* San Francisco, CA: Jossey-Bass.

United States Department of Education, (2005, October 10), *No child left behind.*

Vygotsky, L. (1986, 1934). *Language and thought.* Cambridge, MA: MIT Press.

Warren, R., & Warren, R. (2002). *The purpose driven life: What on earth am I here for?* Philadelphia, PA: Running Press Book Publishers.

Whitmore, J. (2002). *Coaching for performance.* Boston, MA: Nicholas Brealey Publishing.

Wong, E., & Heifetz, R. (2009) *Top human technology.* China and Centre for Public Leadership, Harvard University.

Index

CORWIN
A SAGE Company

The Corwin logo—a raven striding across an open book—represents the union of courage and learning. Corwin is committed to improving education for all learners by publishing books and other professional development resources for those serving the field of PreK–12 education. By providing practical, hands-on materials, Corwin continues to carry out the promise of its motto: **"Helping Educators Do Their Work Better."**

Advancing professional learning for student success

Learning Forward (formerly National Staff Development Council) is an international association of learning educators committed to one purpose in K–12 education: Every educator engages in effective professional learning every day so every student achieves.